The Land Agent

Scotland's Land
Series editor: Dr Annie Tindley

Editorial Advisory Board
Dr Calum MacLeod, University of Edinburgh
Dr Malcolm Combe, University of Aberdeen
Dr Iain Robertson, University of the Highlands and Islands
Professor Terence Dooley, Maynooth University
Professor Ewen A. Cameron, University of Edinburgh
Dr John MacAskill, University of Edinburgh

This series presents the latest scholarly work to academic and public readers on Scotland's land issues. Predominantly focusing on the history of Scotland's economic, political, and social and cultural relationships to land, landscape, country houses and landed estates, it also brings in cutting-edge approaches to explore new methodologies and perspectives around this politically contentious but stimulating issue. As an interdisciplinary series, it will necessarily contain a wide range of approaches, including history, law, economics and economic history, philosophy, environment/landscape studies, and human/cultural geography. The aim of the series is to bring together and publish the best work on land issues across a wide range of disciplines for a diverse set of audiences.

Published and forthcoming titles

The Land Agent: 1700–1920
Lowri Ann Rees, Ciarán Reilly and Annie Tindley (eds)

Scotland's Foreshore: Public Rights, Private Rights and the Crown, 1840–2017
John MacAskill

edinburghuniversitypress.com/series/slf

The Land Agent

1700–1920

Edited by Lowri Ann Rees, Ciarán Reilly and Annie Tindley

EDINBURGH
University Press

Edinburgh University Press is one of the leading university presses in the UK. We publish academic books and journals in our selected subject areas across the humanities and social sciences, combining cutting-edge scholarship with high editorial and production values to produce academic works of lasting importance. For more information visit our website: edinburghuniversitypress.com

© editorial matter and organisation Lowri Ann Rees, Ciarán Reilly and Annie Tindley, 2018
© the chapters their several authors, 2018

Edinburgh University Press Ltd
The Tun – Holyrood Road
12 (2f) Jackson's Entry
Edinburgh EH8 8PJ

Typeset in 10.5/13pt Sabon by
Servis Filmsetting Ltd, Stockport, Cheshire
and printed and bound in Great Britain

A CIP record for this book is available from the British Library

ISBN 978 1 4744 3886 5 (hardback)
ISBN 978 1 4744 3888 9 (webready PDF)
ISBN 978 1 4744 3889 6 (epub)

Contents

Figures

Acknowledgements

The editors wish to gratefully acknowledge the financial and moral support of the Institute for the Study of Welsh Estates (University of Bangor); the Centre for the Study of Historic Irish Houses & Estates (Maynooth University) and the Centre for Scotland's Land Futures (University of Dundee, University of Stirling and the University of the Highlands and Islands), which supported the academic workshop in October 2015 at which these papers were (for the most part) first presented. They would also like to thank very warmly all of the contributors to this volume and the anonymous reviewers for Edinburgh University Press for their very useful comments and suggestions.

Notes on the Contributors

Fidelma Byrne is currently the academic coordinator at the Kilkenny campus of Maynooth University, where in 2016 she completed her PhD, entitled 'Estate Management on the Wentworth-Fitzwilliam Core Estates of Ireland and Yorkshire: A Comparative Study, 1815–65'.

Ewen A. Cameron is Professor of Scottish History at the University of Edinburgh. He has long-standing interests in the history of land legislation in Scotland and has published widely on the subject, for example his book *Land for the People?*

Robin K. Campbell is a historian, writer, speaker and contributor to books on the Inner Hebrides. Following an honours degree in History from London University, his research has primarily focused on the clearances in Argyllshire during the nineteenth century, including collecting and recording memories, songs and stories from Gaelic oral tradition-bearers in the islands of Mull and Tiree.

Anne Casement gained a doctorate from the Queen's University of Belfast in 2002 for her study of estate management in Ulster in the mid-nineteenth century. She is now a freelance historian specialising in the study of historic estates and their landscape, architectural and management history, particularly those associated with the Londonderry family of Mount Stewart, County Down. Many of her findings have been published in *Irish Architectural and Decorative Studies* and *Apollo*, and her book on the Irish drawings of Lord Mark Kerr was published in 2010.

Shaun Evans is Director of the Institute for the Study of Welsh Estates at Bangor University, an interdisciplinary national coordinating centre for promoting research into the history, culture and landscapes of Wales through the prisms of estates and the collections they generated over the course of their existence. He has previously worked in the Research Team at The National Archives and is Chair of the North East Wales Heritage Forum.

David Gent is an independent scholar currently working in academic administration and learning enhancement at the University of York. His AHRC-funded PhD at York examined the life of George Howard, 7th Earl of Carlisle (1802–64), a Whig politician and the owner of Castle Howard in Yorkshire, the focus of his contribution to this volume. David maintains active research interests in English politics in the early-Victorian era and the English landed elite and their estates.

Kirsty Gunn created and directs the programme in Writing Practice and Study at the University of Dundee and is an Associate of the Centre for Scotland's Land Futures. Her last novel, *The Big Music*, was set in Sutherland and drew upon her own experience, knowledge and memories of that particular landscape and the culture it inspires. She is published in the UK by Faber and Faber and internationally.

John McGregor holds an MA(Hons) from the University of Edinburgh and a PhD from the Open University and was on the associate staff of the Open University from 1979 to 2013. He has researched and published extensively on Scotland's nineteenth- and twentieth-century railway politics.

Finlay McKichan is a retired Senior Lecturer in the Education School of the University of Aberdeen. He has published two articles on Lord Seaforth in the *Scottish Historical Review* and one in *Northern Scotland*. He is completing a monograph, *Lord Seaforth: Highland Proprietor, Caribbean Governor*, for Edinburgh University Press.

Rachel Murphy is currently working as a postdoctoral researcher on *Deep Maps: West Cork Coastal Cultures*, an interdisciplinary project funded by the Irish Research Council. Rachel recently completed a PhD at University College Cork entitled 'Place, Community and Organisation on the Courtown Estates, 1649–1977'. Her research interests include landed estates, environmental history and spatial humanities.

Lowri Ann Rees is Lecturer in Modern History, School of History and Archaeology, Bangor University. Her research interests centre on eighteenth- and nineteenth-century Wales, in particular the landed elite and their country estates. She has published on paternalism and rural protest, the Rebecca Riots, Welsh sojourners in India, and is currently researching upward social mobility in Wales.

Ciarán Reilly is based at the Centre for the Study of Historic Irish Houses & Estates, Maynooth University and is a historian of nineteenth- and twentieth-century Irish history.

Annie Tindley is a senior lecturer in modern British history at Newcastle University. Her research interests revolve around the interrogation of the aristocratic and landed classes, landed estates and their management from the mid-eighteenth to mid-twentieth centuries, in the Scottish, Irish, British and imperial contexts.

Map of the British and Irish Isles, showing the approximate location of the landed estates discussed in the volume

Introduction

Lowri Ann Rees, Ciarán Reilly and Annie Tindley

THIS EDITED VOLUME IS about a subject of rural history that has often been ignored or reviled: the land agent. Factor, commissioner, manager, steward or agent: call him (and he was until well into the twentieth century universally a 'him') what you will, historians of rural Britain and Ireland have yet to give his role and operational parameters much sustained attention.[1] This blind spot is particularly odd when we remind ourselves of the power – actual and reputational – wielded by land agents over large rural populations until relatively recently. As the representatives of landowners 'on the ground' in a part of Europe where large swathes of land were concentrated into relatively few hands, it is perhaps unsurprising that land agents carry a somewhat mixed – sometimes dark – historical reputation.[2] In parts of Scotland, Wales and Ireland in particular, some agents developed local, regional – even national – reputations as tyrants and oppressors of the poor, to the extent that their names are still remembered today.[3] In some parts of the British and Irish isles, agents did not labour under such burdensome reputations, but they were still generally recognised as powerful, well-educated men; leaders of their local society, often holding a

---

[1] There are honourable exceptions; see, for instance, C. Beardmore, G. Monks and S. King (eds), *The Land Agent in Britain: Past, Present and Future* (Cambridge, 2016), especially pp. 1–16; E. Richards, *Patrick Sellar and the Highland Clearances: Homicide, Eviction and the Price of Progress* (Edinburgh, 1999); C. Beardmore, 'Landowner, tenant and agent on the Marquis of Anglesey's Dorset and Somerset estate, 1814–44', *Rural History*, 26:2 (2015), pp. 181–99.

[2] For general discussion on Scotland, see A. Tindley, '"They sow the wind, they reap the whirlwind": estate management in the post-clearance Highlands, c. 1815– c. 1900', *Northern Scotland*, 3 (2012), pp. 66–85; and for Ireland, C. Reilly, *The Irish Land Agent, 1830–60: The Case of King's County* (Dublin, 2014).

[3] Richards, *Patrick Sellar*, pp. 1–13; Tindley, '"They sow the wind"', pp. 66–7; D. W. Howell, 'The land question in nineteenth century Wales, Ireland and Scotland: a comparative study', *Agricultural History Review*, 61:1 (2013), pp. 104–5.

multiplicity of local and regional political and governmental offices. They were relatively well paid too, often far in advance of doctors, clergy or teachers, fellow members of the rural middle and professional classes.[4] Land agents are not just of interest to historians either; in the twenty-first century, they are still instrumental to the administration of landed estates.[5]

Their role was a challenging one, as the chapters in this collection will demonstrate, in every geographical context. Resident land agents were required to manage almost every aspect of the estate, from the collection of rents and rates, to managing building repairs and improvements, surveying and agricultural science, the sensitive relations between landlords and tenants, as well as strategic planning for the future. All of this was underpinned by their relationship to their employer, the landowner, and their attitude to their estates, investment and consumption. Most land agents also had to have a strong working knowledge of the law; indeed, there was an enduring link between the legal and agency professions throughout the period covered by this volume, and certain law firms became associated with estate management and developed dynastic expertise. This volume covers a period of intense professionalisation and specialisation in estate management practice in Britain, Ireland and the European and colonial contexts, with minimum standards and knowledge, training and experience increasingly expected of land agents.[6] Agricultural revolution and improvement, the diversification of landed investment and interests generated by the Industrial Revolution, and fundamental political adjustment were challenges and opportunities faced by the land agency profession to varying degrees.[7] This volume examines these processes across a wide chronological and

---

[4] For example, the agents for the Sutherland estates were by the 1840s paid £400 per annum and had a sheep farm in hand; the parish doctor was paid £15 per annum by the Duke of Sutherland; Tindley, '"They sow the wind"', p. 68.

[5] S. King, 'The role of the land agent: continuity and continuity', in Beardmore et al., *Land Agent*, pp. 129–50.

[6] G. Monk, 'The path of professionalisation: mechanisation and legislation on the Welbeck estate', in Beardmore et al., *Land Agent*, pp. 39–59.

[7] However, there has not been room in this volume for a sustained discussion of land agent training beyond the case studies presented here. I. H. Adams, 'Economic process and the Scottish land surveyor', *Imago Mundi*, 27 (1975), pp. 13–18; I. H. Adams, 'The agents of agricultural change', in M. L. Parry and T. R. Slater (eds), *The Making of the Scottish Countryside* (London, 1980), pp. 159–60, 167–9; T. M. Devine, 'The transformation of agriculture: cultivation and clearance', in T. M. Devine, C. H. Lee and G. C. Peden (eds), *The Transformation of Scotland: The Economy since 1700* (Edinburgh, 2005), pp. 79, 87.

geographical stage. By broadening our historical perspective to include the 'four nations' of England, Wales, Scotland and Ireland, and as far as possible further out into the imperial context, we hope to make connections and uncover new perspectives on the neglected figure of the land agent.[8] As the ownership of land was often transnational in nature, so was its management.[9] As such, this volume asks a number of comparative questions. How did the nature of the profession change – in terms of expectations of the role, training, career paths and the parameters of local power? What can a focus on the role of the agent, rather than that of the landowner or tenant, uncover for the rural historian? And lastly, how did experiences compare across geographies and chronologies; how uniform was agency experience and why? As well as uncovering the forgotten histories of land agency, this volume seeks to present a collective contribution to these questions through the following chapters, to offer new perspectives as well as identify gaps and future research opportunities.

Although central to the issues that have more effectively captured the sustained attention of historians – landlord–tenant relations, for instance, or protest, improvement, clearance and famine – nuanced understandings of the land agent and their role in post-1700 rural society have been somewhat thin on the ground.[10] We have selected this period because that is broadly when estate management began to professionalise, although this was a process that occurred at different

[8] Comparative studies of the land wars and tenant agitation exist, but no comparative or transnational studies on the role of land agents have been developed. For the former, see Howell, 'Land question', pp. 83–4, 104–5; E. A. Cameron, 'Communication or separation? Reactions to Irish land agitation and legislation in the Highlands of Scotland, c. 1870–1910', *English Historical Review*, 210 (2005), pp. 633–66; A. G. Newby, *Ireland, Radicalism and the Scottish Highlands, c. 1870–1912* (Edinburgh, 2007), pp. 144–5; F. Byrne, 'Estate management practices on the Wentworth-Fitzwilliam core estates of Ireland and Yorkshire: a comparative study, 1815–65' (unpublished PhD thesis, Maynooth University, 2017).

[9] See A. Tindley, 'All the arts of a Radical agitation': transnational perspectives on British and Irish landowners and estates, 1800–1921', *Historical Research* (forthcoming).

[10] General rural histories of the period tend to note the role of the land agent only in passing; for instance, E. Richards, *The Leviathan of Wealth: The Sutherland Fortune in the Industrial Revolution* (London, 1973); T. Williamson, *The Transformation of Rural England: Farming and the Landscape, 1700–1870* (Exeter, 2002); J. Hunter, *The Making of the Crofting Community* (Edinburgh, 1976); C. O'Gráda, *Ireland before and after the Famine: Explorations in Economic History, 1800–1925* (Manchester, 1993); E. A. Cameron, *Land for the People?: The British Government and the Scottish Highlands, c. 1880–1925* (East Linton, 1996).

rates in different places. This emphasises an important point, however: that although the aim of this volume is to expose themes, differences and comparisons across boundaries, the specificity of time and place must underpin any transnational perspective.[11] To set this into context, the existing historiography for the four nations will be concisely outlined, so that the chapters that follow, which are organised thematically, are securely situated within the framework of current thinking.

The land agent in Scotland (normally called a factor) has a fundamentally contradictory reputation. On the one hand, factors are – rightly, in many cases – seen as the vanguard of the Agricultural Revolution and both the ideology and practice of improvement in the later eighteenth and early nineteenth centuries.[12] Establishing improved methods in the wake of the last Jacobite Rising in 1745–6, the Forfeited Estates appointed a number of factors to oversee improvement on the land annexed by the state from rebellious landowners, and thereby established a new set of expectations and parameters for factors.[13] They were to maintain and manage properties, but they were also expected to improve and diversify them too; to commercialise, to lead by example in farming practice and to maintain social and moral discipline over the people. On the other hand, the Scottish factor is persistently dogged by a dark reputation; that he is an oppressor, a tyrant. Perhaps he is a rack-renter, or an evictor or simply a bully who preys on a vulnerable and poverty-stricken small tenantry.[14] Neither contemporaries nor historians have as yet satisfactorily considered how and why – and with what concrete results – this dual *Jekyll and Hyde* conception of the land agent developed in Scotland, as the historiography demonstrates.

There are book-length studies of some Scottish land agents, motivated in part by their infamous reputations: studies of Patrick Sellar, the great clearance agent and sheep farmer, who was tried for his life in 1816; or Donald Munro, the hated 'Beast' who was factor for Matheson of Lewis for many years.[15] Work has been completed on another domineering

[11] E. Delaney, 'Our island story? Towards a transnational history of late modern Ireland', *Irish Historical Studies*, 37 (2011), p. 603.

[12] Adams, 'Agents of agricultural change', pp. 159–60, 167–9.

[13] S. Nenadic, *Lairds and Luxury: The Highland Gentry in Eighteenth-Century Scotland* (Edinburgh, 2007), pp. 1–2; F. McKichan, 'Lord Seaforth and Highland estate management in the first phase of clearance (1783–1815)', *Scottish Historical Review*, 86 (2007), p. 53.

[14] Tindley, '"They sow the wind"'.

[15] J. Shaw Grant, *A Shilling for your Scowl: The History of a Scottish Legal Mafia* (Stornoway, 1992), pp. 137–41; J. Macleod, *None Dare Oppose: The Laird,*

figure, Evander McIver, the 'King of Scourie' so-called, and on the reputation of agency profession in Scotland more broadly.[16] The questions
occupying these historians circulate around the nature of reputation, and
whether agents were constrained – or not – by their often difficult reputations. What is missing from the scholarship is an external perspective.
We might remind ourselves that Scottish land agents working in other
parts of the British and Irish isles often enjoyed a very good reputation
– as business-like, honest, active and improving men, particularly in
Ireland.[17] As these chapters will demonstrate, there were some structural
reasons why this was so, embedded in differing land law and practice,
but as this minor example demonstrates, taking a wider perspective can
throw new light on old historiographical questions.

The Scottish historiography is also somewhat curtailed by the long-
standing focus on landlord–tenant relations and protest, land reform
and land war.[18] Of course, the land agent had a central role in all of the
themes, but this has been sidelined by historians who have developed a
somewhat polarised view of rural Scotland – large, aristocratic landlords
on the one side; a mass of poverty-stricken small tenantry on the other.[19]
The land agent occasionally gets a walk-on role in the great set-piece
clashes between the landlord and tenant, but is generally regarded as
a one-dimensional landlord proxy rather than a figure of power and
influence in his own right. This volume seeks to complicate this historiographical view, not least by exposing and discussing the Scottish land
agent's international reputation.

Of the four nations primarily under consideration in this volume,
perhaps the English land agent or steward has the least controversial
reputation. England, unlike Scotland or Ireland, suffered no outright

the Beast and the People of Lewis (Edinburgh, 2010), p. 256; Richards, *Patrick Sellar*.

[16] E. Richards and A. Tindley, 'After the clearances: Evander McIver and the "Highland Question", 1835–73', *Rural History*, 23:1 (2012), pp. 41–57; E. Richards and A. Tindley, 'Turmoil among the crofters: Evander McIver and the "Highland Question", 1873–1903', *Agricultural History Review*, 60:2 (2012), pp. 191–213.

[17] This was particularly the case in Ireland, where Scottish land agents (and land-owners) had a generally more positive reputation than their home-grown brethren.

[18] See, for example, Richards, *Patrick Sellar*; Richards, *Leviathan of Wealth*; Hunter, *Making of the Crofting Community*; Cameron, *Land for the People?*; T. M. Devine, *The Great Highland Famine: Hunger, Emigration and the Scottish Highlands in the Nineteenth Century* (Edinburgh, 1988); I. Robertson, *Landscapes of Protest in the Scottish Highlands after 1914: The Later Highland Land Wars* (London, 2013).

[19] See the classic account in Hunter, *Making of the Crofting Community*.

rural catastrophe in the eighteenth or nineteenth centuries; instead there were the longer processes of enclosure and agricultural improvement. That these caused suffering, generated protest and have maintained a hold in the popular and historical memory there is no doubt. However, their relatively long time frame, the availability of alternative employment sources and the relative wealth of the country meant that the levels of protest and residual resentment seen elsewhere – and the land agent's association with that – were not evident in England. Although the land question as broadly conceived was a stark political and social reality in England, there is no land war to rival those of Ireland or the Scottish Highlands. Protest, poaching, politics and speeches there are, however, and more recent historiography has shifted away from monotone constructions of the nature of protest and deference in the English countryside to expose the hidden or coded ecologies underlying social relations.[20] As such, a more rounded historiography of the land agent has been possible, with key work examining their role in economic diversification in the eighteenth and nineteenth centuries.[21] As landowners sought to accelerate the commercial opportunities of their landed properties, developing mining or quarrying, canals and railways where possible, land agents were in the vanguard of England's industrial (and imperial) revolution. In some places we are as likely to find agents worrying over transportation charges for mineral cargoes as over arable yields, and in many cases they led their employers into risky – if sometimes rewarding – commercial and industrial ventures.[22] English agents were the ultimate multitaskers, undertaking the ordinarily recognisable tasks of all agents such as rent setting and collections, and managing agricultural improvement and innovation, alongside more unusual roles, such as organising workforces for mines or learning about the latest

---

[20] C. Beardmore, 'The rural estate through the eyes of the land agent: a community in microcosm c. 1812–1844', *Family & Community History*, 19:1 (2016), pp. 17–33; C. Griffin and I. Robertson, 'Moral ecologies: conservation in conflict in rural England', *History Workshop Journal*, 82:1 (2016), pp. 24–49.

[21] S. Daniels and S. Seymour, 'Landscape design and the idea of improvement, 1730–1900', in R. Dodgshon and R. Butlin (eds), *An Historical Geography of England & Wales* (2nd edn, London, 1990), pp. 487–520; S. Wilmot, *The Business of Improvement: Agriculture and Scientific Culture in Britain, c. 1700–1870* (Reading, 1990); S. Wade Martins, *Farmers, Landlords and Landscapes: Rural Britain, 1720–1870* (Macclesfield, 2004); Williamson, *Transformation of Rural England*; J. Finch and K. Giles (eds), *Estate Landscapes: Design, Improvement and Power in the Post-Medieval Landscape* (Woodbridge, 2007).

[22] D. Cannadine, 'The landowner as millionaire: the finances of the Dukes of Devonshire, c. 1800–c. 1926', *Agricultural History Review*, 25 (1977), pp. 77–97.

technologies.[23] They were less traditional perhaps than their colleagues in the Celtic fringe, and were perhaps more plugged into the social mores and diversified networks of the urban and industrial world. As such their historiography focuses less on protest and conflict, and more on their contribution to the development and diversification of estate economies, and ensuring that the English landed classes were amongst the most economically, politically and socially resilient in Europe.[24]

The role of the land agent in Wales is under researched, despite the growing and healthy rural historiography.[25] This is not due to a dearth of archival material; repositories are full of extensive estate collections that contain documentation and correspondence between landlord and agent. Of the historiography which does exist, the emphasis is on the day-to-day administrative role of the agent on the estate, with some consideration as to the difficulties of the role.[26] There is therefore scope for further exploration of challenges to the power and authority of the land agent; for instance, how they reacted during times of rural unrest and agitation.[27] The gulf between landlord and tenants was deepening

[23] S. Webster, 'Estate improvement and the professionalisation of land agents on the Egremont estates in Sussex and Yorkshire, 1770–1835', *Rural History*, 18:1 (2007), pp. 47–69; G. Monks, 'Land management: Welbeck and Holkham in the long nineteenth century' (PhD thesis, University of Leicester, 2015).

[24] D. Roberts, *Paternalism in Early Victorian England* (London, 1979), especially pp. 129–48; M. Cragoe, *An Anglican Aristocracy: The Moral Economy of the Landed Estate in Carmarthenshire, 1832–95* (Oxford, 1996); F. M. L. Thompson, *English Landed Society in the Nineteenth Century* (London, 1963), pp. 184–211.

[25] See, for example, W. Linnard, '"Lord" Forrest of St Fagans: estate agent extraordinary', *Morgannwg*, 33 (1989), pp. 55–68; R. J. Colyer, 'The land agent in nineteenth-century Wales', *Welsh History Review*, 8:4 (1977), pp. 401–25; see also sections of D. W. Howell, *Land and People in Nineteenth-Century Wales* (London, 1977) and D. W. Howell, *Patriarchs and Parasites: The Gentry of South-West Wales in the Eighteenth Century* (Cardiff, 1986).

[26] See, for example, Colyer, 'Land agent in nineteenth-century Wales'; see also sections of Howell, *Land and People* and Howell, *Patriarchs and Parasites*.

[27] On enclosure riots in Wales, see, for example, E. Jones, *The War of the Little Englishman: Enclosure Riots on a Lonely Welsh Hillside* (Talybont, 2007); S. Howard, 'Riotous community: crowds, politics and society in Wales, c. 1700–1840', *Welsh History Review*, 20:4 (2001), pp. 656–86; R. J. Colyer, 'The gentry and the county in nineteenth-century Cardiganshire', *Welsh History Review*, 10 (1981), pp. 497–535. For Rebecca Riots, see Rh. E. Jones, *Petticoat Heroes: Gender, Culture and Popular Protest in the Rebecca Riots* (Cardiff, 2015); L. A. Rees, 'Paternalism and rural protest: the Rebecca Riots and the landed interest of south-west Wales', *Agricultural History Review*, 59:1 (2011), pp. 36–60; D. J. V. Jones, *Rebecca's Children: A Study of Rural Society, Crime and Protest* (Cardiff, 1989); D. Williams, *The Rebecca Riots: A Study in Agrarian Discontent* (Cardiff, 1955).

in a number of ways, with different political affiliations emerging from the mid-nineteenth century adding to the growing sense of division that already existed along religious and linguistic lines.[28] In this climate, a Royal Commission was set up in 1893 to investigate the Land Question in Wales, with its results published three years later.[29] A prominent strand in the attacks on landlords was absenteeism, an important issue with regards to the land agent, often the most senior representative of the landowner. David W. Howell, however, argues that the issue was inflated by the radical press, fuelling the image of Anglicised landlords fleeing with their rental income, which was invested elsewhere. The situation in Wales was very different to Ireland, and as the nineteenth century progressed, with improving transport infrastructures, absentee-ism became less frequent.[30] Nonetheless, landlords still acquired the services of land agents to manage their estates.

Later in the nineteenth century, the role of the land agent was discussed in the report of the Welsh Land Commission, with recommendations as to training, possession of agricultural experience and power of authority, and advice not to interfere in matters of religion or politics.[31] Allusions were made in the report to cases of estate mismanagement by land agents.[32] Earlier nineteenth-century examples of unscrupulous agents include Charles Hassall and Richard Jones of Pantirion, who acted on

For Tithe Wars, see S. E. Jones, 'Hanes y degwm yng Nghymru yn ystod y bedwaredd ganrif ar bymtheg, gyda sylw arbennig i "Ryfel y Degwm"' (unpublished PhD thesis, Bangor University, 2017); M. Jones, 'Y lleol a'r cenedlaethol: Rhyfel y Degwm yn Llangwm', *Transactions of the Denbighshire Historical Society*, 57 (2009), pp. 64–82; D. C. Richter, 'The Welsh police, the Home Office, and the Welsh tithe-war of 1886–91', *Welsh History Review*, 12 (1984), pp. 50–75; F. P. Jones, 'Rhyfel y degwm 1886–91', *Transactions of the Denbighshire Historical Society*, 2 (1953), pp. 71–105. For more on the landlord–tenant relationship on smaller estates, see M. Benbough-Jackson, '"Landlord Careless"? Landowners, tenants and agriculture on four estates in west Wales, 1850–75', *Rural History*, 14:1 (2003), pp. 81–98.

[28] J. Davies, *A History of Wales* (London, 1993), pp. 410–11.

[29] D. Lleufer Thomas, *Welsh Land Commission: A Digest of its Report* (London, 1896). For more on the 'land questions' and the Welsh Land Commission, see Howell, 'Land question', pp. 83–110; J. Graham Jones, 'Select Committee or Royal Commission? Wales and "the land question", 1892', *Welsh History Review*, 17 (1994), pp. 205–29.

[30] Howell, *Land and People*, pp. 45–6. Cragoe draws attention to Richard Moore-Colyer's argument concerning the over-emphasis on the detrimental impact of absenteeism; Cragoe, *An Anglican Aristocracy*, p. 16.

[31] Thomas, *Welsh Land Commission*, pp. 456–9.

[32] A tenant farmer in the Vale of Glamorgan stated how land agents had behaved harshly and unjustly towards tenant farmers by increasing rents. Although he gave a

the behalf of their employer, Augustus Brackenbury, who had purchased enclosed land in Cardiganshire. The linguistic barrier between English-speaking land agents and monoglot Welsh tenants also presented problems. Whilst the findings of the Land Commission noted it was unfair to describe land agents in Wales as cruel oppressors, there were clearly systemic issues at play.

Since the early 1970s the study of Irish landed estates, landlordism and the land question has received a new impetus. Indeed, the last decade alone has witnessed a number of important studies including those by, Terence Dooley, Gerard Lyne, Ciarán Reilly and others, which has begun to shift understandings of the role and reputation of landowners, as well as their agents.[33] However, for the most part the careers of Irish land agents still remain buried in the archives of the estates which they served. It is little wonder then that Irish land agents are depicted as being rapacious, dishonest and the villains of the Irish countryside. Social memory is particularly unkind to the agent and his team of estate officials. The oft-quoted nineteenth-century verdict that the 'landlords were sometimes decent men but the agents were devils one and all' is perhaps more typical of how the agents of landed estates were traditionally represented in Irish nationalist historiography or indeed by contemporary commentators, travellers and writers of fiction.[34] These assumptions were drawn largely from works of fiction. Writers such as the celebrated nineteenth-century author William Carleton were particularly condemnatory of agents, believing that 'a history of their conduct would be a black catalogue of dishonesty, oppression and treachery'.[35] Without any defence, these charges 'assumed the status of canon in Irish

number of examples, these were not deemed worthy of note in the report. Thomas, *Welsh Land Commission*, p. 285.

[33] For studies on the role of the Irish land agent, see, for example, Reilly, *Irish Land Agent*; T. Dooley, *The Big Houses and Landed Estates of Ireland: A Research Guide* (Dublin, 2007); W. A. Maguire, The Downshire Estates in Ireland, 1801–1845: The Management of Irish Landed Estates in the Early Nineteenth Century (Oxford, 1972); J. S. Donnelly Jr, *The Land and the People of Nineteenth Century Cork: The Rural Economy and the Land Question* (London, 1975); R. McCarthy, *The Trinity College Estates, 1800–1923: Corporate Management in an Age of Reform* (Dundalk, 1992); G. Lyne, *The Lansdowne Estate in Kerry under W. S. Trench 1849–72* (Dublin, 2001).

[34] Quoted in K. Trant, *The Blessington Estate, 1667–1908* (Dublin, 2004), p. 79. See Postscript for more on the land agent in fiction.

[35] W. Carleton, *The Works of William Carleton* (2 vols, New York, 1880), vol. 1, p. 112; see also M. Chesnutt, *Studies in the Short Stories of William Carleton* (Gothenburg, 1976), pp. 112–13.

history'.[36] From Fenian rhetoric to Land League platforms, land agents as well as landlords were blamed for the social ills of Irish society. This was also reflected in the files of the Irish Folklore Commission gathered in the 1930s and 1940s, which found that agents were remembered as 'mischief makers and always out to make the most out of every situation to feather their own nests'.[37] Tales regarding notorious figures such as Marcus Keane, agent of the Westby and Conyngham estates in County Clare are omnipresent. Indeed, one such account notes how Keane's body was dug up and his coffin thrown outside the walls of the cemetery.[38] In more recent times the avaricious, cruel and oppressive land agent has been portrayed in television and drama.[39] Even Irish children's stories and legends are critical of the agent and landlord.[40]

Land agents themselves left little account or defence of their actions. Only the memoirs of men such as Samuel Hussey and William Steuart Trench offer any defence of this much-vilified position. That one of these men, Hussey, was referred to by a contemporary as 'the most abused man in Ireland' is perhaps evidence of the need to investigate their character afresh.[41] As W. A. Maguire suggested, if we are to truly understand Irish agrarian history, then a proper appreciation of the role of the agent is necessary.[42] Land agents were central to the Irish rural world in the nineteenth century as they dealt with tenants on a daily basis and in most cases were aware of the inherent problems that existed in the countryside.[43] As the County Down landlord, Lord Dufferin argued, 'if the landlord was the father of his tenantry then the agent was their nurse'.[44]

---

[36] W. Crawford, *The Management of a Major Ulster Estate in the Late Eighteenth Century: The Eighth Earl of Abercorn and his Irish Agents* (Dublin, 2001), p. 1.

[37] C. Póirtéir, *Famine Echoes* (Dublin, 1995), p. 216.

[38] Póirtéir, *Famine Echoes*, pp. 222–3.

[39] See, for example, *The Hanging Gale* (TV series, produced by Robert Cooper and James Mitchell. Ireland: BBC Northern Ireland and Irish Film Board, 1995), produced as part of the sesquicentenary commemoration of the Great Famine.

[40] See, for example, F. Trotman, *Irish Folk Tales* (Dublin, 2008), p. 14.

[41] S. M. Hussey, *Reminiscences of an Irish Land Agent* (London, 1904), preface.

[42] Maguire, *Downshire Estates*, p. 183; see also Dooley, *A Research Guide*, p. 222.

[43] Both C. O'Gráda and L. M. Cullen have asserted this; see C. O'Gráda, 'Irish agricultural history: recent research', *Agricultural Historical Review*, 38:2 (1990), p. 164.

[44] Quoted in A. L. Casement, 'The management of landed estates in Ulster in the mid nineteenth century with special reference to the career of John Andrews as agent to the third and fourth Marquesses of Londonderry from 1828 to 1863' (unpublished PhD thesis, Queens University of Belfast, 2002), p. i.

As the case of Ireland illustrates, the management of a landed estate was a complex role and did not simply refer to the collection of rent. Among the other numerous duties land agents performed were the collection of tithes up to c. 1838 (and in some cases beyond), making leases, surveying land, corresponding with the landlord, keeping accounts and allotting work on the demesne. Others were charged with the task of representing the landlord on special committees and as magistrates, organising agricultural shows and instructing tenants on new farming methods. These were onerous tasks and many had neither the qualifications nor the interest to carry them out efficiently. Eric Richards's argument for the Victorian English case that 'some agents had the grace and tact of the landlord' was not often the case in Ireland. Some were patriarchal towards their tenants, while others mirrored Richards's 'rougher breed', who 'managed to tyrannise entire rural populations creating riot and an undying legacy of hatred'.[45]

Now that the existing historiography on the land agent according to national understandings has been outlined, the four key themes that this volume is structured around can be introduced. These themes arose organically from the chapters included here, and we have endeavoured to promote a geographical spread for each, although naturally there is a great deal of overlap, the connections and interactions being made clear throughout.

The first theme interrogates power and its constructions on landed estates, and how land agents instrumentalised power. They occupied a particularly powerful position within the estate framework. They represented the interests of their employer in overseeing the management of the estate; some landowners would offer direct instructions, but more often than not, the agent was expected to exercise their best judgement when acting on their employer's behalf. The power dynamics in the relationship between agent and the wider estate community is explored by David Gent in his chapter on the career of John Henderson, agent to the Earls of Carlisle at their Castle Howard estate, in Yorkshire, from 1827 until the late 1860s. In doing so Gent highlights how the agent, as well as the landlord, could play an influential role in agricultural and commercial improvement. He also illustrates the important point that agents played a role in shaping the communities resident on their estates – the very behaviour of people – in the face of real or imagined threats to the moral and social order of rural society. This was something that

---

[45] E. Richards, 'The land agent', in G. E. Mingay (ed.), *The Victorian Countryside* (London, 1981), vol. 2, pp. 439–56 (quote at p. 439).

exercised Henderson's overseer, James Loch, one of the most influential land agents in Britain in the first half of the nineteenth century, and who appears elsewhere in this volume in his position as commissioner for the Sutherland estates.

To the tenants, the agent was the collector of rent and enforcer of rules. It comes as no surprise therefore that with such influence the agent was generally not a popular figure on the estate, as highlighted in Ewen Cameron's chapter on the Scottish factor at the end of the nineteenth century. Cameron draws attention to the traditional image of the unpopular factor, even when transposed to more unusual contexts. By introducing us to a number of such individuals, Cameron explores the tensions and difficulties facing the agent, but also, in parallel, the tremendous degree of power they held in Highland society. This could encompass political power, and extend beyond the rural, into the urban sphere.

Staying in Scotland, the might of the railway companies, and the restrictions and opportunities they represented for Scottish estates, is explored in John McGregor's chapter. During this period there were opportunities for factors to exercise power and influence at local and national levels, negotiating the demands of their employers with the railway companies. McGregor considers the awareness of rights and obligations within such power dynamics, with the factor very much acting as the middleman.

The second theme considers understandings around the networks, comparisons and differences that geographies created around land agency. How were estates and landed interests managed across the four nations and beyond, and what do the similarities and differences tell us? Estate management was in many cases a fundamentally trans-national endeavour, reflecting the multinational nature of much British and Irish landownership. How new ideas and expertise translated between contexts and how concepts of political economy, imperialism and improvement manifested themselves differently (or not) in different places are the key areas for discussion. Three authors offer different perspectives in this part, each tackling estates which cross different jurisdictions. Fidelma Byrne explores the case study of the Wentworth-Fitzwilliam estates, split between the north of England and Ireland, focusing on the inter-managerial conflict that dogged the land agency across the two locations. It provides us with a stark example of how estates under the same ownership and management systems diversified in terms of economic, social and political focus, with problematic consequences for the land agents trying to direct and manage those processes. Economic diversification came early to the Yorkshire estates in the form of mining interests, and the land agents there had to adapt to this change, managing what was early and innovative technological change, with the financial and social risks that came with that. In contrast, the Irish estates remained dependent upon agricultural activity, of a relatively unimproved type; they also had to battle the horrors of the Great Irish Famine. As Byrne argues, the land agents overseeing these processes were committed to their employer's paternalistic mode of thinking, which while admirable, led to internal fissures which over time widened to reveal the fundamentally flawed management system on the estate.

Rachel Murphy tackles similar themes and geographies in her chapter, examining the management of the estates of the Earl of Courtown, in Cheshire, England and Carlow, Ireland. She interrogates the quite surprising level of differences between how the land agency role was conceived in England and Ireland, what their powers and responsibilities were and how they were perceived. She also unpicks the strata of management that sat below the land agent – the bailiffs and sub-agents – to argue that despite relatively large numbers of personnel, it was extremely difficult to own or manage a large, dispersed estate from a geographical distance, particularly during a period of political upheaval and protest. In this case, the construction of power on the landed estates was personified by the head agents and the bailiffs and sub-agents, and as anti-landlord agitation swept across the Irish estates in the later nineteenth century, they faced the sharp edge of tenant anger.

Finlay McKichan provides the last chapter in this part, a case study in the transnational transfer of land agent skills. Peter Fairbairn was first chief factor on the Seaforth estate in Ross-shire, where his ability, energy and honesty were much admired by his employer. From 1801 he was attorney of the Seaforth cotton plantations in Berbice, the results of which were so disappointing that by 1811 Lord Seaforth for a time considered dismissing him. This chapter compares his performance in Ross-shire and Berbice, examines how far his skills as a land agent were transferable between the two locations and considers how far the problems in Berbice were due to issues beyond his control. The transnational comparison in this case is of particular interest due to the opportunity it provides for a consideration of colonial constructions of power. We are thereby able to think about whether and what the nature of transnational understandings of power were and whether there was any cross-over between land agency in the heart of empire and in the colonial territories themselves. Was estate management the same in Ross-shire and Berbice – and if not, why and in what ways was it different?

The third theme addresses the challenges and catastrophes faced and managed – successfully or not – by land agents in the modern period. These challenges might constitute political, social or economic shifts and difficulties, ranging from Europe's worst nineteenth century peacetime disaster, the Great Irish Famine and its aftermath, to political agitation, rioting and attack – both physical and reputational. No part of the British or Irish isles escaped acute rural pressures in the period covered by this book, and four contributors uncover case studies to explore this theme.

First, Anne Casement discusses the tenant right agitation that afflicted Ulster in the nineteenth century, examining the responses of the Londonderry family and estate as a case study to explore the ways in which land agents reacted to the challenge of agitation for the reform of land tenure. This chapter discusses the resulting management crisis, unparalleled in the career of an agent of twenty-two years' standing, which was not amenable to solution by conventional methods. Although in each part of the British and Irish isles, a crisis might have different roots and expressions, similar themes and questions emerge for the historian: how did land agents respond, and how effectively? Were they flexible enough to adjust to change, or did they make situations worse? Lastly, how and in what ways did their behaviour reflect the needs and interests of their landed employers?

These questions are also explored in Lowri Ann Rees's chapter, taking the analysis to Wales, exploring the Rebecca Riots of the 1840s, a period of intense agitation and strife. This chapter utilises the extensive correspondence of the Middleton Hall land agent, Thomas Herbert Cooke, as he became drawn into upheaval and protest, examining its impact on the estate, and in particular, his role. His correspondence is also revealing of the attitude of a newcomer to the local area, with Cooke critical of the use of the Welsh language in church, the agricultural practices of the tenantry and poor quality of the land he was expected to manage. Whilst he appears as a rather melancholic character, pessimistic and critical, his tendency to worry was completely justified during the summer of 1843, when he witnessed at first hand the Rebecca Riots. This chapter will reveal how the land agent and his employer became targets of Rebecca's wrath, highlighting the difficult position estate middlemen held within society.

Ciarán Reilly's chapter takes us to Ireland and back to the eighteenth century, in order to track the evolution of the land agency profession and underpin discussion of its functionality. It focuses on the management of the 14,000-acre Blundell estate during the period 1700–80, and in particular, the career of father and son combination Henry and John Hatch, agents between them for over fifty years. Their agency of the Blundell estate offers an insight into the complexities and evolution of the business in eighteenth-century Ireland and argues that any simplistic moral analysis is not viable. Eighteenth-century land agents in Ireland – and elsewhere – were largely left to their own devices. Lacking the necessary skills and business acumen, it was hardly surprising that many foundered, or like John Hatch, wished to resign. It was only in the nineteenth century (and by then too late for some) that landlords began to closely scrutinise the management of their estates.

Shaun Evans takes us back to Wales and one of the largest, richest and most controversial of its landed estates: Penrhyn, and the career of Pennant A. Lloyd, land agent for eighteen years for the Douglas-Pennant family. Lloyd was far more than a land manager, however; he negotiated the political priorities of his employer, as well as the enormous slate quarries and their workforces that contributed so much to the family's great wealth. As in other parts of Wales, and the British and Irish isles, issues around language, religion, culture and changing social conditions and expectations all presented Lloyd with a set of sometimes insurmountable challenges. His record and approach in combating these is analysed by Evans in this chapter.

The final theme of the book is that of social memory and the land agent, and two chapters, both using Scotland as their focus, explore the legacies – short, medium and long term – of the reputation of the land agent. Robin Campbell's chapter highlights the power of oral tradition in perpetuating the villainous images of a Scottish land agent in nineteenth-century Argyllshire through the generations to the present day. It explores the criticisms levelled at Campbell's administration of the Duke of Argyll's island estates, which included the forced eviction of local communities, the underlying external influences affecting that policy and the considerable pressures facing Campbell in managing such a large estate. Oral tradition and contemporary sources provide an illustrative insight into this powerful and much-feared man.

Annie Tindley's chapter also deals with one of the great ducal estates of Scotland, that of the Dukes and Earls of Sutherland. By 1861, the Sutherland estates were the largest landed estates in western Europe: covering over one million acres in the county of Sutherland and bolstered by a private family fortune, the Sutherland estates and the ducal family that owned them were one of the great patrician establishments of Victorian Britain. They were, however, haunted by their reputation as clearance landlords, a reputation that intruded on their rarefied London existence, and more pressingly, on relations between them, their estate managers and their tenantry in the north of Scotland. This chapter explores a number of key themes in relation to the drivers and philosophies of estate ownership and management in post-clearance Sutherland.

In a final Postscript part, this discussion of the land agent and social memory is extended into an analysis of the land agent in fiction, a discussion framed by Kirsty Gunn's short story, 'Poor Beasts', exploring the past, present and future of the land agent and the land question. The Postscript also gives an overview of the land agent in modern fiction across the four nations, building on the framework provided by the four core themes of the book.[46]

In conclusion, this book presents an interdisciplinary and transnational picture of the evolving nature of one of the most challenging and challenged roles in British and Irish rural society. Reviled in social memory and popular and fictional accounts, the land agent was nonetheless one of the most powerful tools in the armoury of the British and Irish landed classes and their territorial, political and social dominance in the modern period. As such, the scope of the volume is broad, geographically, chronologically and thematically, so that the wider significance of the land agent is made apparent; not least their continuing influence on contemporary estate management, land use and rural policy, including land reform. Analysis and understandings of the land agent have been somewhat neglected by historians, creating an unhelpful polarisation in the historiography between the figure of the landlord, and the communities of tenants and occupiers of land. This book seeks to understand and unpack the nature, purposes and processes of power in rural society, as mediated by land agents, particularly around the themes of land management, landlord–tenant relations, protest and deference in a four nations context.

---

[46] C. Dakers, 'Land agents: fact and fiction in the long nineteenth century', in Beardmore et al., *Land Agent*, pp. 59–86.

PART I

Power and its Constructions on Landed Estates

1

'Stirring and advancing times': Landlords, Agents and Improvement on the Castle Howard Estate, 1826–66

David Gent

INTRODUCTION

IN LATE AUGUST 1857, ninety men from around the Castle Howard estate in North Yorkshire gathered in a tent outside a local inn. They were there to give a testimonial dinner to John Henderson (c. 1790–1875), the resident agent on the estate since 1826. He was presented with a silver tea service, purchased for £170 by his friends and the estate tenants, to commend 'the advantages which he has personally conferred on the tenantry and others'.[1] Henderson served as agent throughout the ownerships of both George Howard, 6th Earl of Carlisle (1773–1848) and his son George W. F. Howard, 7th Earl of Carlisle (1802–64), the Whig politician better known to historians by his courtesy title of Lord Morpeth.[2] Although his career ultimately came to a discreditable end, for forty years Henderson was a successful agent. His working life is well detailed in the voluminous estate papers, which reveal both the wide range of his activities as an agent and something of his motivations and beliefs.[3] This study explores his multifaceted attempts to 'improve' the estate in conjunction with Lord Morpeth and James Loch, the most prominent estate commissioner of the period, who from 1823 until his death in 1855 remotely supervised all the Howard holdings from his office in London.

The ideal of 'improvement' led to a significant reordering of landed estates in Britain in the eighteenth and nineteenth centuries. To improve

---

[1] *York Herald*, 29 August 1857, p. 10.

[2] In order to avoid confusion, the title of Lord Morpeth is used throughout this chapter to refer to the 7th Earl of Carlisle. References give the correct title for that particular date, with Morpeth becoming 7th Earl of Carlisle in October 1848.

[3] In addition to the activities discussed in this chapter, Henderson also had a key role in shaping garden design at Castle Howard; see C. Ridgway, 'Design and restoration at Castle Howard', in C. Ridgway (ed.), *William Andrews Nesfield (1794–1881): Victorian Landscape Architect* (York, 1996), pp. 39–52.

an estate was to restructure its landscape, to enhance its order and utility; but also, as Daniels and Seymour have noted, to restructure 'the conduct of those who lived in, worked in and looked upon it'.[4] By the early nineteenth century agricultural improvement had become associated with a culture of progress, which celebrated the nation's social, economic, moral, technical and intellectual advancement. Sarah Wilmot and others have shown how the adoption of 'improving' methods on landed estates reflected the aristocracy's involvement in this culture, being viewed as a public-spirited contribution to the development and productivity of the nation.[5] Recent research has, however, also begun to reveal the important contribution land agents made to this process of improvement, through strategic management of estates and encouragement of new methods and techniques.[6] Crucial here has been work illustrating the proactive role of Loch and his subordinates in propelling agricultural change and new forms of industry on the Scottish and English estates of the Dukes of Sutherland, the former including the notorious clearances. Steeped in the culture of the Scottish Enlightenment, Loch regarded improvement as a duty, something that would bring the benefits of progress to backward rural communities.[7]

This study underscores and extends this work. The first half of the chapter illustrates Henderson and Loch's significant role in improving agriculture on the estate through the encouragement of 'high farming' and developments in infrastructure. By the 1840s this was done in

[4] S. Daniels and S. Seymour, 'Landscape design and the idea of improvement, 1730–1900', in R. Dodgshon and R. Butlin (eds), *An Historical Geography of England & Wales* (2nd edn, London, 1990), pp. 487–520 (quote at p. 487).

[5] For the culture and impact of improvement, see S. Wilmot, *'The Business of Improvement': Agriculture and Scientific Culture in Britain, c. 1700–1870* (Reading, 1990); S. Wade Martins, *Farmers, Landlords and Landscapes: Rural Britain, 1720–1870* (Macclesfield, 2004); T. Williamson, *The Transformation of Rural England: Farming and the Landscape, 1700–1870* (Exeter, 2002); J. Finch and K. Giles (eds), *Estate Landscapes: Design, Improvement and Power in the Post-Medieval Landscape* (Woodbridge, 2007).

[6] S. Webster, 'Estate improvement and the professionalisation of land agents on the Egremont estates in Sussex and Yorkshire, 1770–1835', *Rural History*, 18:1 (2007), pp. 47–69; G. Monks, 'Land management: Welbeck and Holkham in the long nineteenth century' (PhD thesis, University of Leicester, 2015).

[7] See A. Tindley, *The Sutherland Estate, 1850–1920* (Edinburgh, 2010); J. Bowen, 'A landscape of improvement: the impact of James Loch, chief agent to the Marquis of Stafford, on the Lilleshall estate, Shropshire', *Midland History*, 35:2 (2010), pp. 191–214; E. Richards, *The Leviathan of Wealth: The Sutherland Fortune in the Industrial Revolution* (London, 1973), especially pp. 25–34 for Loch's views.

conjunction with Lord Morpeth, a man who fully embraced the coming of 'progress' to rural society, enthusing about what he referred to as 'stirring and advancing times'.[8] This work, partly an attempt to secure the Howards' financial position, reflected the centrality of the ethos of improvement in the beliefs of the three men and their strategy for the estate. This was, however, only one of Henderson's responsibilities as agent. He also managed relations with the estate residents. Whilst Carol Beardmore's recent study of the estates of the Marquess of Anglesey has suggested that agents played an essential part in the operation of rural communities, this remains an under-studied aspect of land agency in England in this period.[9]

The second half of the chapter addresses this theme by exploring Henderson and Morpeth's attempts to shape the lives and behaviour of the estate population. Such approaches to estate communities have most commonly been analysed by historians within the framework of early-Victorian paternalism, under which landlords were seen to have a responsibility towards the welfare and conduct of their tenants.[10] In contrast, it will be suggested here that the estate's approach to its community is best understood in the context of ideas about progress and improvement. Morpeth and Henderson pursued a number of projects to improve the morality and living conditions of the estate villagers and worked to remove threats to the estate's moral order. These actions reflected both Morpeth's progressive religious beliefs and anxieties created by perceived immorality and disorder, against a backdrop of rural protest.

IMPROVING THE ESTATE

The Castle Howard estate consisted of just over 13,000 acres on the border of the North and East Ridings of Yorkshire. It encompassed a mixture of

---

[8] *York Herald*, 25 April 1846, p. 7. Lord Morpeth's encouragement of improvement is also detailed in D. Gent, 'The Seventh Earl of Carlisle and the Castle Howard estate: Whiggery, religion and improvement, 1830–1864', *Yorkshire Archaeological Journal*, 82:1 (2010), pp. 315–41.

[9] C. Beardmore, 'The rural estate through the eyes of the land agent: a community in microcosm c. 1812–1844', *Family & Community History*, 19:1 (2016), pp. 17–33.

[10] D. Roberts, *Paternalism in Early Victorian England* (London, 1979), especially pp. 129–48; M. Cragoe, *An Anglican Aristocracy: The Moral Economy of the Landed Estate in Carmarthenshire, 1832–95* (Oxford, 1996); F. M. L. Thompson, *English Landed Society in the Nineteenth Century* (London, 1963), pp. 184–211; Beardmore, 'Rural estate'.

enclosed arable farmland, pasture and productive woodland, in addition to the villages of Welburn, Bulmer, Coneysthorpe, Terrington and Slingsby.[11] Whilst Castle Howard was their main residence, the Howards also owned a London townhouse as well as over 47,000 acres in Cumberland and nearly 18,000 acres around the Northumberland town of Morpeth. In the early 1830s they enjoyed an annual income of around £40,000, with the Yorkshire estate yielding £10,000. Yet this masked considerable outgoings, not least on the colossal debts of the 5th earl, which totalled over £220,000.[12] The financial crisis caused by this profligacy led to Loch's appointment as estate commissioner in 1823, the Howards having been impressed by his work for the Sutherlands. Loch believed he had three key duties: to provide a suitable standard of living for the family; pay off the creditors; and ensure the long-term viability of the estates.[13] He set about overhauling the Howards' finances, cutting their household expenditure and applying improvements to increase the value of their holdings. By the mid-1840s the family's income was £50,000 a year, with the Castle Howard estate bringing in around £15,000 of that total.[14]

Whilst Loch provided strategic oversight of the estates, he left their day-to-day running to resident agents like Henderson, whom he installed at Castle Howard. It is likely that Henderson, like Loch a Scot, was recruited from an agricultural background, as his elder brother was tenant of a large farm in his native Forfarshire.[15] Although regularly reporting to Loch, Henderson's position was one of considerable autonomy, with responsibility for all practical operations on the wider estate as well as the family's accounts. Henderson was, it seems, both energetic and stubborn in his work. The 6th earl had occasion to think that he did 'too much' and was 'resolved upon following his own way', whilst also complaining that Loch was too busy to properly supervise his work. Yet he held a 'good opinion of [Henderson] in several respects' and was generally happy to entrust him and Loch with his estate dealings.[16]

---

[11] Carlisle MSS, Castle Howard [hereafter CH], F5/18/5, 1831 survey of the estate. Papers from this collection are cited by kind permission of the Howard family.

[12] CH/F6/7–8, papers on overall financial position of the Howard estates.

[13] CH/F6/3, James Loch to Lord Morpeth, 15 May 1836.

[14] CH/F5/5, Castle Howard accounts; CH/F6/7, estimate of receipts from estates (1844).

[15] This is evident from census returns and the notice of the marriage of Henderson's niece in the *Malton Messenger*, 11 June 1859.

[16] CH/F6/3, 6th Earl of Carlisle to Loch, 25 December 1835; CH/J18/1/48/41, Carlisle to Georgiana Carlisle, 11 September [1833].

As a result of his father's incapacitating illness, Lord Morpeth took increasing control of the estate from the early 1840s, inheriting in 1848. Morpeth was a highly engaged proprietor: in 1843, for instance, he reminded Henderson to let the Widow Coates 'have the bit of ground with the apple trees', a level of detail surely above most landlords' notice.[17] Yet he was also a busy politician in Westminster and, from 1855, Dublin as Lord Lieutenant of Ireland and hence often absent from Yorkshire. In 1846 Morpeth explained that he would route all estate business through Henderson, whilst emphasising that he reserved the right to involve himself in matters directly.[18] This vague arrangement relied on Henderson drawing attention to matters of importance, with the two men's correspondence consequently tending to focus on issues that had caught Morpeth's interest rather than on operational detail. The upshot was that Henderson was vital to the estate: Loch noted to Morpeth that he was nearly indispensable due to his 'knowledge of all those parts of your affairs that require the most attention'.[19]

One of Henderson's main responsibilities was to act as an intermediary between the Howards and their eighty or so tenant farmers. Land agents were expected to represent the views of tenants without compromising the interests of their employers.[20] Henderson periodically advocated rent reduction on the tenants' behalf in times of economic distress. One such attempt in 1835 was resisted by the 6th earl, who noted that 'resident stewards always recommend the reduction of rents, it is more agreeable for them to be well with the tenants', forcing Loch to defend Henderson's sense of duty. Loch seems to have pressed on regardless, for the 6th earl ('lost in surprise') was forced to command him to cease reductions. As Loch explained, adjustment of rent was a necessary response to poor economic conditions that were leading 'respectable' tenants to quit. As the estate could not attract new tenants to replace them without an expensive outlay on the farms, to prevent reduction was self-defeating.[21] This episode aside, Henderson was generally able to secure a response from the Howards to tenant demands. A speaker at his testimonial praised that he had been 'open to the cry of distress ... ever ready to administer relief'. In reply, Henderson noted

---

[17] CH/F5/3, Lord Morpeth to John Henderson, 14 June [1843].

[18] CH/F5/3, Morpeth to Henderson, 14 October 1846.

[19] CH/J19/24, Loch to 7th Earl of Carlisle, 26 January 1849.

[20] Beardmore, 'Rural estate', p. 20.

[21] CH/F6/3, Carlisle to Loch, December 1835 and undated; Loch to Carlisle, December 1835; Loch to Morpeth, 15 May 1836, November 1836.

that he had 'endeavoured . . . to do what I considered was right, between landlord and tenant'.[22]

This flexibility over rent was consistent with Loch and Henderson's aim to raise the estate's value through agricultural improvement. By the 1830s this had become associated with 'high farming': a high-input and high-output system involving an increased use of manufactured and imported material such as fertilisers, oilcake for fodder, drainage and more generally the application of new scientific knowledge and technology.[23] Contemporary guides to estate management emphasised the importance of tenant farmers in this process. High farming required investment from tenants and a willingness to adopt new practices, something felt to be unlikely if landlords did not provide their tenants with a sense of security in their lease. As the application of improving methods would ultimately benefit the landlord by increasing the worth of the land, it was argued that it was sensible for agents to take a long-term view and avoid the folly of driving good tenants away in times of distress.[24]

However, not all the Castle Howard farmers were felt capable of such improvement. In 1836 Loch noted his determination to change as many tenancies each year as the Howards' precarious financial position allowed.[25] He had drawn from his work for the Sutherlands the lesson that improvement required tenants who were 'active, industrious and skilful' and 'intelligent'.[26] In emphasising such qualities he was not alone. The mid-century land agent J. L. Morton, for instance, argued that it was vital to have tenants who were both open-minded enough to try new methods and sufficiently skilled and resourceful to succeed in using them. In this, Morton felt, agents had to exercise 'great care' when selecting tenants.[27] Henderson seems to have been guided by such views. His record of changes on the estate between 1845 and 1854 shows that he offered tenancies to new farmers he considered to be 'industrious',

[22] *York Herald*, 29 August 1857, p. 10.

[23] Williamson, *Transformation of Rural England*, pp. 139–54.

[24] See, for instance, J. L. Morton, *The Resources of Estates, being a Treatise on the Agricultural Improvement and General Management of Landed Property* (London, 1858), pp. 9–19, 100; D. Low, *On Landed Property and the Economy of Estates* (London, 1844), pp. 5–16.

[25] CH/F6/3, Loch to Morpeth, 15 May 1836.

[26] J. Loch, *An Account of the Improvements on the Estates of the Marquess of Stafford in the Counties of Stafford and Salop on the Estate of Sutherland, with Remarks* (London, 1820), appendix II, pp. 101–2.

[27] Morton, *Resources of Estates*, pp. 9, 119–21.

'good manager[s]' and of 'active habits', characteristics he linked to improvements on their farms.[28]

Whilst setting the conditions for improvement by tenants, Loch believed that landlords' 'proper line of duty' was to encourage this through capital investment.[29] James Bowen has shown how he introduced new farm buildings on the Sutherland estate in Staffordshire in the 1820s, designed to attract tenants with the resources to spend on improvement and laid out to accommodate improving methods.[30] The Castle Howard accounts indicate that regular expenditure was applied to farm buildings: for instance, £777 was spent on such work at Slingsby in 1840.[31] Yet these sums were far more restrained than the equivalent expenditure for the super-wealthy Sutherlands. Loch noted in 1836 that a 'large outlay on buildings' was not practical given the Howards' relatively constrained finances.[32] Henderson could complain that the farm buildings were a barrier to agricultural improvement as late as 1858.[33]

The main area of investment Loch prioritised on the Howard estates was drainage. He and Henderson were both strong proponents of drainage, which was widely seen as a necessary basis for other improving methods: 'the first principle of agriculture', as Henderson put it.[34] Jon Finch has detailed how the two men developed irrigation around Castle Howard in the late 1820s.[35] In the 1830s the estate also supplied tiles for tenants to use in under-draining.[36] After success on the Northumberland estate, Loch pressed the case for greater expenditure on draining at Castle Howard, but the 6th earl proved unreceptive, doubting its profitability on his cornfields.[37] From 1846 there was, however, a step-change in investment in this area. This reflected Morpeth's increasing control of the estate. He had become versed in the benefits of drainage through

[28] CH/F5/18/12, account of changes on the estate (1854).

[29] Loch, *Account of the Improvements*, appendix II, pp. 101–2.

[30] Bowen, 'A landscape of improvement'.

[31] CH/F5/5, Castle Howard annual accounts.

[32] CH/F6/3, Loch to Morpeth, 15 May 1836.

[33] CH/F5/3, Henderson to Carlisle, 5 May 1858.

[34] J. Henderson, 'Report upon the Rye and Derwent Drainage', *Journal of the Royal Agricultural Society*, 14 (1853), pp. 129–42 (quote at p. 129); Loch, *Account of the Improvements, passim*.

[35] J. Finch, 'Pallas, Flora and Ceres: landscape priorities and improvement on the Castle Howard estate, 1699–1880', in Finch and Giles (eds), *Estate Landscapes*, pp. 19–37.

[36] CH/F6/3, Loch to Carlisle, 5 December 1839; CH/F5/5, Castle Howard annual accounts.

[37] CH/F6/1, Loch to Carlisle, 17 May 1836; Carlisle to Loch, 12 November 1841.

managing Crown lands as First Commissioner of Woods and Forests in Lord Russell's government and by serving as one of the Commissioners who administered the 1846 Public Money Drainage Act. He exploited this Act to obtain a £10,000 loan for his Yorkshire and Northumberland estates in 1848. Henderson used this to construct a set of 'deep drains', drawing on the advice of the leading drainage engineer Josiah Parkes.[38]

This loan worked in tandem with another development secured by Morpeth in Parliament: the Rye and Derwent Drainage Act of 1846. This Act allowed for the purchase and removal of mill dams along these two rivers, a response to flooding which regularly devastated the crops of the Howards' tenants near Slingsby as well as those of other local landowners such as the Earl Fitzwilliam. Henderson was the inspiration behind this legislation, a product of his repeated attempts from the late 1820s to get the region's landowners to coalesce on this matter. He was also a leading actor on the committee empowered by the Act, working closely with Fitzwilliam's agent. He then contributed a detailed account of his work to the *Journal of the Royal Agricultural Society*. Although the motive behind all this drainage was partly financial – estate papers suggest that the drained land increased in value and yielded higher rent – Henderson downplayed any economic motives in his account, instead presenting the work as a community-spirited act of 'great public utility'.[39]

In contributing to the Royal Agricultural Society, Henderson was participating in the main contemporary forum championing 'high farming', drainage and the application of scientific principles to agriculture.[40] Henderson positioned his work within this movement, beginning his article with a discourse on modern knowledge of the management of rivers and explaining that he had applied 'the deductions of scientific agriculture'.[41] Morpeth was likewise an enthusiastic advocate of this scientific approach. In 1845 he founded the York Yeoman School, which provided a moral and technical education to the sons of local farmers. One of its aims was to promote the uptake of new agricultural methods, with Morpeth arguing that 'new scientific views' and 'recent discoveries and experiments' made this vitally important. The Yeoman School was a product of Morpeth's leadership of York's philanthropic culture, being

---

[38] CH/F5/91, drainage papers.

[39] CH/F5/2, Henderson to W. Allen [Fitzwilliam's agent], 17 November 1829; Henderson, 'Derwent Drainage', p. 131; CH/F5/91, drainage papers.

[40] Wilmot, *Business of Improvement, passim.*

[41] Henderson, 'Derwent Drainage', p. 129.

directly connected to an Anglican teacher training college in the city of which he was the chief patron. Morpeth sought subscriptions from other members of Yorkshire's landed elite, presenting the initiative as a benevolent contribution to local agriculture.[42] The Yeoman School rather assumed that young farmers could not obtain the knowledge necessary for agricultural improvement on their family farms. The notion that farmers would not take up improving methods without education and leadership from enlightened superiors was prevalent in the movement for agricultural improvement in the first half of the century.[43]

On the estate farmers were educated in new practices through the showcasing of new techniques and methods at the 1,200-acre Castle Howard Home Farm, under Henderson's management. Home farms were seen as an important way in which land agents could spread knowledge of improving methods.[44] Henderson was particularly involved in the selective breeding of livestock, especially Shorthorn cattle, tapping into something of a craze for pedigree Shorthorns among the elite. This fashion has been seen to reflect landlords' eagerness to demonstrate their 'improving' credentials.[45] At Castle Howard, however, it was Henderson who was the driving force. The 6th earl was sceptical about the profitability of Henderson's 'fancies', noting in 1835 that 'I see from the York Paper he has been occupied with fathering an ox – his farm accounts will require a close investigation'.[46] Yet by 1839 Henderson was able to sell his stock for over £5,000, which he applied to reduce the Howards' debt. The 6th earl conceded that his 'success is very great'.[47] Henderson also permitted tenant farmers to breed their own animals with his herd, producing larger and more productive cattle. His testimonial praised his 'exertions' in this area and pointed to the pride felt by tenants in the 'noble' blood of their livestock: indeed, the tea service presented to Henderson on this occasion was symbolically topped with a model of a Shorthorn.[48]

---

[42] CH/J19/1/111/77, York Yeoman School papers; speech reported in *Morning Chronicle*, 3 February 1845, pp. 2–3.

[43] See Wilmot, *Business of Improvement*, pp. 40–6.

[44] Morton, *Resources of Estates*, p. 9.

[45] J. R. Walton, 'The diffusion of the improved Shorthorn breed of cattle in Britain during the eighteenth and nineteenth centuries', *Transactions of the Institute of British Geographers*, 9:1 (1984), pp. 22–36.

[46] CH/F6/3, Carlisle to Loch, 25 December 1835.

[47] CH/F6/3, Loch to Carlisle, 3 January 1839; Carlisle to Loch, 10 September 1839.

[48] *York Herald*, 29 August 1857, p. 10.

Beyond stockbreeding, Henderson also used the Home Farm to encourage the use of other modern practices. He maintained an agricultural laboratory known as 'The Manure' where he conducted experiments in fertilisers. One trial in 1843 involved the addition of sulphuric acid to other chemicals.[49] Henderson was thus directly participating in the practice of scientific agriculture, engaging in the field of agricultural chemistry in its infancy. He may have taken inspiration here from the Yorkshire Agricultural Society, which encouraged this practice at a very early stage. Morpeth was a patron of the Society and Henderson regularly attended its shows to exhibit his cattle.[50] Progress in adopting fertilisers on the estate may have been slow: one correspondent in 1850 suggested that tenants were reluctant to use nitrates for fear that Henderson would raise their rent.[51] Yet there is some evidence to suggest that Henderson was successful. In 1845 an account of Slingsby recorded that 'new systems of agriculture', including fertilisers and threshing machines, had been 'extensively introduced' during his time as agent.[52] By 1858 Henderson could assure Morpeth that the estate was the equal to any in its farming practices. He took credit for establishing the use of seed drills and double-moulded ploughs by distributing this equipment among tenants, reporting that this had led to the introduction of turnip cultivation.[53] As this shows, the estate promoted the use of new agricultural technology. At least one threshing machine was purchased by Henderson in the 1830s, whilst he and Morpeth bought a reaping machine in 1854. Despite judging the latter an 'impractical ... failure', Morpeth nevertheless found it 'ingenious'.[54] Such technology could be adopted not because it was practical, but because it exemplified modernity.[55]

The estate aimed to further stimulate farming by developing the com-

[49] CH/J19/8/1, Morpeth diary, 11 October 1843, 27 December 1843.

[50] V. Hall, *A History of the Yorkshire Agricultural Society 1837–1987* (London, 1987). For attendance at the Society's shows, see reports in *York Herald*, 1 September 1838; *Hull Packet*, 5 August 1842; *Leeds Intelligencer*, 4 August 1855.

[51] CH/F5/3, 'A Traveller' to Carlisle, November 1850.

[52] Rev. W. Walker, *Some Account of the Parish and Village of Slingsby in Yorkshire* (York, 1845), p. 7.

[53] CH/F5/3, Henderson to Carlisle, 5 May 1858.

[54] CH/F5/2, Henderson to Mr Crosskill, 19 September 1838; CH/19/8/31, 7th Earl Carlisle diary, 8 September 1854.

[55] On this theme, see the account of the adoption of similarly erratic technology in A. Tindley and A. Wodehouse, 'The role of social networks in agricultural innovation: the Sutherland reclamations and the Fowler steam plough, c. 1855–c. 1885', *Rural History*, 25:2 (2014), pp. 203–22.

mercial infrastructure of agriculture in the region. Henderson played an important role in establishing new cattle and wool fairs at Malton, the nearest market town, in 1845. He and Lord Morpeth also attended the opening of the Malton corn exchange in 1846 (founded by Earl Fitzwilliam), with Morpeth waxing lyrical that the many 'signs of improvement' in the district were representative of national progress.[56] These two initiatives were seen to allow the region's farmers to exploit the opportunities offered by railway development in the region, in which the estate again played a key part. The 5th and 6th earls had been pioneering developers of railways in Cumberland, whilst Castle Howard had a station on the York to Scarborough line from 1845.[57] Morpeth continued this tradition by founding, in 1845, the Malton and Driffield Junction Railway Company, which aimed to produce a line linking these two towns and ultimately Newcastle to Hull. It was presented as a boon to local farmers, offering up new markets and supplies.[58] Like the Yeoman School, this attempt to develop the region's economy reflected Morpeth's sense of duty and leadership of local society: he noted that he never invested in railways except where 'I feel an interest in the district'.[59] Henderson became a director of the Company, regularly attending meetings of its Board.[60] It is unclear how much he invested, but sums of £1,000 for other directors were not uncommon. Sadly for Henderson, the Company had vastly underestimated the cost and difficulty of the project. In 1848 it attempted to resolve these troubles by calling in liabilities imposed on shareholders. This must have been a large financial blow as Henderson, facing 'ruin', had to plead with Morpeth to deduct his debts from his salary. Estate papers indicate he was paid just £300 a year in the mid-1850s; likely the result of this episode, for this was a very low salary for an agent.[61] The line was not completed until 1853, and it is unlikely that Henderson saw a return on his investment.

[56] *York Herald*, 10 May 1845, p. 8; 25 April 1846, p. 7.

[57] B. Webb and D. Gordon, *Lord Carlisle's Railways* (Lichfield, 1978).

[58] The details of the Company provided here are taken from W. Burton, *The Malton and Driffield Junction Railway* (Halifax, 1997), pp. 5–24.

[59] CH/J19/8/9, Morpeth diary, 3 November 1845.

[60] Reports of the Company's meetings in *York Herald*, 6 December 1845, p. 7; 29 August 1846, p. 7; 16 April 1853, p. 7. See Chapter 3 in this volume by John McGregor for more detail on land agents and railways.

[61] CH/F5/116, Henderson to Carlisle, 5 December 1848; CH/H1/1/24, servants' wages.

THE ESTATE COMMUNITY

Henderson's work on the agricultural and economic aspects of estate management was just one part of his role as agent. He also acted as the representative of the Howards in dealings with the estate community, which comprised over 500 households and 2,600 people. Henderson included not just tenants but also freeholders within these figures, considering both to come within the boundaries of the estate.[62] The majority of the estate populace were labourers, the elderly or widows, leasing little more than a humble cottage and a small plot of land.[63] The Howards felt a strong duty of care to these 'cottagers', granting nominal rents alongside free coal, wood, clothing, milk and ale and pensions for many of the poorest villagers.[64] Morpeth supplemented this charity with his personal attention, touring the villages and visiting the sick. This reflected the sense of duty he felt as a landlord, but also, and primarily, as a highly committed Christian whose faith dominated his actions.[65]

Henderson helped to discharge the Howards' duties to the community. His testimonial noted that he had performed 'many kind and considerate acts' at the family's behest.[66] He certainly had a high awareness about the circumstances of families on the estate. In 1845 he compiled an extensive survey for Morpeth listing detailed information about the size and sources of income of each household, alongside a judgement as to whether they were deserving of charity.[67] This knowledge was built not only through Henderson's role as agent but also his membership of the Malton Poor Law Union (a post he filled alongside Morpeth). David Spring has suggested this was a common position for land agents, encouraging them to become guardians of morality within their districts.[68] Henderson kept a close watch on the conduct of the estate villagers and was prepared to take severe steps with those he saw as guilty of disorderly or immoral behaviour. We find, for instance, that he used legal measures to ensure that a 'vagabond named Potter' left his cottage (he was 'a disgrace to the estate'); removed an 'idle, drunken' cottager

---

[62] CH/F5/98, survey of the estate (1845); Henderson to Loch, 27 July 1854.

[63] CH/F5/98, survey of the estate (1845).

[64] CH/F5/5, Castle Howard annual accounts; CH/F5/30/1, rent rolls; CH/F5/96, papers relating to village charities.

[65] Gent, 'Seventh Earl of Carlisle', pp. 326–8.

[66] *York Herald*, 29 August 1857, p. 10.

[67] CH/F5/98, survey of the estate (1845).

[68] CH/N, civil administration papers; D. Spring, *The English Landed Estate in the Nineteenth Century: Its Administration* (Baltimore, 1963), pp. 119–20.

from the hamlet of Ganthorpe; and spent years trying to persuade a family to quit on the grounds that they were 'not the most reputable people', ultimately resorting to paying them £60.[69] In 1836 he worked to remove the pauper Rose Blakey, a 'base strumpet' whose house in Bulmer ('a scene of vice and immorality') had reportedly been 'the ruin of many very decent young men'. Blakey had allegedly also encouraged poaching on the estate, and Henderson remained worried about 'poachers and disorderly characters' amidst the cottagers into the 1850s.[70] In similar vein, in 1837 he endeavoured to prevent a beer house at Bulmer from obtaining a spirit licence on the grounds that it was a 'harbour for all sorts of wicked and disorderly persons'.[71] These can all be seen as attempts to address perceived dangers to the stability, propriety and order of the estate.

Thus far, the estate's relationship with its resident community appears highly paternalist: authoritarian, controlling, but guided by a strong sense of responsibility. David Roberts, for one, has seen Morpeth as a characteristically paternalist landlord.[72] Yet Morpeth in fact rejected contemporary expressions of paternalism such as the 'Young England' group as being too backward looking and 'nostalgic', at odds with national progress.[73] The background to community relations on the estate can arguably be more immediately located in the reaction to the 'Captain Swing' movement: the spate of rioting, incendiarism and machine-breaking that swept rural England in 1830 in protest at underemployment, low wages and restrictions on poor relief and customary uses of land. Although largely focused in the South, there were a number of acts of protest in the North. The latter part of 1830 saw rick-burning and riots around the city of Carlisle, close to the Howards' Cumberland estate. From 1830 to early 1831 there were also several incidents of incendiarism, threatening letters and the destruction of threshing machines in the East and North Ridings, some not far from Castle Howard. Although it is doubtful that these acts were connected

[69] CH/F5/3, Henderson to Carlisle, 2 November 1855; CH/F5/18/12, observations by Henderson on changes on the estate 1845–1854; see also A. Tindley, '"Actual pinching and suffering": estate responses to poverty in Sutherland, 1845–1886', *Scottish Historical Review*, 90:2 (2011), pp. 236–56.
[70] CH/F5/2, Henderson to Mr Lewis, 17 November 1836; CH/F5/118, papers relating to the case of Thomas Coates, 1853–4.
[71] CH/F5/2, Henderson to Rev. W. Preston, 30 August 1837.
[72] Roberts, *Paternalism*, pp. 232–6.
[73] G. W. F. Howard, 7th Earl of Carlisle, *Lectures and Addresses in Aid of Popular Education* (London, 1852), p. 79.

to the movement in the South, they were certainly associated in the York press with the threat of 'Swing'.[74]

The Howards were highly aware of these events, both as landlords and through their wider political roles. The 6th earl was Lord Lieutenant of the East Riding and a member of the Cabinet that suppressed the protests, whilst Morpeth, then Member of Parliament for Yorkshire, spoke in the Commons in support of the repressive special commissions established to try the Southern protestors.[75] The family's agents, too, reacted. Warned by an alarmed Loch to be on guard against incendiarism, Henderson consulted the magistrates on how best to address disorder, but decided not to take measures such as forming a band of special constables or otherwise evince any 'distrust in the working classes', whom he felt were 'here more comfortable than they have been for some time'.[76] Morpeth likewise noted to Loch that, although some of their neighbours had been 'scorched', Henderson had offered reassurance as to the 'disposition' of the Castle Howard tenants.[77] The estate thus reacted to the prospect of unrest by putting faith in the stability of its community: as the 6th earl put it to Loch, 'if the population be sound, the alarm need not be so great'.[78]

Nevertheless, although never reaching the heights of 1830, acts of protest, often covert, remained endemic in rural England into the 1850s. At times these directly affected Howard lands. In 1834 rails surrounding plantations on the Cumberland estate were pulled down in a dispute over enclosure. There were also a number of suspected incendiary fires on farms in the East and North Ridings across the 1830s and 40s, including, in 1838, an alleged incident at Appleton-le-Street, within the Castle Howard estate. These were acts which directly threatened the process of 'improvement'. Incendiarism in particular was feared, constituting a direct threat to farmers' livelihoods.[79] In this context,

[74] K. Navickas, *Protest and the Politics of Space and Place, 1789–1848* (Manchester, 2016), pp. 251–76; *York Herald*, 11 December 1830, p. 3.

[75] Hansard, *Parliamentary Debates* (HC), Third Series, 8 February 1831, vol. II, cols 295–6.

[76] CH/F6/1, Henderson to Loch, 11 December 1830 (emphasis in original).

[77] CH/F6/3, Morpeth to Loch, 6 January [by internal context early 1831].

[78] CH/F6/3, Carlisle to Loch, 19 January 1831.

[79] Navickas, *Protest*, p. 264; *York Herald*, 7 April 1838, p. 2. Other alleged incidents of incendiarism reasonably close to Castle Howard are recorded in the *York Herald*, 24 October 1835, p. 2 (Murton, near York); 14 April 1838, p. 3 (Market Weighton); 2 March 1839, p. 2 (Driffield); 6 February 1841, p. 3 (Easingwold); 23 October 1841, p. 3 (Grimston, near York); 4 May 1844, p. 6 (Stillington). For the

Henderson's concern to uphold the stability of the estate and rid it of 'disorderly' characters becomes more explicable.

The primary influence of 'Swing' on Castle Howard was, however, a more benign one. It helped convince Morpeth of the need for the landed elite to work to reform the lives of the working classes and give them opportunities for moral and social advancement. On this, he argued, the 'tranquillity and prosperity' of the country depended.[80] In the 1830s he became a leading patron of the Labourers' Friend Society, part of a national movement to provide allotments to labourers formed in a reaction to 'Swing'. The Society highly appealed to progressive aristocrats, holding out the prospect that rural social problems could be resolved through the benevolent encouragement of self-improvement.[81] Morpeth representatively argued that allotments would reduce reliance on poor relief, encourage independence and industriousness and tackle immorality and drunkenness by offering an alternative to the alehouse.[82] In 1832 he duly instructed Henderson to construct allotments in the estate villages. Henderson reported that they had a beneficial effect on tenants' 'industry', noting that 'it is not easy to imagine a more happy, contented or, comparatively, a more comfortable peasantry than on this Estate'.[83] Yet, as we have already seen, the reality of life around Castle Howard could be rather messier and less decorous than this rosy picture suggests. The impression of a satisfied estate population was shattered in 1844 when an unknown protagonist set fire to the wheat stacks belonging to William Brigham, the leading tenant farmer at Slingsby. Morpeth recorded 'great concern' at this event in his diary.[84]

The allotment project was the first of a number of initiatives promoted by Morpeth with the aim of reforming the behaviour and social condition of the labouring classes. In the 1840s such reforms dominated

ongoing practice and fear of incendiarism, see C. Griffin, *Protest, Politics and Work in Rural England, 1700–1850* (Basingstoke, 2014), pp. 110–17.

[80] Speech reported in *Proceedings of the Labourers' Friend Society at its First Public Meeting* (London, 1832), pp. 4–6.

[81] J. Burchardt, *The Allotment Movement in England, 1793–1873* (Woodbridge, 2002), pp. 51–94.

[82] *Proceedings of the Labourers' Friend Society* (1832), pp. 4–6; speech reported in *Morning Chronicle*, 20 March 1834, p. 4.

[83] CH/J19/1/6/22, Henderson to Morpeth [n.d.]; CH/F5/2, Henderson to Morpeth, 4 January 1832.

[84] CH/J19/8/4, Morpeth diary, 10 August 1844. If this was, as Morpeth thought, a deliberate act, the reasons for it are unknown. Speculatively, given their introduction to Slingsby, Brigham likely used a threshing machine, something that led farmers to be targeted elsewhere.

his actions as a politician, philanthropist and – more importantly here
– landlord. This reforming spirit reflected his religious beliefs. Raised
as an evangelical, Morpeth felt that man had an inherent tendency
towards sin, corrupting both the self and others. Yet he also became
convinced that such sin could be overcome. He took from incarnational
theology (which stresses the humanity of Christ) the idea that mankind
might reach an almost divine level of moral and social advancement.[85]
Instances of immorality and disorder concerned Morpeth because they
prevented this progress by exercising a negative influence on others: the
'mass of the population', he warned, was 'too likely to be corrupted by
evil associations and bad companionship'.[86] For Morpeth, progress was
best achieved within an organic society in which each person worked to
improve himself and others. There was, he thought, 'scarcely anything
that might not be attained' if only each person could 'rise up to what
he might be' and 'aid the general welfare and advancement of his spe-
cies'.[87] At Castle Howard, he worked with Henderson to pursue such
improvement in three main areas: education, sanitation and housing.[88]

   The Castle Howard estate contained a number of schools established
by the Howard family. Morpeth was a keen patron, doubling expenditure on schooling during his ownership and founding new schools in
Slingsby and Welburn.[89] Schooling was important to him partly because
it helped the poor to access the Gospel: his papers include an account
of his distribution of Bibles to the estate cottagers in 1843, an exercise
which he simultaneously used to check their literacy.[90] As Morpeth's
representative, Henderson exercised oversight of the schools. In the
1840s this led him to become embroiled in a long-running dispute
between the Rev. Walker of Slingsby and the village schoolmistress,
whom Walker attempted to dismiss: an affair which caused 'turmoil' in
the village. Henderson believed that Walker did not adequately supervise the school and his intervention seems to have earnt his enmity,
as Morpeth felt it likely that Walker was behind an anonymous letter

   [85] See D. Gent, 'Aristocratic Whig politics in early-Victorian Yorkshire: Lord
Morpeth and his world' (PhD thesis, University of York, 2010).
   [86] Howard, *Lectures and Addresses*, p. 95.
   [87] Howard, *Lectures and Addresses*, p. 61.
   [88] Beyond the activities listed here, Morpeth also built a church in the village
at Welburn and constructed a reformatory for juvenile criminals on the estate; see
Gent, 'Seventh Earl of Carlisle'.
   [89] CH/F5/5, Castle Howard annual accounts; CH/J19/8/21, 7th Earl Carlisle
diary, 12 September 1849; CH/J19/8/33, Carlisle diary, 16 November 1855.
   [90] CH/J19/7, papers on distribution of Bibles, 1843.

complaining about his conduct as agent.[91] Walker's involvement arose from the fact that early-Victorian schools were as much sites of moral and religious instruction as places for education in reading and writing. Morpeth was a firm believer in the idea that school staff would positively mould the behaviour of their charges, believing that they trained 'the rural population to habits of industry, sobriety and order'.[92] Henderson seems to have shared this belief, hoping that one schoolmaster would work a 'great reformation' in the villages.[93]

Morpeth also focused his attention on living conditions within the villages, taking periodic tours of the estate to check on this personally. Henderson traced these inspections to 1845, when Morpeth began to take 'a greater interest . . . in the social condition of the resident population'.[94] He was particularly interested in the health of the cottagers. A response to all too common incidents of disease on the estate, this also reflected his political interest in public health. He was responsible for the pioneering 1848 Public Health Act and thereafter headed the General Board of Health, working closely with the sanitary reformer Edwin Chadwick. Soon after Morpeth inherited he noted that he was 'anxious about the sanitary condition of the villages' and would see it as a 'personal discredit' to learn of 'fever' in them. This, he ordered Henderson and Loch, was a priority for expenditure, an issue upon which his agents should take 'ingenious steps'. Henderson quickly commenced this work, hoping to make a 'great improvement'.[95] At Morpeth's instigation he replaced the 'unwholesome pond' at Terrington with a healthier water supply; identified and removed 'nuisance' smells then thought to carry disease; and encouraged vaccination among tenants.[96] He likely needed no encouragement in this work, for in June 1847 two of his children died from 'fever'. Poignantly, only months later Morpeth instructed him to implement regulations to avoid typhus.[97]

---

[91] CH/F5/2, Henderson to Morpeth, 13 March 1845; Morpeth to Henderson, 3 March 1845, 15 May 1847; CH/J19/8/24, Carlisle diary, 20 November 1850.

[92] CH/J19/1/63/93, script for a speech to schoolmasters, 1856.

[93] CH/F5/3, Henderson to Morpeth, 14 January 1841.

[94] CH/F5/98, Henderson to Loch, 27 July 1854.

[95] CH/F5/3, Carlisle to Henderson, 3 November 1848; Henderson to Carlisle, 14 November 1858; CH/F6/1, Carlisle to Loch, 7 November 1848.

[96] CH/F5/3, Carlisle to Henderson, 3 November 1848, 17 October 1854; CH/F5/98, estate survey (1854), remarks on Terrington; CH/C28/10, 'List of Nuisance Smells' (1853).

[97] CH/J18/1/44/1, Georgiana Carlisle to Morpeth, June 1847; CH/F5/3, Morpeth to Henderson, 29 September 1847.

Morpeth also directed Henderson's attention to housing. For instance, in 1854 he remarked that a set of houses at Terrington was 'wretched, and not creditable to the village, to me, or to you'. A wounded Henderson explained that the houses in question were not, in fact, his property. As he pointed out, the estate expended large sums on cottage repairs, typically over £500 each year.[98] Nevertheless, Morpeth ordered that further investment should be regularly applied 'to the improvement of the villages'.[99] Although it was widely accepted that overcrowded cottages encouraged the spread of disease, this process of improvement also had wider ends. Henderson paid attention to the aesthetic of the cottages. For instance, he constructed new cottages at Slingsby which he hoped would make a 'great improvement to the look' of the village.[100] Morpeth's interest in the cottages also likely had a moral purpose. It was a commonplace among the public health movement, most forcefully articulated by Chadwick, that overcrowded housing encouraged bad moral habits such as intemperance, incest, prostitution and violence.[101] As a philanthropist Morpeth was actively involved in a number of moralistic associations which sought to improve the housing of the working classes for precisely this reason; he also asked Chadwick's advice when constructing new cottages in Northumberland in 1849.[102] It is thus probable that building at Castle Howard was influenced by these ideas. To improve housing on the estate was, by extension, to improve its people.

CONCLUSION

The conclusion to Henderson's career was an ignominious one. In 1866 he was dismissed for misappropriation of funds. Speculatively, this may have been the product of the financial difficulties he faced through his poor railway investments.[103] As Annie Tindley has detailed in a Scottish context, land agency was a difficult profession; it was

[98] CH/F5/98, Henderson to Carlisle, replies to comments arising from inspection of the estate; CH/F5/5, Castle Howard annual accounts.

[99] CH/F5/3, Carlisle to Henderson, 8 November 1854.

[100] CH/F5/98, estate survey, remarks on Slingsby cottages (1854).

[101] C. Hamlin, *Public Health and Social Justice in the Age of Chadwick: Britain, 1800–1854* (Cambridge, 1998), pp. 165–78.

[102] Gent, 'Aristocratic Whig politics', pp. 171–2; Chadwick Papers (University College London, Special Collections), 1055, V, fo. 578, 7th Earl of Carlisle to Edwin Chadwick, 9 April 1849.

[103] Ridgway, 'Design and restoration', p. 48.

not uncommon for agents' careers to collapse in mental or physical breakdown or due to deliberate or unintentional mismanagement.[104] Henderson's dismissal should not overshadow the contribution he had made to the estate. This study has shown that he and Loch helped to create the conditions for agricultural improvement at Castle Howard, both through strategic management in areas such as tenant relations and investment and by directly encouraging improving methods. Whilst this process was strongly encouraged by Lord Morpeth as he took control of Castle Howard in the 1840s, this was building on work already started by his agents. This serves to confirm recent historiography emphasising the important role of land agents in 'improvement' in this period. Henderson's active involvement in areas such as drainage, fertilisers and stockbreeding indicates that the culture of improvement belonged to agents as much as aristocrats. Given Loch's controversial role in Highland history, the view from Castle Howard is of further interest in confirming that the precepts of agricultural improvement were core to his approach to estate management and not specific to the much better-studied Sutherland context.

Henderson's example, however, also suggests that studies of English land agents could profitably be expanded to more fully encompass their relationship with the residents of landed estates. Castle Howard, like other great estates, was more a community than an economic unit, and as such Henderson was embedded in a complex set of social relationships. Both Morpeth and Henderson were highly concerned with the conduct and living conditions of the estate villagers. Managing the Castle Howard estate also meant 'managing' its people: shaping and monitoring their behaviour, seeking to make them more moral and better housed. Against accounts which have rooted such involvement in landlord paternalism, this study has suggested that the interaction between the estate and its residents should be viewed as occurring within a framework of 'improvement'. Just as Henderson and Morpeth sought to promote economic and technological advancement on the estate farms, they also sought to bring order and moral and social progress to the estate labourers. Their actions occurred against a backdrop of perceived immorality and the threat of disorder: something which made 'improvement' seem all the more imperative. As for Henderson, the census return for 1871 shows that despite his dismissal,

---

[104] A. Tindley, '"They sow the wind, they reap the whirlwind": estate management in the post-clearance Highlands, c. 1815–c. 1900', *Northern Scotland*, 3 (2012), pp. 66–85, especially pp. 76–8.

he remained on the estate as the farmer of a smallholding in Ganthorpe. He died there in 1875, seemingly a fixture in the landscape he helped to create.

2

'Not a popular personage': The Factor in Scottish Property Relations, c. 1870–1920

Ewen A. Cameron

THE BAPTISM OF ANGUS MACKINTOSH, 1910

IN HIS IMPORTANT POEM about history and memory in the crofting township in which he was brought up – Idrigill on the Kilmuir estate in the north end of the island of Skye – Aonghas MacNeacail tells of the day

> cha b' eachdraidh ach cuimhne
> an latha bhaist ciorstaidh am bàillidh
> lu mùn à poit a thug i bhon chulàist
>
> (it wasn't history but memory / the day kirsty baptised the factor / with piss from a pot she took from the backroom).[1]

The context for this singular anointment was a dispute between the crofters and the estate management over part of a farm, Scuddaburgh, which the crofters claimed for their own use, against the wishes of the proprietors. The lease of the farm tenant, Murdo Gillies, came to an end in 1907; the crofters demanded the whole of the farm, while the proprietors offered them only part of it and wished to retain the rest as a small model farm. The dispute was long-running and, remarkably, was only settled with the personal intervention of Lord Pentland, the Secretary for Scotland, who convened a meeting in the Free Church in Uig. The unfortunate factor was a man called Angus Mackintosh, a Gaelic speaker, who had been brought in by the proprietors in the hope that he would have the skills and outlook to be able to communicate in an effective manner with the crofters. Mackintosh came from Daviot, south of Inverness, and after studying law at the University of Edinburgh held factorial posts in Fife and for Lady Gordon Cathcart in South Uist,

---

[1] A. MacNeacail, *dèanamh gàire ris a' chloc, dàin ùra agus thaghte: laughing at the clock, new and selected poems* (Edinburgh, 2012), pp. 164–5.

Benbecula and Barra.[2] Things did not go according to plan. Indeed, the bitterness of the dispute can be explained, at least in part, by the widespread feeling that the land of Scuddaburgh farm had been 'promised' to the crofters of Idrigill by Mackintosh. The crofters had taken illegal possession of the disputed part of the farm and the landowner had taken out interdicts against them. When these were breached, Mackintosh was called upon to identify to the Sheriff Officer those whom he thought had broken their terms. This put him in an enormously difficult position, as it made it almost impossible for him to work with the tenants after the events that ended with Kirsty's actions; indeed, his superiors felt that 'his residence at Uig will be made extremely difficult and his work among the crofters marred'.[3]

Alongside MacNeacail's account – written many years after the event but based on his intimate knowledge of the oral tradition of the township and his direct knowledge of, and kinship with, those involved – we also have Mackintosh's account, written for his employers. In this account he emphasised the role of the women of the township, 'some of whom behaved like furies. It was hardly to be expected that in the circumstances I should escape and a good deal of dirty water and divots came my way.'[4] The dirty water may equate with the 'piss' in Kirsty's pot and it is not impossible that the 'divots' could have been a euphemistic reference to human or animal faeces. The Sheriff Officers declared themselves deforced and left the scene of the action. In Mackintosh's words: 'They were followed by a howling mob of men and women who marched them right up past the hotel shouting and yelling and blowing horns all the time.'[5] Mackintosh concluded that the crofters blamed him for helping the representatives of the landlords and the authorities identify those involved in the raid and, hence, the breach of interdict and felt that both his job and his life would be impossible as a result.

So what? The crofting areas of the Highlands and islands were frequently disturbed by this kind of protest from the early 1870s to, at least, the mid-1920s. The island of Skye was the epicentre of protest during the 1880s with seminal events taking place at Braes in 1882, Glendale in 1883 and, indeed, on the Kilmuir estate throughout the 1880s. That

---

[2] D. Shaw, *The Idrigill Raiders* (Ullapool, 2010), pp. 7–8; I. MacDonald, *A Family in Skye, 1908–1916* (Stornoway, 1980), pp. 15, 64, 148.

[3] National Records of Scotland [hereafter NRS], AF42/7570, Henry Cook to R. R. MacGregor.

[4] NRS, AF42/7574, Mackintosh to the CDB, 23 August 1910.

[5] NRS, AF42/7574, Mackintosh to the CDB, 23 August 1910.

estate had been seen as one of the worst managed of all private estates in the Highlands with the landowner infamous for his harsh estate management and, particularly, his rack renting of the tenants. These protests induced the Liberal government to appoint a Royal Commission under Lord Napier to investigate the grievances of the crofters and then, along lines somewhat different to Napier's recommendations, to legislate to grant security of tenure and other rights for crofters in the seven most northerly counties of Scotland. This did not bring an end to the protests. Governments continued to legislate on the Highland land question, in 1897, in 1911 and in 1919. Protest was perhaps less common in the 1890s but it certainly recurred in the 1900s and then again after the conclusion of the Great War; in the latter period the main focus of land raiding was in the island of Lewis. [6]

What makes the events sketched out above of some significance in the long history of protest on the Highland land question is that the landowners of the Kilmuir estate in 1910 were not a long-established Highland family with clan heritage, nor an English industrial magnate who had bought into Highland land in the mid-nineteenth century, as so many did, but the state, in the form of the Congested Districts Board (CDB). This body had been established in 1897 to further the policy of land purchase in the Highlands of Scotland. The Board was based on an Irish body of the same name established in 1891. [7] The aim in Scotland was to provide facilities for crofters to purchase their holdings and become owner-occupiers of their land. This was based on Conservative ideological premises of creating stability in society by spreading the benefits of property ownership to a wider section of the population. [8] The principal purchases of the board were two estates in Skye: Glendale and Kilmuir, both secured in 1904. These estates had seen intense land agitation in the 1880s. Glendale was purchased by the crofters in a model transaction and they paid off their loans in the mid-1950s. The inhabitants of Kilmuir were much more troublesome, as we have seen. One of the ways in which they expressed this was to oppose the idea of turning them from tenants into owners. They did not

[6] I. M. M. MacPhail, *The Crofters' War* (Stornoway, 1989); I. J. M. Robertson, *Landscapes of Protest in the Scottish Highlands after 1914: The Later Highland Land Wars* (Farnham, 2013).

[7] C. Breathnach, *The Congested Districts Board of Ireland, 1891–1923* (Dublin, 2005).

[8] NRS, AF42/1782, Memo by Sir Reginald MacLeod to Lord Balfour of Burleigh (Secretary for Scotland), on the Scottish and Irish Congested Districts Boards, 4 September 1903.

want to lose rating concessions and they felt that the Crofters Holdings (Scotland) Act 1886 recognised their customary ownership of the land, rendering unnecessary and vexatious the requirement to borrow money to pay for something which they felt they already possessed. The context required to analyse this point requires an awareness of the way in which national and local politics related to each other. When the Kilmuir estate had been purchased by the CDB the Conservative government was still in power. That government resigned in late 1905 and was replaced by a Liberal government that won a massive general election victory in January 1906 and had its own plans for Scottish land reform. Liberals were resistant to the idea of transferring property to crofters but wished to address one of the key weaknesses of the crofting system by extending the amount of land available to crofters. They aimed to do this by forcing private landowners to let more of their land as smallholdings and providing support and finance to equip such holdings and the holders, who would remain as tenants. Their legislative vehicle to achieve this policy goal was delayed by internal party divisions and the opposition of the House of Lords, who spotted a weak Liberal bill on which they could successfully prey. This gave the CDB and its policy a stay of execution and indicated to the politically aware crofters of Kilmuir that they had an opportunity to sustain their position as tenants. The government capitulated to them in this regard and found themselves with a sizeable estate on their hands and a population of crofters to manage.[9] This was, effectively, unintended land nationalisation.[10] The next stage of the crofters' campaign was to focus on the farms on the estate. These were under lease for various terms and could not be used to extend the crofters' holdings or to give them additional arable or grazing land until the end of the leases. This caused frustration and presented a management problem for the CDB when the crofters took action to try to secure access to one of these farms, Scuddaburgh.[11] It was in the course of the protests surrounding this farm that Mackintosh was baptised by Kirsty.

In 1904 the CDB had considered the appointment of a factor for Kilmuir and Glendale and Hugh MacDiarmid, the factor for the Duke

---

[9] The wider context is dealt with in E. A. Cameron, *Land for the People?: The British Government and the Scottish Highlands, c. 1880–1925* (East Linton, 1996), pp. 83–123.

[10] C. Stewart, *The Highland Experiment in Land Nationalisation* (London, 1904).

[11] E. A. Cameron, '"They will listen to no remonstrance": land raids and land raiders in the Scottish Highlands, 1886 to 1914', *Scottish Economic and Social History*, 17 (1997), pp. 43–64.

of Argyll on Tiree was thought to be a 'suitable' candidate for the post.[12] In an interesting note, Angus Sutherland, former Crofter Member of Parliament and now member of the CDB as Chairman of the Fishery Board for Scotland, argued: 'I think we should exhaust every other means before determining to appoint a factor. Unfortunately, the factor, as such, is not a popular personage in the highlands.'[13] He also felt that the population of these estates should be encouraged to develop their own methods of estate management as they were being 'set up to go on on their own resources and responsibility'.[14] Another member of the CDB was against the appointment of a factor, as, strictly speaking, the holders were the proprietors – the CDB was not the landlord and certainly did not anticipate becoming so in the long term; the aim was to encourage purchase by the holders. As we have seen, this broke down in Kilmuir. His view was that the Board 'should think twice before they employ any official under the name of a factor'.[15]

When the policy of purchase broke down an official did have to be appointed. This turned out to be the unfortunate Mackintosh. He was consistently uncomfortable in his role in Kilmuir. In November 1907 he wrote to the Secretary of the Board requesting a move to Edinburgh, where he could carry out his work more efficiently:

> When I was appointed it was clearly understood that I was not to be known as the Board's 'factor' but while I am resident here and doing the work of a factor the people look upon me simply in that capacity and they are apt to think that nothing I say or do is final until it has been remitted to Edinburgh.[16]

Thus he felt that he had all the unpopularity and attracted all the opprobrium traditionally directed towards a factor but that he had none of the power wielded by officials of that name.[17] He was not helped by the fact that it seemed that the crofters were egged on in their campaign over Scuddaburgh by one John MacKenzie, the ground officer for Colonel William Fraser, the former proprietor.[18] If the John MacKenzie who was assisting the crofters in 1909–10 was the same person as the

---

[12] NRS, AF42/1891, Memo by David Brand (Chairman of the Crofters Commission), 2 February 1904.
[13] NRS, AF42/1891, Angus Sutherland, 23 February 1904.
[14] NRS, AF42/1891, Angus Sutherland, 23 February 1904.
[15] NRS, AF42/1891, William MacKenzie, 4 March 1904.
[16] NRS, AF42/4270, Mackintosh to Macgregor, 21 November 1907.
[17] NRS, AF42/4270, Mackintosh to Macgregor, 21 November 1907
[18] Shaw, *Idrigill Raiders*, p. 16.

former ground officer to Fraser, this would represent a major shift from his former position. Investigation of the Kilmuir estate papers reveals MacKenzie's troubled reaction to the crofters' protests of the 1880s. In one letter to Alexander Macdonald in Portree he remarked that 'there are some pretty nasty things going on at present which certainly no person would like to hear of' and in another letter he condemned the leadership of the crofters' movement in the district for the malign influence they had over the crofters.[19] Twenty-five years later, however, he seems to have been willing to foment opposition to Mackintosh. Perhaps he disagreed with the concept of state ownership of land and was embittered by the loss of position when the estate changed hands; perhaps he was scarred by the experience of working on an estate where the relationship between landowner and tenant had been as bitter as anywhere in the Highlands. Given the depth of the tensions on the estate in the 1880s, it is perhaps not surprising that the memory of the agitation was alive and well only a generation later. The tactics used in the dispute of 1909–10 were very reminiscent of the 1880s: the blowing of horns to attract attention, the deforcement of officers of the law, the raiding of land and, of course, the denunciation of, and violence towards, factors. It was the build-up of tension in Kilmuir that led to poor Mackintosh's unfortunate baptism in 1910 but it was clear that he had identified the problematic nature of his role some years earlier. Interestingly, the state had been critical of private estate managers, for example in Vatersay, for not enforcing interdicts against raiders but in 1910 the Uig riot showed them some of the practical difficulties of Highland estate management.[20]

The hostility towards factors on the Kilmuir estate goes further back than the 1880s. Fraser quickly became one of the hate figures in the Highlands after his purchase of the estate in 1855. This was clearly shown by a curious event in 1877. During that year a flood in Uig washed away a burial ground and the factor's house, taking with it the factor, David Ferguson, who had remained in the house, against the 'remonstrances' of his family.[21] A striking report in John Murdoch's *Highlander* asserted:

> it is strange that nearly all the dead buried in Uig during the last five hundred years should be brought up ... against the house, as if the dead in their

[19] Inverness, Highland Archive, Kilmuir Estate Papers, AG INV/10/73, John MacKenzie to Alexander Macdonald, 2 April 1884, 23 November 1884.

[20] NRS, AF42/4127, Minute by the Under Secretary for Scotland (Reginald MacLeod), 25 April 1906.

[21] *Scotsman*, 22 October 1877, p. 5.

graves arose to perform the vengeance which the living had not the spirit to execute . . . [A]lthough the living would not put forth a hand themselves against the laird, they do not hesitate to express their regret that the proprietor was not in the place of the manager when he was swept away.[22]

This episode is another of the key moments in the history of Uig and, by extension, of the Highlands, dealt with by Aonghas MacNeacail in the poem with which this chapter began:

cha b' eachdraidh ach cuimhne
là na dile, chaid loids a' chaiptein
a sguabadh dhan tràigh
nuair a phòs sruthan rà is chonain
gun tochar a ghabhail
ach dàthaidh an sgalag
a dh'fhan 'dileas dha maighstir'
agus cuirp nan linn às a' cladh

(it wasn't history but memory / the day of the flood, the captain's lodge / was swept to the shore / when the streams of rha and conon married / taking no dowry / but david the servant / who 'stayed true to his master' / and the corpses of centuries from the cemetery).[23]

It was one of John Murdoch's constant themes during the 1880s that the crofters did not have the confidence to be able to mount opposition to the factors and the landlords. As the events dealt with here show, they had clearly acquired that confidence in the 1880s and the same forms of protests were deployed again against the state, as opposed to a private landlord, in the 1900s.

THE FACTOR IN HIGHLAND HISTORY

Kilmuir, of course, was not unique in its identification of the factor as a target for the protests of crofters and cottars. This set of relationships had been a constant theme of Highland history since the middle of the eighteenth century. Colin Campbell of Glenure, the victim of the Appin Murder in 1752, was, after all, a factor for the Forfeited Estates Commission (which was, in some of its developmental objectives, similar to the CDB, although certainly not interested in transferring ownership

---

[22] *Highlander*, 3 November 1877. As a result of this article Fraser sued the *Highlander* and the substantial damages awarded in his favour were injurious to the newspaper, which never enjoyed robust financial health.

[23] MacNeacail, *dèanamh gàire ris a' chloc*, pp. 164–5.

of the land to the people).[24] On the Sutherland estate in the early nineteenth century, where some of the most concerted protests during the first
phase of the Highland clearances took place, it was those who managed
the estate, especially Patrick Sellar, who attracted the contempt of the
people to a much greater extent than the Sutherland family themselves.[25]
Factors were vitally important figures who provided a bridge between
the strategic outlook of the landowner and 'Commissioners' (chief
executive-like figures on larger estates like Sutherland, where James
Loch acted in this capacity) and the ground officers who related most
closely to the tenants.[26]

There were, however, different models of factorship on Highland
estates. The image that has come down to us is akin to that of a popular
understanding of Sellar – the unfeeling agent of the landlord's policies
and his own interests (Sellar was a sheep farmer on his own account,
as well as agent for the Sutherlands). Although this image of Sellar has
persisted through novels and plays, there was more tension between him
and his employers than is often acknowledged in the popular account.[27]

The key moment at which the role of the factor was exposed came
much later in the century, in 1874, on the island of Lewis. In that year
a group of crofters from Bernera were put on trial in Stornoway after
a dispute with the estate management had ended with a violent event.
The so-called 'Bernera Riot' has been seen as one of the key events in
the development of protest that presaged the outbreak of concerted and
widespread protest in the 1880s. For our purposes it is the trial that is
more important because the defence agent, Charles Innes, exposed the
dominant role of Sir James Matheson's factor, Donald Munro.[28] At

[24] J. Hunter, 'The Appin Murder – Historical Context', paper presented at The
Royal Society of Edinburgh, RSE @ Lochaber, 3 September 2013, Ben Nevis Hotel,
Fort William, Report by Kate Kennedy, available at <https://www.royalsoced.org.
uk/cms/files/events/reports/2012-2013/The-Appin-Murder-Historical-Context.pdf>
(last accessed 17 November 2017).

[25] J. Hunter, *Set Adrift upon the World: The Sutherland Clearances* (Edinburgh,
2015); E. Richards, *Patrick Sellar and the Highland Clearances: Homicide, Eviction
and the Price of Progress* (Edinburgh, 1999); I. Grimble, *The Trial of Patrick Sellar*
(London, 1962); Sellar-like figures, drawn from the popular memory of the clearances, feature prominently in Scottish novels such as N. M. Gunn, *Butcher's Broom*
(Edinburgh, 1934); F. MacColla, *And the Cock Crew* (Glasgow, 1945); I. Crichton
Smith, *Consider the Lilies* (London, 1968).

[26] See Chapter 1 in this volume by David Gent for more detail on Loch.

[27] Hunter, *Set Adrift*, p. 201.

[28] *Report of the Trial of the So-Called Bernera Rioters at Stornoway on the 17th
and 18th of July 1874* (n.p., 1874; reprinted facsimile edn, Edinburgh, 1985); a

the trial it became clear that he wielded power over the crofters and cottars of the island not only as factor but also through the possession of many local offices: Chairman of the Parochial Board and the School Board, Procurator Fiscal, Director of the Gas and Water Companies in Stornoway as well as senior positions in the Harbour Trust and the Road Trust.[29] This extensive influence was an important source of unpopularity. Munro was bitterly excoriated by the seminal Lewis poet John Smith in his famous poem 'The Spirit of Kindliness', which looked forward to Munro's death:

'N sin molaidh a' chnuimh shnàigeach thu
Cho tàirceach 's a bhios d'fheòil,
Nuair gheibh I air do chàradh thu
Gu sàmhach air a bòrd.

(Then the crawling worm will praise you, / For the tastiness of your flesh, / When it finds you stretched straight out / On its board without a breath).[30]

A Glasgow poet, Murdo MacLeod, described Munro's rule in Lewis as 'Gur sàrachadh le ainneart / Aoin de ainglibh dubha Shàtain' ('The tyranny of one of Satan's black angels').[31] Although it was not Munro who was on trial but three crofters – Angus Macdonald, Norman MacAulay and John MacLeod, all of whom were acquitted – Innes shone a light on his management, and his rule over the island was brought to an end.[32] In 1875 he was replaced as factor by one William Mackay, a more emollient figure but one who did little to alter the fundamentally weak position of the island's tenantry.[33] Although the Munro example was an egregious one, it was replicated in less intensive fashion in other areas of the Highlands.

A slightly different model of factorship can be seen in the island of Skye at the same period. In this case the key figure was Alexander

recent account which very helpfully sketches in the wider context is R. J. Grace, *Opium and Empire: The Lives and Careers of William Jardine and James Matheson* (Montreal and Kingston, 2014), pp. 308–35.

[29] MacPhail, *Crofters' War*, p. 13.

[30] D. E. Meek (ed.), *Tuath is Tighearna: Tenants and Landlords. An Anthology of Gaelic Poetry of Social and Political Protest from the Clearances to the Land Agitation* (Edinburgh, 1995), p. 88.

[31] Meek, *Tuath is Tighearna*, p. 97.

[32] The trial and Munro's humiliation were widely reported; see *Scotsman*, 21 July 1874, p. 6.

[33] J. Shaw Grant, *A Shilling for your Scowl: The History of a Scottish Legal Mafia* (Stornoway, 1992); J. MacLeod, *None Dare Oppose: The Laird, the Beast and the People of Lewis* (Edinburgh, 2011).

Macdonald, a solicitor based in Portree. He exerted wide-ranging powers through his position as factor for a range of estates across the island, including those of Lord Macdonald, Fraser of Kilmuir and a range of smaller estates.[34] It was his pervasive influence that was called into question by the opening exchanges of the Napier Commission at Braes in 1883 when the first witness raised the question of whether his bearing witness on matters of estate management would result in his victimisation by Macdonald. Lord Napier asked Alexander Macdonald to assure Stewart and other witnesses that they would not be victimised. The exchange with Macdonald, who was unwilling to give more than a very heavily qualified assurance, is suggestive of a factor determined to retain the means of keeping the crofters in a vulnerable position. Stewart was reassured to a sufficient degree to allow him to continue with his statement and to answer the Commissioners' questions.[35] This represents a very subtle shift of relations in a Highland estate context. Factors certainly perceived the intervention of the state into their business to be an erosion of the powerful position that they held in Highland society. This was seen clearly in the events in Uig in 1909: even as the state became a landowner it required the employment of a factor but the long political agitation over the land question on the Kilmuir estate had conditioned the crofters to view the CDB as a less intimidating proprietor than previous, private, owners of the estate. The wider political situation after the election of the Liberals in 1906 meant that the CDB was on borrowed time, placing local managers like Mackintosh in a very difficult position.

THE PUBLIC ROLES OF FACTORS

So far we have considered the factor in terms of his role on the Highland estate, managing the relations between the landowner and the tenants, but factors often had much wider roles. One of the notable points about

[34] Alexander Macdonald's influence runs through the archives of the key Skye estates: Clan Donald Centre, Lord MacDonald MSS, Bundle 3129, items 3–4, Lady MacDonald to Alex Macdonald, 19 February 1886; Lord MacDonald to Alexander Macdonald, 26 February 1886. Dunvegan Castle MSS, 2/721 and 2/722 contain correspondence between MacLeod of MacLeod and Macdonald on a wide range of subjects over the period 1885–6. Macdonald also factored the smaller Strathaird estate in southern Skye; Highland Archive, Strathaird Estate Papers, AG INV/12/3–8 has his correspondence relating to that estate from 1886 to 1889.
[35] *Report of the Commissioners of Enquiry into the Condition of the Crofters and Cottars in the Highlands and Islands of Scotland*, 1884, C. 3980-I, Qs 13–21.

Alexander Macdonald's correspondence with Fraser of Kilmuir was his interest in politics, especially during the highly contested election of 1885 when the franchise was extended to include most male crofters. In Inverness-shire the election contest included a Crofter candidate, Charles Fraser Mackintosh, and Reginald MacLeod of Dunvegan, the Conservative candidate. Macdonald acted as factor for MacLeod's father. Prior to the introduction of the secret ballot in 1872 and the reforms of 1884–5 the factor would have had a lot of political work to do. Even in the new context the factor was an important political player. A legally qualified factor, such as Macdonald, would have had a lot of work to do in the Registration Courts. Fraser was a Liberal but in 1885 MacLeod was seen as a stronger challenger to the threat of Fraser Mackintosh, so he was favoured by the estate management, including Macdonald.[36] This election was an interesting one from the point of view of the history of the Highland factor because Fraser Mackintosh, who had been in business as a solicitor in Inverness, was accused of having acted as a factor for some small estates around Inverness, possibly having conducted evictions, and thereby, in the eyes of his opponents, was a hypocrite in coming forward in the Crofter interest. His Liberal opponent, the landowner Kenneth MacKenzie of Gairloch, condemned him for his actions as a factor and there was hostile correspondence in the *Inverness Courier*, a Liberal paper. The local Conservative organ, the *Northern Chronicle*, also gave prominence to the issue, reporting a hostile meeting at no less a place than Roy Bridge in the Braes of Lochaber, where there was criticism of his role as a factor for The MacKintosh, a local landowner and a Conservative.[37]

So, wherever one turns in this most interesting election there were landowners and their factors but it was highly significant that Fraser Mackintosh's opponents thought that exposing him as a 'factor' was likely to attract a particular degree of opprobrium among the new small-tenant voters. Fraser Mackintosh, it should be recorded, won the election and remained as Member of Parliament for the county until 1892. This was a fairly predictable form of electoral mud-slinging as for many lawyers working in Highland towns such as Inverness, Dingwall, Portree or Fort William, acting as a factor for local landowners was a

---

[36] Highland Archive, Kilmuir Estate Papers, AG INV/10/14, John MacKenzie (Ground Officer) to Macdonald, 6 March 1884, 21 November 1885; AG INV/10/31, William Fraser to Macdonald, 22 November 1885, 5 December 1885.

[37] *Inverness Courier*, 6 August 1885, 20 August 1885; *Northern Chronicle*, 9 September 1885, 7 October 1885.

common form of business. Investigation of the archives of Highland estates reveals factors of this kind not only hard at work on the detailed business of estate management – rent collection, dispute resolution, dealing with tenant grievances – but also engaging in wider activities such as observing the political interests of the landowner and liaising with other local notables such as clergymen and schoolmasters. Before the introduction of county councils in 1888 factors of larger estates were 'Commissioners of Supply' and involved in the raising of income from the rates and the provision of local services. As all of this work involved detailed knowledge of the law of property, agriculture and local government, men like Macdonald, Fraser Mackintosh and many others were ideally placed to provide this service.[38]

There was a small group of factors who took a wider role in debates over the land question but who owed their public prominence to their position in estate management. James Loch, Commissioner for the Sutherland estates in Scotland and England, was a perfect example. Loch served the 1st and 2nd dukes from 1812 until his death in 1855, overseeing the strategy of the massive programme of removals conducted on the dukes' Scottish estates. He was Member of Parliament for an English seat prior to his long tenure (1830–52) of the Wick Burghs constituency. He was very prominent in public offices in London and Scotland and a zealous defender of the interests and reputation of his employer. He developed a reputation for sagacity in matters of estate management that spread to other great landowners, such as the Bedfords. As such, he became a public advocate for the defence of the rights of private property and in some ways a key figure in the development of the facto-

---

[38] The correspondence of Allan Macdonald, an Inverness solicitor who acted as factor for The MacKintosh, can be found in the MacKintosh Muniments in the NRS; see GD176/2630, John Kennedy to Allan Macdonald, 6 July 1883; GD176/2644, MacKintosh to Macdonald, 5 May 1886, 30 May 1886; GD176/2666, MacKintosh to Macdonald, 22 July 1886; GD176/2674/46, MacKintosh to Macdonald, 20 March 1887; GD176/2702/22, MacKintosh to Macdonald, 10 January 1889; these letters range over national events, such as the Napier Commission and the Crofters Act, and local detail, such as the awkward demands for lower rents of the crofters of Inveroy. In Caithness a Thurso solicitor, George Logan, acted for Sinclair of Ulbster; see Thurso Estate Office, Sinclair of Ulbster MSS, Letters to Proprietor, George Logan to Sir Tollemache Sinclair, 14 March 1885, 8 April 1885, 23 May 1885, 29 May 1885, 24 January 1886. In the west, William MacKenzie acted for MacKenzie of Kintail; see NLS, Acc. 8838/1, William MacKenzie to MacKenzie of Kintail, 19 April 1887; MacKenzie of Kintail to William MacKenzie, 25 July 1887, 18 October 1889. The material in this small and under-used collection has a more local focus and concentrates on the day-to-day running of the estate.

rial profession. He must be one of the few estate managers who have had a monument raised to them by the landowners whom they served, in this case at Uppat, overlooking Dunrobin Castle, one of his favourite spots.[39]

In the late nineteenth century the key figure in this model of factorial activity was George Malcolm. His principal role as a factor was on the Glengarry and Glenquoich estates of Edward Ellice (Whig Member of Parliament for St Andrews Burghs, 1837–80), although he also managed the Corrour estate of John Stirling Maxwell, but he took energetic part in a wide range of public activities. He was an Inverness-shire county councillor, an agent for the Caledonian Bank and a notable advocate of the extension of railways in the Highlands, especially the West Highland Railway to Fort William and its later Mallaig extension and the ill-fated branch line from Spean Bridge to Invergarry.[40] Malcolm's principal public role, however, was as defender of the sporting economy of the Highland landed estate, of which both Glengarry and Glenquoich, and Corrour were prime examples.[41] He published widely and spoke publicly on this theme on any and every opportunity with which he was presented, including both the Napier Commission of 1883–4 and the Deer Forest Commission of 1892–5, both key investigations into the issues around the Highland land question. In these statements and writings he argued that sporting estates did not encroach on the interests

[39] E. Richards, 'Loch, James (1780–1855)', in *Oxford Dictionary of National Biography*, Oxford University Press, 2004, available at <http://www.oxforddnb.com/view/article/16883> (last accessed 17 November 2017); J. Loch, *An Account of the Improvements on the Estates of the Marquess of Stafford in the Counties of Stafford and Salop on the Estate of Sutherland, with Remarks* (London, 1820); 'Uppat James Loch Memorial, Reference: LB7026', Historic Environment Scotland, available at <http://portal.historic-scotland.gov.uk/designation/LB7026> (last accessed 17 November 2017).

[40] J. McGregor, *The West Highland Railway: Plans, Politics and People* (Edinburgh, 2005), pp. 221–2; *Scotsman*, 11 August 1913, p. 6. It is a striking reflection on the success of Malcolm and his fellow railway promoters among the landed and factorial class in the Highlands that King Edward VII, a keen sportsman and, in that capacity, frequent visitor to the Ellice estates could travel from Invergarry to Ballater, for Balmoral, in an unbroken rail journey; see *Scotsman*, 27 September 1904, p. 4; 26 September 1905, p. 5; and see Chapter 3 in this volume by John McGregor for further details.

[41] Indeed, the former might be seen to be the archetypal sporting estate as it may have formed the background for Edwin Landseer's *Monarch of the Glen*, although the magnificent example of *Cervus elaphus* depicted in the painting was in no danger from the artist, a hopeless shot; see R. Ormond, *The Monarch of the Glen: Landseer in the Highlands* (Edinburgh, 2005), pp. 14, 108, 125.

of the small tenants in that the former only occupied land at higher
altitudes that could not be usefully grazed or farmed, and that the
employment and local income provided by such estates far outweighed
any perceived disadvantages.[42] He was deeply concerned by the Deer
Forest Commission, chaired by David Brand (Chairman of the Crofters
Commission, of whom and which he was very suspicious). Stimulated
by this threat to the future of the sporting estate, he was very active in
trying to establish the Highland Property Association, in some ways
a forerunner of the Scottish Land and Property Federation (later the
Scottish Landowners Federation and Scottish Land and Estates). Many
archives of Highland estates contain representations from Malcolm
drawing the attention of his fellow factors and their employers to the
challenge posed to the sporting estate by Sheriff Brand and his radical
Commissioners.[43]

THE URBAN FACTOR

To return to the poem with which we started this chapter, MacNeacail
notes in an English note to the poem: 'no scot, from croft or tenement,
needs to be told that the factor is the landlord's agent or rent-collector'.[44]
Actually, the factor was more than just a rent collector but the implication of the phrase 'from croft or tenement' is very important. In urban
Scotland, as was seen most obviously during the urban rent strikes of
1915, it tended to be the factor who was the target of opprobrium rather
than the rentiers who owned the houses.[45] These protests were a direct
result of changes in the housing market at the beginning of the Great
War. Two convergent forces placed enormous pressure on this market:
the virtual cessation of house building as labour, capital and materials
were directed towards the war effort and an increase in rent due to this

[42] G. Malcolm, *Population, Crofts, Sheep Walks and Deer Forests* (Edinburgh,
1883); *Royal Commission (Highlands and Islands) 1892*, C. 7681, Qs 52296–551.

[43] Ardtornish House MSS, AH11/5, George Malcolm to Walter Elliot, 20 March
1893, 7 April 1893; Dunvegan Castle MSS, 2/712/18/2,3 George Malcolm to
MacLeod, 25 March 1893; Inveraray Castle MSS, George Malcolm to Argyll, 19
April 1895 (in this letter Malcolm complains to the duke about the partisan nature
of the work of the 'Deer Forest Commission'); for general background, see W. Orr,
*Deer Forests, Landlords and Crofters: The Western Highlands in Victorian and
Edwardian Times* (Edinburgh, 1982).

[44] MacNeacail, *dèanamh gàire ris a' chloc*, p. 167.

[45] N. J. Morgan and M. J. Daunton, 'Landlords in Glasgow: a study of 1900',
Business History, 25 (1983), pp. 264–86.

shortage; and the fact that in areas affected by munitions industries there was a large influx of workers earning high wages. This meant that certain groups, especially the families of serving soldiers, were in a weak position. The separation allowances paid to these families were not sufficient for these market conditions.[46] The Independent Labour Party and local organisations, often led by women, quickly became active and, as in the Highland land war of the 1880s, the rent strike became their key weapon. The dispute culminated in a concerted action in Glasgow on 17 November 1915 when a large number of rent strikers were threatened with legal action in the Sheriff Court. This precipitated industrial protest in the shipyards and munitions works and threatened a general crisis on the Clyde. The protestors aimed to capture the moral and patriotic high ground. In a dramatic gesture in June 1915 during the attempted eviction of the McHugh family from their house in Shettleston in the east end of Glasgow a Union Jack was nailed across the mouth of the tenement close. A large crowd present in the street were inflamed by a speech from John Wheatley and their action was to go to the office of the factor and have him burned in effigy.[47]

These factors wielded very considerable power over a large population. Although the property relations in the urban landscape were less homogenous than on a large Highland estate, the range of the factor's power was often very considerable. For example, John M'Fie, one of the leading factors in Glasgow in the Edwardian period, was responsible for 4,100 houses and 555 shops. Archibald Stewart and John Marr, of the Partick and Govan House Factors' Association, had over 5,000 houses on the books of their firms and estimated that 90 per cent of all the property in Govan and Partick (at the centre of the rent strikes in 1915) was in the hands of factors.[48] Thus in the urban landscape, where ownership of property was not concentrated, it was the factor who was the focus of power as he aggregated the many different house-owners whom he represented. The house-owners themselves were anonymous as far as the tenants were concerned. Thus the factor became the focus also of protest.

One of the results of the rent strikes was an act which restricted the right of house-owners in munitions areas to raise rents; this restriction

---

[46] S. Pedersen, 'Gender, welfare and citizenship in Britain during the Great War', *American Historical Review*, 95 (1990), pp. 983–1006.

[47] J. Melling, *Rent Strikes: People's Struggle for Housing in West Scotland, 1890–1916* (Edinburgh, 1983), pp. 66–7; I. Wood, *John Wheatley* (Manchester, 1990), pp. 54–7.

[48] *Report of the Departmental Committee on House-Letting in Scotland, vol. II, Minutes of Evidence and Appendices*, 1907, Cd. 3792, Qs 186, 261, 1290–2, 1350.

was to apply until the end of the war. This might be seen in some senses as cognate with the effect of the Crofters Act in restricting the landowners' right to set rents on Highland estates. In the urban case, however, the stakes were higher in that the government was induced to intervene by the need to maintain munitions production; in time of war this was more important than the property rights of house-owners.[49] Indeed, when this form of rent control was introduced to some urban areas in 1915, urban factors, like their rural Highland counterparts of thirty years earlier, felt that it was their role that was being eroded in urban property relations. This remained a grievance for factors and they continued to chafe at the restrictions in the free market for rented property, which remained in place well into the post-war period.[50] This raises a very important point in that the disputes about property that affected both rural and urban Scotland in the period from about 1880 to 1930 were much more complicated than a mere argument between owner – whether of house or landed estate – and tenant.

CONCLUSION

In conclusion, it can be seen that the 'factor' was indeed an unpopular personage in the rural areas of the Highlands but also in industrial districts of urban Scotland. This reflects the fact that issues of property were vital to politics and social relations in the period from 1880 to 1920. The factor's unpopularity stemmed, obviously, from his role in carrying out the dirty work of the landowner – especially evictions but also transactions around rent and the enforcement of estate regulations such as the prohibition of subdivision. The matter goes further, however. As the state intervened in the land issue it was the factor's role that was most obviously usurped. This weakened position was exposed in more open political conditions and with a more confident, and legally secure, tenantry. There was no residual deference to the factor and shorn of his former power there was the prospect of contempt and ridicule. Landowners could express their dissatisfaction with the new state of affairs by selling land and retiring to London or the empire; the

[49] The National Archives, Kew, CAB37/137/29, The Increase of Rents of Workmen's Dwellings, Thomas McKinnon Wood, 17 November 1915; CAB37/138/3, Increase of Rents and Mortgage Interest, Walter H. Long, 23 November 1915.

[50] House of Lords Record Office, Andrew Bonar Law MSS, Box 22, Folder 3, fo. 47, James Stewart (House Factor) to Messrs Russell and Duncan (Writers), 30 June 1922.

factor had no such luxury. It is odd, however, that the unpopular factor has not been accorded more attention by historians. There is a rich anti-landlord literature in the Scottish polemical tradition but the role of the factor, other than in special cases like Patrick Sellar or Donald Munro, has not been analysed in the same way as Irish historians have looked at the role of land agents in rural Ireland in the nineteenth century.[51] This is a strange gap since the popular memory of the iniquities perpetrated by factors is quite rich. We have seen that there were different models of factorial activity. Some were loyal servants of a particular landlord, others sold their professional services across a range of landed estates; some confined themselves to the day-to-day business of estate management, others adopted a public role and advocated causes related to the defence and interests of private property. The institution of landownership changed over the late nineteenth and early twentieth centuries. The state intervened and imposed institutions, such as the Crofters Commission, to occupy the space between the landowner and the tenant, thereby eroding the role of the factor. State intervention developed and moved ultimately towards outright ownership of land. This effectively placed the state in need of factors to manage its land. Men who adopted this role, such as the unfortunate Angus Mackintosh, were placed in a much more difficult position than their colleagues who worked for private landowners. Although the latter were not always fixed in their approach, few changed their policy towards estate management in quite the way that the state did in the period after 1905. This volte-face left poor Mackintosh in a vulnerable position and, although there were very specific and local reasons behind his baptism, his fate can be seen as a tribute to the factorial profession as a whole.

---

[51] C. Reilly, *The Irish Land Agent, 1830–60: The Case of King's County* (Dublin, 2014); J. McEntee, 'The state and the landed estate: order and shifting power relations in Ireland, 1815–1891' (unpublished PhD thesis, National University of Ireland, Galway, 2012).

3

The Factor and Railway Promotion in the Scottish Highlands: The West Highland Railway

John McGregor

INTRODUCTION

THE LATE NINETEENTH-CENTURY western Highlands saw a surge of railway promotions. Estate factors became activists and parliamentary witnesses; they were caught up in railway construction, and they made use of the new railways. This chapter examines and contextualises their involvement, highlighting their important role in the development of railway infrastructure in rural Britain.

The West Highland Railway was promoted as a 130-mile line from Craigendoran on the lower Clyde to a new harbour at Roshven (Loch Ailort). The 100 miles to Fort William were authorised in 1889, completed five years later, and a short branch to Banavie on the Caledonian Canal was added in 1895. This was the only section that saw the light of day. With Mallaig (at the mouth of Loch Nevis) substituted for Roshven, the 40-mile West Highland Extension was approved in 1894 but awaited state assistance, finally granted in 1896: the route was finished to Mallaig in 1901. Contemplated but not pursued was a link from Glen Spean, by Loch Laggan, to the Highland Railway in Strathspey. Likewise, authorised but unbuilt was the West Highland Ballachulish Extension, south from Fort William (unlike the Callander & Oban Company's Connel Ferry–Ballachulish branch, which was built and opened in 1903). The Loch Fyne Light Railway, from West Highland Arrochar & Tarbet to St Catherine's opposite Inveraray, though approved under the Light Railways Act of 1896, was allowed to languish.

By agreeing to guarantee, work and maintain the West Highland, the North British Company could invade the territory of the Caledonian Company, their great rival, who worked the Callander & Oban Railway (completed to Oban in 1880). Moreover, the Highland Company were alarmed, in that first Roshven and then Mallaig threatened their traffic through Strome Ferry, terminus of the Dingwall & Skye line (opened in 1870). More alarming still was the prospect that a West Highland (that is, North British) advance up the Great Glen would breach the Highland's monopoly at Inverness. The much-contested Invergarry & Fort Augustus Railway, diverging from the West Highland at Spean Bridge, was authorised in 1896 and opened in 1903; but the 30-mile gap onward to Inverness was never filled, and the Invergarry & Fort Augustus would remain a West Highland appendage.[1]

CREATING THE WEST HIGHLAND LINE

The West Highland derived in some degree from the ambitious, blatantly speculative Glasgow & North Western Railway – a 160-mile direct line to Inverness, via Loch Lomond, Glen Coe and the Great Glen – promoted in 1882–3, at which date the Highland Company's Tay-and-Spey main line still detoured via Forres (the Aviemore cut-off was not completed until 1898). Moreover the Glasgow & North Western would have intersected the Callander & Oban route. The promoters counted on embroiling Caledonian, North British and Highland so that at least part of their scheme would be taken up; but, save in Lochaber, the proprietors along the route proved hostile.[2] Many enthusiastic but ill-organised witnesses were deployed, including estate factors Thomas Armstrong (Ardnamurchan), William Hossack (Appin) and William Martin (Poltalloch).[3] In the then climate of distress and unrest across much of the western Highlands and islands, it was urged that transport improvements would stimulate economic development; and the promoters promised the early addition of a branch westward to a new harbour on the Arisaig seaboard, serving mail steamers and fishery.[4]

George Malcolm, factor for the Ellice Trustees' Glen Garry, advised the Glasgow & North Western engineer on the best route along the middle reaches of the Great Glen.[5] William Tait, factor for the Sinclairs of Caithness and a director of the Caithness Quarry Company, argued for

---

[1] D. Ross, *The North British Railway* (Stenlake, 2014); J. McGregor, *The West Highland Railway: Plans, Politics and People* (Edinburgh, 2005).

[2] McGregor, *West Highland Railway*, pp. 27–33.

[3] National Records of Scotland [hereafter NRS], BR/PYB(S)/1/325, Glasgow & North Western Railway Bill, 1882–3, evidence, 7 May 1883, 10 May 1883.

[4] NRS, BR/PYB(S)/1/325, Glasgow & North Western Railway Bill, 1882–3, speech for the bill, 30 April 1883.

[5] NRS, BR/PYB(S)/1/325, Glasgow & North Western Railway Bill, 1882–3, evidence by Thomas Walrond-Smith, engineer, Glasgow & North Western Railway, 8 May 1883.

Figure 1 Nigel B. Mackenzie, factor and
railway promoter. Image courtesy of
J. McGregor.

salutary competition – a second, shorter route to Inverness would remedy
the Highland Company's alleged mistreatment of the Far North.[6] Daniel
McLeish, Fort William solicitor and factor for Mrs Cameron-Campbell
of Callart, the burgh's feudal superior, testified to local eagerness for
the scheme. It was a dazzling prospect that a town long disappointed
of rail connection might become principal intermediate centre on a new
trunk route to Inverness. Fort William's existing railheads, reached by
coach or steamer, were Inverness or Kingussie (Highland Company),
Oban or Tyndrum (Callander & Oban), all 40–65 miles away.[7] Nigel
MacKenzie, another prominent local solicitor, was factor for the properties of Cameron of Lochiel, south and west of the town (see Figure 1).
Member of Parliament for Inverness-shire since the 1860s, Lochiel was
serving on the Napier Commission (1883–4) and could not attend at
Westminster, where MacKenzie gave evidence on his behalf.[8]

Though the grandiose Glasgow & North Western was defeated, it
had intensified the mutual suspicions of Caledonian and North British,
while awakening press and parliamentary sympathy for the districts
distant from the Highland Railway or poorly served by the cross-country
Callander & Oban line. If local endeavour could be demonstrated, if

    [6] NRS, BR/PYB(S)/1/325, Glasgow & North Western Railway Bill, 1882–3,
evidence, 8 May 1883.
    [7] NRS, BR/PYB(S)/1/325, Glasgow & North Western Railway Bill, 1882–3,
evidence, 7 May 1883.
    [8] NRS, BR/PYB(S)/1/325, Glasgow & North Western Railway Bill, 1882–3,
evidence, 7 May 1883.

landowners stood united, then a more modest venture might succeed. The Clyde, Ardrishaig & Crinan Railway, approved in 1887, met this prescription, not without input from estate factors. Led by Colonel Edward Malcolm of Poltalloch, the proprietors of South Argyll engaged with the North British Company on terms which foreshadowed the North British agreement with the West Highland promoters two years later. Disadvantaged by water breaks (across the Firth of Clyde and then across Loch Fyne), the line remained unbuilt. In 1892, with the West Highland under construction, the Clyde, Ardrishaig & Crinan Company would be wound up.[9] Protagonists of the West Highland were able to cite the Napier Report's particular (if tentative) recommendation that any railway reaching Fort William would merit limited government assistance, encouraging its continuation to the Atlantic coast.[10]

The building of the West Highland (1889–94) closely concerned William Dunn, who was factor for the Marquess of Breadalbane. Through Glen Falloch and Strathfillan into Glen Orchy, then by Strathtulla into Rannoch, it traversed the Breadalbane lands for 30 miles. Dunn dealt repeatedly with contractors Lucas & Aird, with engineers Formans & McCall, with John Robertson of Old Blair, arbiter under the West Highland Railway Act 1890, with Davidson & Syme, Breadalbane's Edinburgh solicitors; and with all Breadalbane's tenants who faced severance.[11] Dunn, based at Kenmore, devoted five days to a thorough inspection of the route (staying one night at Ardlui and two at Tyndrum) in company with William Copland, the independent engineer who costed Breadalbane's compensation claims. Details of acreages and leases were painstakingly assembled, to sustain Breadalbane's case before the arbiter.[12]

More than fifty accommodation works were finally settled – bridges, creeps, private level crossings and associated fencing. One farmer held out for a modified award; a large sheep-fank was partially rebuilt rather than replaced. In Strathfillan, where the line usefully divided the rough hill grazing from the better grass below, existing lengths of dyke, now

    [9] NRS, BR/CAC/3/2, Clyde, Ardrishaig and Crinan Railway Act, 1887; related materials and Abandonment Act, 1892.
    [10] McGregor, *West Highland Railway*, chs 3, 4; NRS, C.3980, Report of the Royal Commission into the condition of the crofters and cottars in the Highlands and Islands of Scotland, 1884.
    [11] NRS, GD112/53/100, Davidson and Syme, expenses, Breadalbane Reference, West Highland Railway, 1890–3.
    [12] NRS, GD112/53/100; GD112/53/97, William Dunn to Davidson and Syme, 2 October 1891, and arbiter's hearing, Breadalbane Reference, 16 November 1891.

crowned with iron standards and strands of wire, came to form the railway boundary. Opportunity was taken to improve Crannach Wood in Strathtulla, where the contractors, besides clearing the railway right-of-way, thinned the trees on either side. To stabilise the formation on Rannoch Moor, drainage ditches outside the railway fences were required, which the factor at first resisted, as hazardous to sheep.[13] The tenants of Auch and Achallader were able to take advantage of the contractor's sidings, which remained in use after the railway opened.[14]

By contrast, the West Highland Mallaig Extension, engineered by Simpson & Wilson and built by Robert McAlpine, just touched the northern edge of the Earl of Morton's Conaglen estate – at Craigag, near Kinlochiel. An opponent of the Roshven line but reconciled to its successor, Morton sought recompense for loss of income – Craigag Lodge could not be let during the years of construction (1897–1901) – and for the wages of an additional gamekeeper, to contain the depredations of McAlpine's navvies. More dubious and ultimately unsustainable was his claim that the railway would cause irreparable damage, permanently impeding the movement of deer through the pass between Loch Eil and Loch Shiel, with consequent inbreeding and degeneration of stock. Thomas Telford's road to Arisaig took the same course but, unlike the railway, was not closely fenced. With a natural history 'expert' and two experienced gamekeepers in support, factor George Glendinning made the best case he could. Morton's underlying but unadmitted concern was the loss of deer to a new forest in neighbouring Ardnamurchan.[15]

It was politic to indulge substantial tenant farmers and even more so to oblige powerful landowners and sporting lessees. Sir Alfred Bass, who in 1886 became Lord Burton, held a long lease of the Ellices' Glen Quoich, where George Malcolm doubled as factor. In the spring of 1894 Lucas & Aird made special arrangements to carry Burton and his house party over the West Highland, still five months from opening and in places distinctly impermanent. On several occasions during the summer of 1901, when the Invergarry & Fort Augustus Railway was almost ready, coaches and horse boxes were added to the overnight London–

---

[13] On Lord Abinger's Inverlochy estate in Lochaber, existing deer fences were similarly adapted: NRS, GD112/53/116, Marquess of Breadalbane to Charles Forman, 25 March 1895; Formans and McCall to Breadalbane, 2 April 1895; NRS, BR/NBR/8/1764/4, Davidson and Syme to John Conacher, general manager, North British Railway, 12 December 1895.

[14] McGregor, West Highland Railway, p. 198.

[15] NRS, GD150/3686, Morton Reference, West Highland Mallaig Extension, 1898: proofs, and Earl of Morton to George Glendinning, 2 June 1898, 3 June 1898.

Fort William service and transferred at Spean Bridge for the convenience of the Ellice family and their guests, after the factor had made sure that contractor James Young's pug engine would convey them to Invergarry station.[16] Discretion was necessary, because the Board of Trade had not yet passed the Fort Augustus line for traffic. For Lord Burton's journey south at the end of the 1901 season, so that he need not drive to Spean Bridge, the North British Company provided a locomotive and rolling stock; by then the Invergarry & Fort Augustus had been inspected and approved, though railway politics would delay its public opening two years more. When the widowed Mrs Ellice was refused this privilege, Malcolm at once penned a minatory letter: the North British general manager was reminded how much West Highland traffic was generated by the Invergarry estate.[17]

As on earlier railways in the Highlands, cooperation no doubt became the norm. Factors negotiated line-side delivery of supplies for farms, shepherds' cottages and shooting lodges remote from public stations. Factors endorsed request stops at landowners' private platforms. Corrour, owned by Sir John Stirling-Maxwell on the West Highland proper, Lechavuie, estate of the Cameron-Heads of Inverailort and the Nicholsons of Arisaig's Beasdale estate on the Mallaig Extension, were at first in this category, and Lechavuie so remained. Timetables were slender over much of the year and railway managers permitted estate employees – factors included – to travel by goods trains, sometimes with a formal 'brake-van pass'.[18] However, frictions were not lacking. In Glen Spean The MacKintosh demanded that the West Highland station first designated 'Inverlair' be renamed 'Tulloch', as it would be from 1895: Inverlair Lodge was Abinger, not MacKintosh, property. To this end factor Alan MacDonald, previously at odds with the railway builders, went enthusiastically into battle, threatening to interdict all construction on the Brae Lochaber estate.[19] In western Perthshire Sir John Menzies of Weem, whose prime concern was sporting lets, sparked a quarrel when

---

[16] Malcolm reminded one visitor to 'give a few shillings' to the contractor's enginemen; *Highland Railway Society Journal*, 90 (2009), items from George Malcolm's correspondence.

[17] *Highland Railway Society Journal*, 90 (2009), items from George Malcolm's correspondence.

[18] NRS, BR/TT(S), North British Railway traffic notices and working timetables (see also similar materials for the Caledonian Railway and Highland Railway).

[19] The quarrel was less petty than appears; any future Spean-to-Spey line would need The MacKintosh's goodwill; see McGregor, *West Highland Railway*, p. 220; NRS, BR/WEH/4/4, Tulloch.

he instructed his factor to restrict public use of the new road from Loch
Rannoch to Rannoch station – for which the West Highland Company
had paid – until the local authorities intervened.[20]

Corrour Forest had been purchased by Stirling-Maxwell on the
assurance of access by rail. George Malcolm, in addition to his Glen
Garry and Glen Quoich duties, became factor for the estate, in which
capacity he oversaw the building of an imposing new lodge by Loch
Ossian. In railway terms Corrour was a passing place, dividing the
long single-track section between Rannoch and Inverlair. As a private
station it posed problems. Goods and postal deliveries were at first
contentious, and a cumbersome procedure continued to govern passenger use. Tempers were not improved when Fort William tradesmen
bound for Corrour asserted that Malcolm's name could stop any train,
while Stirling-Maxwell was outraged when the North British insisted
that he vouch for all his employees and intended guests. Having allowed
Lucas & Aird to take sand and gravel without charge, besides engaging
to obtain his coals 'from North British pits' (that is, the mines on the
North British network), he now threatened second thoughts.[21] North
British intransigence stemmed from anxiety that the Board of Trade
might prescribe expensive improvements and safeguards if Corrour's
status were redefined. That passengers were charged 'next station' fares
became Malcolm's especial grievance, and he finally forced the issue by
refusing to pay the excess. An acrimonious correspondence ensued, until
the North British solicitor advised that legal action to recover the small
sum at stake would be folly. By making Corrour a very basic public
station, a solution was eventually found.[22]

Safeguards for Lord Breadalbane's Blackmount deer and River Orchy
salmon were scheduled to the West Highland Railway Act.[23] In planning to re-establish a drove stance at Bridge of Orchy he was in accord
with the West Highland promoters, who counted on intercepting livestock traffic bound for Callander & Oban Tyndrum. When the railway
opened, summer coaches from Ballachulish to Glen Coe and Glen
Etive would be extended to Glen Orchy, creating new circular tours.
Breadalbane stipulated (perhaps illogically) that his lessees at Bridge of

[20] McGregor, *West Highland Railway*, p. 220; NRS, BR/NBR/8/1764/4, Forman
to Conacher, 14 December 1894.

[21] McGregor, *West Highland Railway*, pp. 223–4.

[22] McGregor, *West Highland Railway*, pp. 223–4; NRS, BR/NBR/8/1764/7,
'excess' and other disputes: correspondence, May–June, September 1897.

[23] NRS, BR/PYB(S)/1/342, West Highland Railway Bill, 1888–9, protection
clauses.

Orchy Hotel and Inveroran Inn should not be encouraged to undertake seasonal coaching, because their main interest was the sale of 'alcoholic beverages' to travellers. His pet scheme was a temperance refreshment room, for drovers and summer tourists alike, at Bridge of Orchy station. But the North British had already fixed on Crianlarich, midway between Glasgow and Fort William, as the West Highland's locomotive servicing and 'refreshment' stop. It was another disappointment that the Board of Trade approved a Bridge of Orchy level crossing on the then parliamentary road, although Breadalbane pressed for a bridge.[24]

The North British Company's relations with the marquess deteriorated once traffic on the West Highland began. He threatened to join with opponents of the Treasury Guarantee on which the West Highland Mallaig Extension depended, unless the Callander & Oban-to-West Highland connection at Crianlarich, included in the West Highland Act, was speedily brought into use. The mutual antagonism of Caledonian Company and North British would keep the spur lying idle into 1897.[25] In return for water rights at Crianlarich and Bridge of Orchy he demanded that factor William Dunn be granted free travel over the entire West Highland line. Breadalbane entertained exaggerated fears that North British subterfuge would turn Gorton passing-place (which split the section Bridge of Orchy–Rannoch) into a more-or-less public station, and he insisted on a new agreement prohibiting passenger facilities within his Blackmount preserves. His commissioner, John Blair of Davidson & Syme, was instructed to pursue both water-rights dispute and Gorton dispute to the Court of Session. Assembling evidence and checking facts on the ground meant more labour for Dunn. Conflicts arose too because the North British had sited their surfacemen's cottages (some half a dozen between Ardlui and Gorton) without consulting farmers, foresters or factor.[26]

[24] McGregor, *West Highland Railway*, p. 171; NRS, GC112/53/100; BR/1764/2, Breadalbane to Conacher, 23 October 1893, 28 February 1894; GD112/53/100, Formans and McCall, memorandum, [n.d.] October 1890.

[25] NRS, BR/PYB(S)/1/342, protection clauses; NRS, GD/112/53/112, Davidson and Syme to Formans and McCall, 3 June 1894; NRS, GD/112/53/116, Breadalbane to Marquess of Tweeddale, chairman, North British Railway, 19 February 1895; *Scotsman*, letter to the editor from Breadalbane, 'Crianlarich Junction', 19 September 1896; NRS, GD/112/53/118, revised agreement and Breadalbane to Conacher, 30 October 1896.

[26] NRS, BR/NBR/8/1764/4, Breadalbane to Conacher, 26 October 1895.

LANDOWNERS' LINES

The constituent companies of the Highland Railway (formed by amal-
gamation) were 'landowners' lines' and obtained relatively little outside
finance.[27] In origin the Callander & Oban Railway was similarly a 'landowners' line', though it became the client of the Scottish Central Railway
and thus of the Caledonian Company, who would absorb the Scottish
Central.[28] A landowners' venture which did not prosper was the Fort
William Railway of 1862–3, proposed as a feeder to the Perth–Inverness
trunk route. An early Spey-and-Spean project, it would have run from
Etteridge or Newtonmore by Loch Laggan into Lochaber. Realising that
costs must far outstrip their own resources, the proprietors retreated,
though cajoled by their engineer – Thomas Bouch, later of first Tay
Bridge notoriety – to look elsewhere for capital.[29] The key ingredient
of the Clyde, Ardrishaig & Crinan and West Highland promotions, a
quarter of a century later, was the chronic feuding of Caledonian and
North British; and in pushing these and other schemes, engineer Charles
Forman (see Figure 2) would play adeptly on inter-company rivalries,
North British and Highland besides North British and Caledonian.
Nevertheless, at least the appearance of landowner initiative was needed
and their active backing thereafter was indispensable.

A carefully crafted landed alliance helped the West Highland Bill
through Parliament, softening the speculative interest of Formans &
McCall and Lucas & Aird, while partially disguising the expansion-
ist intentions of the North British Company.[30] Lord Abinger and
Cameron of Lochiel, veteran railway campaigners, secured pledges of
support or, at worst, promises to stand neutral along the entire route
to Fort William and Banavie. Lord Breadalbane, despite his Highland
Railway and Callander & Oban directorships, had reluctantly conceded
'public need'. At the southern end of the line the Luss Trustees, who
wanted railway extension to Garelochhead or Arrochar, were recruited.

---

[27] P. Fletcher, 'Railway capital in northern Scotland, 1844–1874', *Journal
of Scottish Historical Studies*, 30:2 (2010), pp. 146–74; P. Fletcher, *Directors,
Dilemmas and Debt: The Great North of Scotland and Highland Railways in the
Mid-Nineteenth Century* (York, 2010).

[28] J. Thomas, *The Callander and Oban Railway* (Newton Abbot, 1966), pp.
24–8.

[29] McGregor, *West Highland Railway*, pp. 24, 43–4; Highland Council Archives,
Lochaber, Cameron of Lochiel Papers, CL/A/3/2/73/5, correspondence on the proposed Fort William Railway, 1863.

[30] McGregor, *West Highland Railway*, ch. 3.

Figure 2 Charles Forman, with thanks to
the late Rev. Diana Forman.

Edinburgh solicitor Colin MacRae, of MacRae, Flett & Rennie, acted for
the West Highland promoters and subsequently for the West Highland
Company, with Fort William's Nigel MacKenzie in a subordinate role.[31]
Together MacRae and MacKenzie found a formula, in consultation
with engineer Charles Forman, whereby no onerous expense would fall
on Lochiel or the other landed promoters, in the event that the West
Highland Bill had to be withdrawn.[32]

MacRae sought friendly witnesses between Craigendoran and
Crianlarich and assembled the overall West Highland case. For the
districts between Crianlarich and Roshven, MacKenzie precognosed
many of those whose evidence was desirable, then refined what they
should say in Parliament. When the West Highland's Roshven arm was
struck out by the House of Lords Committee (where the West Highland
Bill began), he reassessed the testimony to be offered in the Commons,
when it became the promoters' case that a railway terminating for
the time being at Fort William was a necessary first step towards the
west coast. These heavily annotated proofs survive and can be compared, often revealingly, with the polished parliamentary minutes of

[31] McGregor, *West Highland Railway*, ch. 3.
[32] Highland Council Archives, Lochaber, CL/A/3/2/73/1, Lochiel to J. Brookman,
Lindsay Howe (solicitors), 14 November 1888; Brookman–Mackenzie memorandum, 11 December 1888.

evidence.[33] It was MacKenzie's boast that, during his lengthy career, he represented more landowners across the western Highlands than any other factor-solicitor. He initiated the press campaign from which the West Highland scheme sprang; and, as provost of Fort William and local agent for the British Linen Bank, he readily mobilised the town's hoteliers, merchants and professional men.[34] No one was better placed to bring burgh and 'country' (the Lochaber proprietors and their sporting lessees) together, though others with a foot in both camps contributed too. Distiller Donald MacDonald was Fort William's main employer, but he leased Lord Abinger's Ben Nevis distillery at Lochy Bridge, additional to his own Nevis distillery in the town, and tenanted two farms on Abinger's estate.

One of George Malcolm's many professional roles was secretary of the Highland Property Association; he also claimed a special knowledge of deer management. From experience at Glen Garry and Glen Quoich he argued that, in depressed times for agriculture, sporting estates offered more employment and would yield more railway revenue, year round, than unlet sheep farms. He also prepared tables of the traffic to be generated by movement of livestock and imports of animal feed and other agricultural materials. Witnesses generally emphasised sheep traffic, both the annual shed and the to and fro of wintering; but the possibility of summering store cattle in Brae Lochaber (Glen Spean and Glen Roy) was urged as well. Malcolm, the Caledonian Company complained, had been treacherous. The Lochaber landowners were not unwilling to accept a Callander & Oban branch from Connel Ferry, but Fort William favoured an independent venture and looked instead to the North British. As country spokesman, Malcolm had kept Callander & Oban and Caledonian in play until the West Highland scheme covertly matured and the North British were fully committed. Donald Boyd, Fort William's leading merchant, was Malcolm's partner in deceit.[35]

From Skye, farmer and sometime factor for Lord MacDonald, Donald MacDonald, testified that the Roshven–Glasgow route would attract a useful share of the island's sheep traffic.[36] William Dunn confirmed that Argyll and Perthshire carried large sheep stocks; moreover,

[33] Fort William, West Highland Museum, N. B. MacKenzie Papers; NRS, PYB(S)/1/342, West Highland Railway Bill, 1888–9, evidence, Lords and Commons.

[34] McGregor, *West Highland Railway*, pp. 50–6.

[35] NRS, BR/PYB(S)/1/342, West Highland Railway Bill, evidence, 27 March 1889, 4 July 1889, and speech for the Caledonian Railway, 2 April 1889.

[36] NRS, BR/PYB(S)/1/342, West Highland Railway Bill, evidence, 29 March 1889.

Breadalbane's tenant farmers expected to have two routes at their disposal, once exchange of traffic at Crianlarich was effected.[37] Those already served by the Oban line, which ran east–west through Glen Dochart, Strathfillan and Glen Lochy, would gain a new, shorter route to Glasgow. Those to be served by the West Highland anticipated in addition easier access eastwards, via Crianlarich, to the auction marts of Stirling and Perth and the wintering grounds of Strathmore. James Wilson, the Luss factor, testified that the West Highland would stimulate 'residential' development between Helensburgh and Arrochar, as Sir James Colquhoun and his Trustees desired.[38] In the event new feuing proved sluggish and there were other recriminations, because the promised station at Whistlefield, serving Lochlongside and the Colquhouns' Glen Mallan lodge, was delayed into 1896. Nevertheless, a siding at Glen Douglas passing place, between Garelochhead and Arrochar & Tarbet stations, would liberate several Colquhoun tenants from dependence on the steamers plying Loch Lomond and Loch Long. Further north, one proposal remained unfulfilled. John Scott, factor for the Meggernie estate in Glen Lyon, had suggested that the bridle path by Auch be made a metalled road for access to West Highland Bridge of Orchy – so supplementing the existing railheads at Aberfeldy (Highland Company) and Killin (Callander & Oban and Killin Companies).[39]

MacRae and MacKenzie prepared a draft petition-in-favour, distributed all along the West Highland route (see Figure 3). The form of words invoked by the Napier Report rejected any alternative Callander & Oban scheme as inadequate and dismissed the Highland Company's fears. Sceptical parliamentary committees might have scant regard for inflated and formulaic petitions, but these submissions were a measure of any railway bill's prospects. John Scott covered Glen Lyon. Other canvassers included Alexander Craig, estate manager for Colonel Gustavus Walker at Lochtreighead, and farmer William Menzies, Breadalbane's tenant at Keilator (Crianlarich). Distiller MacDonald, who farmed at Keppoch (Roy Bridge), obtained signatures in Glen Spean and Glen Roy. Duncan MacDiarmid of Camus Ericht, farmer and cattle dealer, a tenant of Sir Robert Menzies, covered the Rannoch district.[40] These were men of local influence, prospective parliamentary witnesses, who formed a tight

[37] NRS, BR/PYB(S)/1/342, West Highland Railway Bill, evidence, 4 July 1889.
[38] NRS, BR/PYB(S)/1/342, West Highland Railway Bill, evidence, 27 March 1889.
[39] NRS, BR/PYB(S)/1/342, West Highland Railway Bill, evidence, 4 July 1889.
[40] Fort William, West Highland Museum, N. B. MacKenzie Papers.

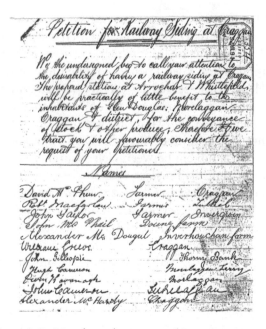

Figure 3 Petition from the tenants of Luss, January
1897[?], to James Wilson, land agent for Luss estates.
National Records of Scotland, BR/NBR/8/1764/5.

network. MacDiarmid, a personal friend of MacDonald, had another
holding in Glen Lyon. Scott had been previously a sub-factor on the
Breadalbane estates. Fletcher Menzies, brother of William, farmed by
Loch Rannoch – he was secretary of the Highland Agricultural Society
and would reinforce George Malcolm's evidence on traffic generated by
sporting estates.[41]

Where witnesses for the Glasgow & North Western Bill had indulged
their unquantified hopes, the orchestrated input of landowners, sporting
lessees, factors and tenant farmers gave the West Highland presentation
in 1888–9 a more disciplined and persuasive tone. Droving across the
western Highlands would be reorganised, in response to the facilities
offered at Bridge of Orchy and Spean Bridge; wintering options would
increase and itinerant livestock dealers would give way to regular local
markets. Besides the annual migration across the Border by the well-
to-do, their movements within the Highlands between mansion and
mansion, shooting lodge and shooting lodge, with paraphernalia and

[41] NRS, BR/PYB(S)/1/342, West Highland Railway Bill, evidence, 27 March
1889.

domestics, would boost both first-class and third-class railway revenue. Local quarrying would expand and wagon-load quantities of granite and other minerals might be sent south – reducing, moreover, the 'empty returns' which kept railway working expenses high. Population was sparse but the lonely West Highland stations would become concentration points, with wide catchments. All this countered the protests of the Highland Company and the Caledonian, founded on hard experience, that the new line's potential revenue was being much exaggerated, especially in respect of the traffic likely to be 'captured from the sea'. In short, factor-witnesses helped sustain a seemingly authoritative and balanced, if in reality overstated, presentation.[42]

Factors were in some sense 'professional witnesses', their expertise in demand, and not thirled to any one landowner or railway project. George Glendinning, who farmed in Midlothian on his own account, spoke *against* the West Highland Mallaig Extension but had earlier been a witness *for* the West Highland Company in respect of Lord Breadalbane's compensation claims.[43] And the broad case made for the West Highland had some substance. On into the twentieth century, the August-to-October season always boosted Scottish railway earnings, despite the early impact of private motoring. Although traditional droving, overtaken by coastal steamer services, had revived when railheads such as Dalwhinnie, Lairg and Tyndrum became available, its final decline was in sight: nevertheless, livestock would be a staple traffic at several intermediate West Highland stations, while Fort William acquired an auction mart (and complementary abattoir) once a rail service was in place. The 'catchment' argument, a more judicious version of the extravagant Glasgow & North Western presentation, proved at least partially valid. West Highland Arrochar & Tarbet, with a local train service from Craigendoran, tapped the Loch Fyne district, in competition with Callander & Oban Dalmally. Remote Rannoch, by serving the whole valley eastward to Loch Tummel, generated a steady, useful income.

The Highland Company and the Callander & Oban could readily demonstrate how the sea 'ruled' their rates for coal and freight. Besides the competing coastal vessels of the Moray Firth and the western seaboard, regular cargo steamers ran both from Glasgow and from Liverpool to Inverness via the Caledonian Canal.[44] The distiller MacDonald, who

---

[42] McGregor, *West Highland Railway*, chs 2, 3 (quote at pp. 50–2).
[43] See NRS, GD112/53/97.
[44] NRS, BR/PYB(S)/1/342, West Highland Railway Bill, evidence: Andrew

owned a steamer and built his own pier at Fort William (subsequently purchased by the West Highland Company), emphasised the convenience and flexibility of wagon-load over ship-load for his barley, draff, fuel and bottled whisky; but he expected rail transport to be no cheaper.[45] James Wilson felt bound to add, when explaining how a railway would benefit the Luss estate, that traffic in domestic coal and timber thinnings was likely to remain with the lighters on the Gare Loch and Loch Long. The promise of a third railway harbour, midway between Oban and Strome Ferry, was the West Highland promoters' best card. Besides boosting the west-coast fishery and helping to professionalise the crofter-fisherman, this must improve mail and passenger services and reduce dependence on sea transport for heavy or bulky goods. In a West Highland 'proof' recorded by MacKenzie, Ardnamurchan factor Thomas Armstrong asserted that 'going past' was the constant complaint of those who relied on David MacBrayne's steamers. When weather or circumstances dictated, passenger landings might be cancelled, with urgent consignments for communities along the west coast carried to Portree, Gairloch or Stornoway and delivered days later, on the vessel's return run to the Clyde. This time Armstrong did not give evidence but other parliamentary witnesses bore him out.[46]

It is arguable, however, that in 1888–9 the West Highland promoters saw their 30-mile Roshven extension as only a marker, a declaration of intent, until government subsidy was certain. The North British Company's guarantee did not reach beyond Fort William, while Lord Morton at Craigag and Professor Hugh Blackburn (the Roshven proprietor), were not won over by Lord Abinger and Cameron of Lochiel. The Roshven line for the moment could not be built and for that reason, besides landowner dissent, it was rejected in the House of Lords. Ranald MacDonald, factor for the Gordon-Cathcart estates in Moray and the Outer Isles, spoke for the proposed harbour; he favoured the short passage from Barra and South Uist to Loch Ailort.[47] But the influential Alexander MacDonald of Portree, factor for several Skye properties, had at once begun a further press campaign urging that Mallaig bay was better situated and better sheltered, especially for fishermen working

Dougall, secretary-general manager, Highland Railway and John Anderson, secretary-general manager, Callander & Oban Railway, 2 April 1889, 3 April 1889.

[45] NRS, BR/PYB(S)/1/342, West Highland Railway Bill, evidence, 4 July 1889.

[46] Fort William, West Highland Museum, N. B. MacKenzie Papers.

[47] NRS, BR/PYB(S)/1/342, West Highland Railway Bill, evidence, 28 March 1889.

the sea lochs of Knoydart and southern Skye. Oban-bound sail boats faced stormy Ardnamurchan Point, Strome-bound boats the tides of Kylerhea; but the rapid increase in steam fishing vessels, able to run at will to any port, would soon overtake all such debate.[48] Earlier, both men had endorsed the Glasgow & North Western promoters' dubious claim that, in the short term, barrelled herring might be carted inland to the railway by existing roads, via either Arisaig to Lochy Bridge or Loch Hourn to Invergarry.[49]

To treat Roshven as expendable risked the whole project but the gamble (if such it was) in the end succeeded. With construction to Fort William in progress, a new westward line, the Loch Eil & Mallaig Railway, was surveyed in 1891, soon retitled the West Highland Mallaig Extension. When a Treasury Guarantee was in place, plus an outright grant towards the cost of Mallaig harbour and the promise of partial relief from local authority rates, the North British rewrote *their* guarantee, to embrace the entire Craigendoran–Mallaig route. Meanwhile the Highland Company had received a parliamentary grant whereby the Dingwall & Skye line was continued to Kyle of Lochalsh – the terminus first intended – while the Caledonian stood to benefit from additional (subsidised) steamer services out of Oban. This roughly equitable outcome followed, after much controversy, from the recommendations of the Lothian Commission (1889–90).[50]

The Loch Eil & Mallaig was on the face of things a latter-day 'landowners' line', commended by the Lothian Commissioners. Ostensibly, John Baird of Knoydart took the initiative – he had welcomed the Glasgow & North Western scheme in 1883, though not the West Highland's Roshven line in 1889 – but Cameron of Lochiel, now a West Highland director, assumed the lead. Lord Abinger, co-architect with Lochiel of the previous landed alliance, died in 1892. It is perhaps not a coincidence that the wider Baird family, Gartsherrie coal and iron masters, had strong ties with the North British Railway and with the engineer Alexander Simpson, who adapted Forman's layout and continued it from Kinlochailort to Mallaig. Radical opinion generally and, more specifically, the Crofter–Liberals Members of Parliament who had swept the constituencies of the western Highlands after 1885 regarded

---

[48] *Scotsman*, letter to the editor, 'proposed West Highland Railway', 18 December 1888. These were largely east-coast boats, fishing the west coast in season.

[49] NRS, BR/PYB(S)/1/325, Glasgow & North Western Railway Bill, 1882–3, evidence, 2 May 1883.

[50] McGregor, *West Highland Railway*, ch. 4.

subsidised transport as only a palliative, whereby proprietors might evade fundamental land reform and railway companies reap undeserved rewards.[51] They saw the landed interest as set on more emigration – a suspicion reinforced when Lord Abinger, in an unguarded moment, declared that the West Highland would encourage the 'paying population' and, by implication, hasten others on their way to Canada.[52] In these circumstances it behoved landlords, sporting tenants and estate factors along the Mallaig line to demonstrate their public spirit-cum-social conscience. The two recalcitrants of 1889–90 came aboard – Lord Morton thought outright opposition useless, while Professor Blackburn was an active supporter. Lord Lovat, as a Morar proprietor, conformed; though a Highland Railway loyalist, he admitted 'public necessity'. Only Mrs Cameron-Head at Inverailort briefly broke ranks.[53]

In Parliament in 1894 all turned on the potential expansion of the west-coast fishery, on government aid and on the adequacy of Mallaig harbour. 'Land' evidence was less needed. Ranald MacDonald was reconciled to Mallaig and testified accordingly. Nigel MacKenzie once more reviewed a range of 'proofs' and gave his own evidence. George Malcolm provided both agricultural and fishing statistics. If light railways were to reach out from Kyleakin, as the Lothian Commission had suggested, the Highland Railway might draw much of Skye's sheep-wintering to Kyle of Lochalsh; but James MacKintosh, Lord MacDonald's new factor, predicted that a remunerative livestock traffic would accrue to the Mallaig Extension.[54] Skye's light lines would not materialise.

The Great Glen Agreement ('Ten Years Truce') of 1889, to which the North British were party, forbad any West Highland thrust through the Glen to Inverness for a decade after traffic to Fort William had begun. On this basis, the Highland Company ceased their Commons opposition to the West Highland Bill, now shorn of Roshven and any immediate threat to Strome Ferry. Undermined by the machinations of Charles Forman, the Agreement was repaired (1894–5), only to be challenged once more by Forman's Invergarry & Fort Augustus scheme (1895–6). Both the Highland Company and the North British loudly condemned this promotion as at bottom speculative, designed to provoke conflict,

[51] E. A. Cameron, *Land for the People?: The British Government and the Scottish Highlands, 1880–1925* (East Linton, 1996). Cameron suggests that landowners under reform pressure saw 'technocratic' measures as usefully diversionary.

[52] NRS, BR/PYB(S)/1/342, evidence; Lord Abinger, 27 March 1889.

[53] McGregor, *West Highland Railway*, chs 4, 5.

[54] NRS, BR/PYB(S)/1/93, West Highland, Mallaig Extension Railway Bill, evidence, 30 April 1894, 11 July 1894, 12 July 1894.

when either Highland or North British could be manoeuvred into buying out the investors.[55] Lord Burton's associations with the Glasgow & North Western project have never been unravelled. The compromise Agreement of 1889, he had reluctantly acknowledged, helped the West Highland to success. But locking up the Great Glen for years ahead was objectionable and he was ready to close with Forman's latest plan. George Malcolm was of similar mind, but his employees, the Ellice Trustees, thought their new West Highland railhead at Spean Bridge quite sufficient.[56]

A comprehensive alliance of landowners along the Invergarry & Fort Augustus route could not be attained. Mrs Ellice was lukewarm, Lord Lovat implacably hostile. The new Lord Abinger was favourable but a frequent absentee and so lent his factor's services in canvassing support. Cameron of Lochiel felt obliged to declare neutrality. However, the 20-mile railway could claim to be a 'sportsmen's line', serving a dozen lodges, with their shootings and fishings.[57] Connecting local communities with the West Highland, it might be incorporated eventually into a through route to Inverness; the ultimate aim, in theory, of both Highland and North British, despite their obvious intent that the Great Glen should remain a no-man's-land. Construction was adequately funded and in the end did not greatly exceed estimated costs; operating expenses were another matter. Highland and North British would fight for working powers, with Burton and his associates by this time at their mercy. Railway matters would increasingly absorb Malcolm's time; persuaded to join the Invergarry & Fort Augustus board, he would see out the unhappy history of the eventually friendless and bankrupt little company.[58]

CONCLUSION

A final glance at Nigel MacKenzie's sometimes buccaneering career is appropriate. MacKenzie persuaded wavering and credulous sporting tenants, who might have opposed the West Highland, that railway

[55] NRS, BR/NBR/8/1764/6, Malcolm to Conacher, 17 August 1896; BR/IFA/4/1/, Keyden, Strang and Girvan (agents, Invergarry & Fort Augustus Railway) to Malcolm, 1 September 1896.

[56] McGregor, *West Highland Railway*, ch. 6.

[57] NRS, BR/PYB(S)/1/386, Invergarry and Fort Augustus Railway Bill: data 'handed in', 1895–6.

[58] NRS, BR/IFA/4/1–12, Invergarry and Fort Augustus Railway letter books, 1895–1914, *passim*.

building would pause during shooting seasons.[59] From his intimate knowledge of Inverailort and adjacent estates, he helped demolish the embarrassing Cameron-Head petition against the West Highland Mallaig Extension Bill. The deer forest which they claimed was already established and much at risk had not been fully fenced and supported few stags.[60] To dispose of this and other grievances the Cameron-Heads' Lechavuie platform became a compensatory sop. And MacKenzie, as Lochaber agent for the West Highland Company, had declined to act for the Invergarry & Fort Augustus syndicate. Briefed 'unofficially' by the North British to deter and discredit the unwelcome Great Glen scheme, he organised bogus local meetings, planting press reports of poor attendance and an indifferent populace; for all the fury of the promoters, he escaped retribution.[61]

As this chapter has demonstrated, factors were essential intermediaries, promoters and resisters to railway development in remote and rural Scotland, as they were in other parts of Britain. In many ways this should not surprise us; factors were well networked, positioned to speak with authority and a degree of expertise to government, as well as titled landowners and railway companies. As the story of the West Highland Line shows, factors at various times were on both sides of the railway debate, at times arguing for the benefits it would bring to their employers and local areas, and at others as passionately opposed if it was seen to damage their interests. On whichever side they were on at any one time, their legal, technical and locally rooted expertise was starkly illustrated, and not to be underestimated.

[59] Highland Council Archives, Lochaber, CL/A/3/2/73/1, Brookman–MacKenzie correspondence.

[60] McGregor, *West Highland Railway*, ch. 5.

[61] NRS, BR/IFA/4/1, Keyden, Strang and Girvan to MacKenzie, 12 March 1896, 16 March 1896.

PART II

The Transnational Land Agent:
Managing Land in the Four Nations and Beyond

4

Divisions of Labour:
Inter-managerial Conflict among the
Wentworth-Fitzwilliam Agents

Fidelma Byrne

INTRODUCTION

IN LATE DECEMBER 1848 Daniel Maude, auditor to the Wentworth-Fitzwilliam estates, wrote to the 5th Earl Fitzwilliam concerning expenditure practices on his South Yorkshire estate. In his correspondence, Maude was highly critical of how certain strands of the commercial enterprise at Wentworth were functioning. He stated: 'I can scarcely with any conscience or satisfaction to myself suggest to your Lordship any measure of economical reform while the extravagant item remains unreformed to some extent at least.'[1] The item to which the auditor was referring was the earl's coal-mining activities, which formed a sizeable portion of the aristocrat's business portfolio.[2] From 1833 this component was managed by Benjamin Biram (1804–57), who also acted as the house steward on the estate.[3] Daniel Maude's contempt for Biram did not suddenly appear. From his appointment in 1841 Maude had uncovered certain defects within Biram's agency, not least of which was the colliery agent's tendency to overspend. Consequently, by the mid-1840s the auditor had amassed a litany of issues arising from Biram's management which he felt warranted intervention, and he was not alone in his thoughts. By this time William Newman, the earl's land agent, had also grown weary of the unregulated and often reckless conduct of Biram, which resulted in large deposits of money amassed through

---

[1] Northamptonshire Record Office [hereafter NRO], Fitzwilliam (Milton) MSS, Daniel Maude to Earl Fitzwilliam, 27 December 1848.

[2] G. Mee, *Aristocratic Enterprise: The Fitzwilliam Industrial Undertakings, 1795–1857* (Glasgow, 1975), p. 4.

[3] The terms 'steward' and 'agent' were used interchangeably during this period to describe the role of the land and house manager at Wentworth. From 1864 both roles were merged and the term 'land agent' was used. For the purposes of this chapter, 'agent' will be used as a term of convenience throughout.

other ventures being used to sustain the industrial arm of the estate enterprises at Wentworth. Newman, akin to Maude, felt that measures should be implemented to mitigate against any further erosion of the estate finances. Amidst their mutual discontent, the auditor and land agent resolved to work together in an effort to convince the earl that in order to make the estate more profitable, Biram needed to be relieved of his duties, or at the very least taken in hand.

In theory this task seemed relatively straightforward; the evidence as presented upheld the claims of both men. However, in practice the complex nature of the power dynamics that existed between the Wentworth-Fitzwilliam agents coupled with their employer's inherent ideology of landlord paternalism rendered this a virtually impossible task. This chapter examines those who occupied positions of authority on the estate and explores the hierarchical structure of the management system by charting how this tripartite agency developed as a consequence of estate expansion. It discusses the agents' background, education and training and in so doing, exposes the core belief system underpinning the Earls Fitzwilliam philosophy. While morally admirable, this ideology had a somewhat negative effect on the estate in terms of economic progression. However, from the mid-nineteenth century the impact of landlord paternalism was minimised by the improved economic climate in South Yorkshire, which also placed Biram in a more favourable position when challenged about his management practices. Unlike the Irish land system, which was chiefly concerned with agricultural land, the South Yorkshire estate was quite distinct, for in addition to its agricultural interests, it contained industrial elements – predominantly coal and ironstone – and thus required a more elaborate administration structure.[4] Perhaps unsurprisingly, in creating an array of roles to oversee the external divisions of labour, internal fissures developed which over time widened to reveal the sometimes flawed management system on the estate.

---

[4] There are of course rare exceptions to this statement. For example, the 20,000-acre Wandesforde estate centred on Castlecomer in County Kilkenny contained the Leinster coalfield. The family mainly leased their industrial holdings although Joseph Dobbs was employed as the colliery agent from 1874 until 1905; see T. Lyng, *Castlecomer Connections: Exploring History, Geography, and Social Evolution in North Kilkenny Environs* (Kilkenny, 1984).

MANAGING THE LANDED INTERESTS

Before examining the complexities of the management structure at Wentworth, it is necessary to provide an overview of the estate at the time of its acquisition by the Fitzwilliam family and its rapid development thereafter, as each of these factors had a profound effect on the style of management that dominated the first half of the nineteenth century. Prior to July 1782 the Wentworth estate in South Yorkshire, which comprised approximately 14,000 acres including the palatial residence of Wentworth Woodhouse, was owned by the aristocratic Marquesses of Rockingham. When the 2nd marquess died without issue on 1 July 1782, the family's vast inheritance passed to his nephew, the 4th Earl Fitzwilliam (1748–1833). It was just one of four properties William Wentworth-Fitzwilliam acquired following the death of his maternal uncle.[5] The Fitzwilliam family were substantial landowners in their own right, owning land in Norfolk, Nottinghamshire and Lincolnshire as well as the family's principal residence, the Milton estate on the outskirts of Peterborough in Northamptonshire. That said, the acquisition of the Rockingham inheritance, and in particular the Wentworth estate, undeniably elevated the family in political and economic terms.[6] In addition to its agricultural land, the Wentworth estate was positioned in the heart of the South Yorkshire coalfield above the Barnsley seam. This industrial situation had been exploited to good effect by the Rockinghams during their tenure. G. E. Mingay notes that 'in 1759 . . . seven collieries produced [an annual income of] £1,094'.[7] It was this industrial element that seemed to capture the imagination of both the 4th and, indeed, 5th Earl Fitzwilliam. Within a relatively short period of time, a number of new pits were opened including New Elsecar colliery in 1795. That same year the 4th earl embraced the Industrial Revolution and was one of the first proprietors in the region to install a Newcomen beam engine at his colliery in Elsecar. This technology, which replaced manual horse-gins,

---

[5] The 3rd Earl Fitzwilliam married Lady Anne Watson-Wentworth in 1744, and William was born in 1748. The other three properties in the Rockingham inheritance included a 3,000-acre estate at Malton in North Yorkshire, land at Higham Ferrers in Northamptonshire as well as a further 66,000 acres of land in Ireland, predominantly in County Wicklow with some satellite areas in Counties Wexford and Kildare; see E. A. Smith, *Whig Principles and Party Politics: Earl Fitzwilliam and the Whig Party, 1718–1833* (Manchester, 1975), pp. 30–1.

[6] Smith, *Whig Principles and Party Politics*, p. 11.

[7] G. E. Mingay, *English Landed Society in the Eighteenth Century* (London, 2007), p. 195.

greatly improved the cost-effectiveness of the pit as it allowed copious amounts of water to be extracted faster, thus improving the productivity of the operation. Such was its success at Elsecar that in 1823 and again in 1843 the estate installed two further engines at Parkgate and Hemingfield collieries respectively to facilitate the deeper workings of the coal seams.[8] In the early years these endeavours required considerable investment, often with very little return. Thus, the agricultural rents remained an integral economic unit as they provided a steady annual source of income to the estate.

When the 4th earl acquired the property in 1782, the management of the estate was divided between Richard Fenton (1708–88) and Benjamin Hall (1721–1805). Fenton resided at Bank Top, in the township of Worsborough, and was an attorney by profession.[9] Aside from his management of the land, Fenton's position also encompassed a number of auxiliary roles including that of legal advisor and auditor over the English estates. Equally, the connection between land and politics provided a political dimension to the role.[10] Sarah Webster contends that this blurred 'occupational pluralism' was a common feature of the time, as attorneys were preferred land agents because of their ability to mediate contentious issues.[11] Conversely, the appointment of Benjamin Hall to the position of house and colliery agent seems to have defied the standard conventions of the time. Hall was born in 1721 in Golcar near Huddersfield. Prior to his agency he served as a soldier in Price's 14th Foot initially although he later attained the rank of lieutenant with the 62nd Regiment of Foot.[12] In 1772, nine years after his retirement from military life, he accepted the position of house agent at Wentworth.

---

[8] Mee, *Aristocratic Enterprise*, p. 23. The Newcomen engine at Elsecar operated from 1795 until 1923. It is the only one in the world to have remained in its original location.

[9] S. J. Wright, *Bretton, the Beaumonts and a Bureaucracy: A West-Yorkshire Estate in the Eighteenth and Nineteenth Centuries* (Wakefield, 2001), p. 51.

[10] R. Robson, *The Attorney in Eighteenth-Century England* (Cambridge, 1959), p. 96.

[11] S. Webster, 'Estate improvement and the professionalisation of land agents on the Egremont estates in Sussex and Yorkshire, 1770–1835', *Rural History*, 28 (2007), pp. 47–69 (quote at p. 49).

[12] See *West Yorkshire, England, Church of England Baptisms, Marriages and Burials, 1512–1812*, St Peter's Huddersfield, baptism dated 25 January 1722, available at <http://www.ancestry.co.uk> (last accessed 1 June 2016). For details of Hall's military service, see Author Unknown, 'The Old Springers: a historical sketch of the 62nd Regiment', in H. Colburn (ed.), *The United Service Magazine and Naval and Military Journal* (174 vols, London, 1870), vol. 122, pp. 317–24.

Hall's role was no less diverse than that of Fenton. In addition to his usual task of managing the house and domestic servants, he catered to the needs of the charity schools, oversaw masonry work on various parts of the demesne and increasingly assumed responsibility for colliery operations.[13]

By 1782 the two men were of advanced years, and each had been assisted in their roles by their respective nephews who would subsequently take over as agents to the Wentworth estate. In 1789 Charles Bowns (c. 1753–1818), who had trained as an attorney and worked in his uncle's practice, took over as land agent, auditor and director of elections following the death of Richard Fenton. In 1805 the apprentice became the master when Joshua Biram (1759–1835) succeeded to the role of house and colliery agent following the death of Benjamin Hall at the age of eighty-four.[14] The positions which Bowns and Biram inherited were considerably more onerous than those held by their predecessors. In addition to auditing the English accounts, Bowns was also responsible for auditing the Irish estates. By 1811 the South Yorkshire estate comprised 17,522 acres and produced an annual income of £40,000. The majority of the money came from farm rentals with the remainder accrued through mining activities and canal developments supplemented by additional revenue.[15] Bowns received an annual salary of £400 from the earl although Fitzwilliam was not his sole employer. The solicitor juggled a number of other agencies, including the Bretton estate near Wakefield, as well as a number of smaller-sized holdings belonging to local gentry. His thriving business exploits led to his training a number of assistants including his nephew, William Newman. By 1811 Bowns was no longer content with his salary and asked for an increment. In a letter to the earl, the agent claimed the job 'necessarily occupied so much of my time that it has not been in my power to pursue the profession of solicitor to that extent which is sufficient to enable me to answer the growing expenses which I experience'.[16] Given Bowns's other business concerns, the agent's claim appears somewhat exaggerated. However, the earl discussed the matter with his accountant who agreed that the £400 a year was of little benefit to the man, and that in light of his

---

[13] See Sheffield Archives [hereafter SA], WWM/A/1380, Benjamin Hall's memoranda book, 1772–84.

[14] See SA, WWM/A/277, West-riding annual estate account, 1789; SA, WWM/F106/98, Joshua Biram Wentworth to Earl Fitzwilliam.

[15] SA, WWM/F106/17, W. Baldwin to Earl Fitzwilliam, 22 June 1811.

[16] SA, WWM/F106/16, Charles Bowns to Earl Fitzwilliam, 11 June 1811.

improvements and loyalty, an increase in his annual income was due. The recommendation was duly approved.[17] This move was significantly telling on numerous levels. First, it resulted in a threefold increase in the land agent's salary, an amount which exceeded that of William Wainwright, the earl's Irish land agent who enjoyed an annual salary of £1,000 for administering the earl's 80,000-acre Irish estate.[18] Perhaps the excessive nature of this pay increase is best contextualised by the fact that some thirty years later, Evander McIver, one of the land agents to the Sutherland estate in north-west Scotland, received an annual salary of just £400 for administering approximately 300,000 acres of the ducal family's vast 1.1 million-acre estate.[19] Second, given the post-war economy of the time, and the shadow of economic depression that prevailed, the granting of such an increase testifies to the wealth of the family. Third, and perhaps most significantly, Bowns had served the estate well and the earl felt morally obliged to grant his request, as later correspondence would demonstrate.[20] This is but one example of how landlord paternalism benefited the employee at the expense of the estate.

Conversely, Joshua Biram's position remained unchanged although the demands of the job from a mining perspective expanded as new seams were worked. His salary was substantially less than that of the land agent. Indeed, by 1830 the elderly house agent received a fixed salary of £150 per annum supplemented by bonus payments from the earl which amounted to approximately £400 per annum. While Joshua Biram did not complain about his situation, his son was more vociferous in his discontent. In a letter dated December 1831 Benjamin Biram claimed his father's wages were 'by no means proportionate to the duties which he had to perform'.[21] His complaint resulted in his father's salary being doubled to £300 per annum, which was to be augmented by a bonus payment.[22] Though much improved, the income was still well below that of the land agent. There is no doubt that the position of land agent was the more superior of the two; it required a professional well

[17] SA, WWM/F106/17, Charles Bowns to Earl Fitzwilliam, 22 June 1811.

[18] SA, WWM/F106/17, Charles Bowns to Earl Fitzwilliam, 22 June 1811; SA, WWM/A/898, Irish estate rental, 1811.

[19] A. Tindley, '"They sow the wind, they reap the whirlwind": estate management in the post-clearance Highlands, c. 1815–c. 1900', *Northern Scotland*, 3 (2012), pp. 66–85, especially p. 70.

[20] SA, WWM/F107/59, Earl Fitzwilliam to Rev. J. Lowe, 19 May 1818.

[21] SA, WWM/G40/24, Benjamin Biram to unidentified individual, 1 December 1831.

[22] SA, WWM/G40/28, Joshua Biram to Lord Milton, 24 December 1831.

versed in legal matters, which was reflected by its higher remuneration. Conversely, the position of colliery agent did not require the same level of education and therefore carried a lower salary. However, in this instance, the higher salary was more a reflection of expertise than a measure of autonomy enjoyed by the agent. These inconsistencies in salary merely reflect the competitiveness of the power dynamic on the estate. Charles Bowns had little time to enjoy his new-found wealth as he died in 1818, while Joshua Biram passed away in 1835. In each instance nepotism once again prevailed. William Newman replaced his uncle Charles in 1818, while Benjamin Biram took over as house and colliery agent in 1833.

ADJUSTING TO CHANGE – A NEW SYSTEM OF MANAGEMENT AT WENTWORTH

Charles Bowns's death heralded a new dawn in how the Wentworth estate would be managed in the future. By 1818 the 4th earl recognised that estate expansion had produced a number of economic units that required a more specialised style of management than had previously existed. The occupational pluralism which combined the role of agent and auditor was now divided into two clearly defined roles. In fact, a letter to the Rev. John Lowe, curate at Wentworth in May that year, appears to suggest that the earl had contemplated change prior to Bowns's death but had been prevented from introducing any modifications by his sense of duty to a loyal friend. In his correspondence the 4th earl stated that he felt the land agent's salary was excessive but admitted he had approved it 'because [he] would not bargain with an old servant with whose activity, intelligence and fidelity [he] was most perfectly satisfied'.[23] Consequently, Newman was offered the position of land agent and took up residence in Darley Hall. However, his job description was greatly reduced when compared with that of his late uncle. Newman continued to manage the agricultural aspects of the business, provided assistance on legal matters and was responsible for reconciling Biram's expenditure. The position carried an annual salary of £600, half that of his predecessor.[24] Conversely, the position of auditor to the Wentworth-Fitzwilliam estates was introduced and subsequently filled by Francis Maude.

Maude (1768–1842) came from a prominent Wakefield family. He had trained as a barrister and resided at Hatfeild Hall, an impressive

[23] SA, WWM/F107/59, Earl Fitzwilliam to Rev. J. Lowe, 19 May 1818.
[24] SA, WWM/F107/59, Earl Fitzwilliam to Rev. J. Lowe, 19 May 1818.

eighteenth-century structure, two and a half miles north-west of
Wakefield. The family also owned Alverthorpe Hall. Maude married in
1797 and was the father of six children.[25] He was an Oxford graduate
and in November 1796 was called to the bar at Gray's Inn. His relationship with the Fitzwilliam family predated his appointment. Held in high
esteem by the family, Maude was asked by the future 5th earl to be
godfather to one of his children in 1807.[26] On other occasions prior to
1818, he offered legal advice on various issues.[27]

By 1822 Benjamin Biram was sharing an office with his father at
Wentworth in preparation for one day assuming the position of house
and colliery agent. This 'on the job' training was a common feature
within the management structure. Each agent took on an apprentice,
generally a younger member of the family, and through practical experience provided them with the necessary skills to assume the role. This
process was not without its merits, as trusted families provided an
unbroken service with relative ease given their insider knowledge of the
estate and its workings. Conversely, it also contained a severe limitation
in that bad practice in one generation was passed down and replicated
in the next. In addition, the landlord's tendency to fill positions from
within families did not necessary enhance the workings of the estate, as
the case of Joshua and Benjamin Biram demonstrates. Of course, this
situation in many respects mirrored the heritable structures within the
landed classes, for while one landlord might be an astute businessman
who contributed enormously to the development of his estate, his successor could be reckless, accruing considerable debts which stunted the
economic development of the estate.

On numerous occasions throughout his agency Joshua Biram was
compelled to request additional funds in order to meet the escalating
overhead costs of running the house and sustaining the family's mining
interests. The amount required often exceeded half of the annual rental
receipts. In 1819 Newman wrote to the earl informing him that Biram
required £7,000 twice yearly in order to finance the mines and house.
Conversely, the remittances paid to Messrs Snow & Co., the London

---

[25] J. Burke, *A Genealogical and Heraldic History of the Landed Gentry; or,
Commoners of Great Britain and Ireland Enjoying Territorial Possessions or High
Official Rank but Uninvested with Heritable Honours* (4 vols, London, 1837), vol.
2, p. 83. For educational and professional details, see S. Urban, *The Gentleman's
Magazine* (New series, London, 1842), vol. 18, p. 330.

[26] SA, WWM/G83/1, Francis Maude to Lord Milton, 15 June 1807.

[27] See, for example, SA, WWM/F127/88, Francis Maude to Lord Milton, 16
February 1809.

bankers, fell short of this amount, totalling just £6,000 at each rental day.[28] By 1824 expenditure relating to the sinking of the New Park Gate colliery, which had opened the previous year, totalled £29,478, the largest capital investment by the estate since Fitzwilliam's acquisition.[29] Despite the obvious deficit between income and expenditure, custom also assisted in pushing up spiralling costs as launches and openings were frequently accompanied by vast displays of extravagance. At the launch of the *Fitzwilliam*, a boat for transporting coals on Greasbrough canal, in 1823, Biram arranged for 'a quantity of roast and boiled beef and bread [to be] taken to the wharf and 2 pipes of ale' for the workmen and concourse of assembled guests to partake in while 'the Rawmarsh Band of Music' entertained the crowd.[30] Biram seemed unperturbed by the overspend and continued to manage his areas safe in the knowledge that should extra finances be required, the estate had sufficient means to transfer funds to area of difficulty. Until 1825 Newman, the man charged with reconciling the annual accounts, himself seemed untroubled by Biram's management. In fact, that year he rather optimistically forecast that: 'the profits of the collieries and the mines should form a regular fund sufficient for the entire supply of Wentworth House and thus enable [him] at rent days to make larger remittances from thence to Messrs Snow'.[31] Newman's optimism was no doubt rooted in the fact that following the end of the Napoleonic wars, Yorkshire was no different to other parts of western Europe in that high inflation exerted pressure on many quarters. However, as the 1820s progressed, shoots of economic recovery were beginning to emerge. Transportation costs had previously impinged on the sale of coal in terms of geographical and economic accessibility, confining the commodity to local markets and those with means. This situation was altered by advances in canal development which resulted in a reduction in transport tariffs and by extension, coal.[32] Alan Birch contends that 1825 'was a period of prosperity when the smallest and apparently, the most inefficient works

[28] SA, WWM/F107/103, William Newman to Earl Fitzwilliam, 23 April 1819.

[29] I. Medlicott, 'Coal mining on the Wentworth estate, 1740–1840', in M. Jones (ed.), *Aspects of Rotherham 3: Discovering Local History* (Barnsley, 1998), pp. 134–53, 141.

[30] SA, WWM/F107/251, Joshua Biram to Earl Fitzwilliam, 27 May 1823.

[31] SA, WWM/F107/153, William Newman to Earl Fitzwilliam, 1 March 1825.

[32] In 1819 the opening of the Sheffield to Tinsley canal allowed Fitzwilliam to transport greater quantities of coal to Sheffield as a consequence of reduced transportation costs; see Medlicott, 'Coal mining on the Wentworth estate', pp. 134–53, 142–3.

could manage to make a living for its owner', hence Newman's cheerful disposition.[33] Despite the brief hiatus, economic depression returned with companies such as Elsecar Ironworks, which was leased to Darwin & Co., experiencing financial difficulty from 1823 and subsequently going into liquidation.[34]

By 1826 rental arrears on the estate stood at £15,354 8s., which further exacerbated the worsening financial situation. The largest expense was a total of £19,600 in fourteen separate payments made to Biram over a six-month period between 29 December 1825 and 30 June 1826.[35] In light of the discrepancy between arrears and overspend, Newman was understandably growing tired of the colliery agent's reckless spending. Correspondence reveals he spoke to the house agent regarding this, and reductions were made in labourers' wages at the mines and ironworks operated by the estate. However, despite the attempts of the land agent to engage with Biram throughout 1830 in an effort to reduce expenditure, by March 1831 the estate was £3,000 overdrawn with the Sheffield and Rotherham Bank.[36] At the same time, unknown to his ageing and infirm father, Benjamin Biram was complaining to Lord Milton that for several years past the workload had far exceeded the capabilities of two people and would benefit from the employment of an additional person, a request that was subsequently granted.[37] The 4th earl died in February 1833 and was succeeded by his only son Charles, the 5th Earl Fitzwilliam. Two years later Joshua Biram died; Benjamin had officially taken over his role in 1833 at which point his title was changed to that of house steward and 'superintendent of the collieries'. As Graham Mee states, Benjamin's first year was a baptism of fire as the collieries were in crisis due to the collapse of the north-eastern coal trade.[38]

LIKE FATHER LIKE SON – REPLICATING BAD PRACTICE

Benjamin Biram's management of the collieries mirrored that of his father with the exception that the younger Biram demonstrated a

---

[33] A. Birch, *Economic History of the British Iron and Steel Industry 1784–1879: Essays in Industrial and Economic History with Special Reference to the Development of Technology* (London, 2006), p. 162.

[34] *London Gazette*, 4 February 1823. The company was subsequently taken over by the 4th earl who appointed a manager.

[35] SA, WWM/A/343, West-riding annual estate account, 1825–6.

[36] SA, WWM/F107/163, William Newman to Earl Fitzwilliam, 18 March 1831.

[37] SA, WWM/G40/13, Benjamin Biram to Lord Milton, 15 March 1831.

[38] Mee, *Aristocratic Enterprise*, p. 36.

sharp scientific mind. During his apprenticeship, he was forever trying to develop new methods of operation to make the pits more efficient and safer for those that worked below ground.[39] Upon succeeding his father, his scientific interests continued with the support of the 5th earl who had a keen interest in all things scientific. Many of Biram's ideas were implemented and subsequently patented, including a mechanical anemometer which measured the volume of air entering and leaving the mine, thus reducing the instances of explosions due to firedamp. Equally, his modifications to the Davy lamp used by miners received national acclaim and led to increased safety standards throughout the Fitzwilliam collieries. These devices were later adopted by mining companies across Britain.[40]

However, when it came to issues of accounting and expenditure, Benjamin Biram seemed to struggle and rarely had the capital to meet demands. In November 1833 he had no money to pay wages and demanded the lessees of Milton Ironworks pay their monthly rent immediately, so that he would have the money to meet his obligations. By December he was threatening to suspend the supply of coal, an essential component for the manufacturing of metal at the works, if the rent was not forthcoming.[41] Again in 1837 he required an additional £1,000 'to meet the half yearly wages, pensions and other payments' which were due to be paid on 1 July and, in the next breath, proceeded to request an increase in his salary from £250 to £300 per annum together with a free supply of coal for domestic use. On the off chance that the earl was not amenable to his suggestion, he proposed that rather than his being paid a fixed annual income, his salary 'might be regulated by the profits of the collieries' so that 'your lordships and my own interests must [sic] uniformly be the same'.[42] Without a doubt, as this communication demonstrates, Biram believed he was above the land agent in terms of the managerial pecking order. Indeed, his language appears to suggest he saw himself on a par with the earl and thus protected from Newman's criticism. Despite his delusional notions of grandeur, on this latter point he was correct.

From the outset of his agency Joshua Biram communicated directly

[39] SA, WWM/G40/26, Joshua Biram to Earl Fitzwilliam, 22 December 1831.

[40] SA, WWM/G49/52a, William Newman to Earl Fitzwilliam, 8 March 1847; for information concerning the lamp, see J. C. Robertson (ed.), *The Mechanics Magazine, Museum, Register, Journal and Gazette, 7 Jul.–29 Dec. 1849* (57 vols, London, 1849), vol. 51, pp. 217–19.

[41] Mee, *Aristocratic Enterprise*, p. 36.

[42] SA, WWM/G40/106, Benjamin Biram to Earl Fitzwilliam, 20 June 1837.

with the landlord, constantly updating him on his mining interests and equally, reverting solely to him with issues of concern. He rarely communicated with Newman concerning any aspect of his administration except, of course, to request additional funds when required. This effectively minimised the land agent's authority over his domain. As an apprentice, Benjamin witnessed first-hand how this technique was advantageous. Thus, the rapport which developed between the Birams and Earls Fitzwilliam acted as a safeguard in the event of attack from other quarters. Though Newman continued to audit the house and colliery expenditure, as far as the Birams were concerned, this was merely a rudimentary exercise rather than a critical appraisal of their management practices. While Joshua used this modus operandi to good effect, Benjamin perfected it, to the point that the 5th earl when corresponding with the agent dispensed with the formalities, addressing him as 'Dear Ben'.[43] This situation understandably riled the land agent but Newman was not prepared to question the earl. Daniel Maude, on the other hand, felt he had nothing to lose and was quite willing to challenge Fitzwilliam over Biram's conduct.

Similar to Benjamin Biram, Daniel Maude (1801–68) served his apprenticeship under his father and took over as estate auditor in 1841. He combined this role with his other profession, that of stipendiary magistrate in Manchester. He was appointed to this role in March 1838, having previously trained as a barrister.[44] Assuming control of the books, he was quick to spot discrepancies in Biram's figures. The principal system of accounting used across the Wentworth-Fitzwilliam estates in the nineteenth century was that of charge and discharge accounting, the precursor to the double entry system. This system, which dated back to the thirteenth century, involved charging the agent with receipts for cash, goods and services rendered, and discharging the charge against him through cash payments derived from sources such as farm rentals and sales of timber. This method was viewed as a good indicator of the agent's management of the estate as arrears of rent outstanding remained as a charge against him until paid.[45] This practice had its merits on landed estates which were administered by a single agent,

[43] Mee, *Aristocratic Enterprise*, p. 99.

[44] C. H. Timperley, *Annals of Manchester; Biographical, Historical, Ecclesiastical, and Commercial from the Earliest Period to the Close of the Year 1839* (Manchester, 1839), p. 98.

[45] D. Oldroyd, *Estates, Enterprise and Investment at the Dawn of the Industrial Revolution: Estate Management and Accounting in the North-East of England, c. 1700–1780* (Aldershot, 2007), p. 18.

but at Wentworth, where responsibility was divided amongst a number of men, the practice seemed to favour the colliery agent at the expense of the land agent, who was left to reconcile the books and explain the deficits to the auditor and earl. Despite Maude's attempts to understand Biram's accounts, their disordered state made it virtually impossible. Nonetheless, he continued to examine the accounts and in December 1846 appeared to have identified the problem. Biram had inflated profit margins in the colliery to the point that while operations appeared profitable on the surface, in reality they were operating at a significant loss.[46] It is difficult to argue that this was a genuine error on Biram's behalf as his salary was intrinsically linked to the annual performance of the collieries. However, when Maude voiced his concerns to the earl in 1848, his protestations were met with a wall of silence.[47]

The earl's lack of interest at this point was arguably due to his preoccupation with his other interests, in particular the Irish estate, which was in the grip of the worst famine in its country's history. A decade prior to its onset, the Irish agent, Robert Chaloner Snr, in correspondence with the future 5th earl requested withholding a portion of a remittance in order to prevent the estate 'from sinking into nothingness'.[48] If anything, the arrival of the famine in 1845 compounded the situation to the point that by 1851 Chaloner Jnr, who had succeeded his father as land agent, could 'see no hope of a lodgement at present . . . as the wages empty the till'.[49] The situation in Yorkshire, although bleak, was not so hopeless. However, there were elements of the estate's industry which were no longer salvageable, most notably the ironworks at Elsecar. For almost twenty years the Fitzwilliams had retained control of this failing business, consistently financing its demise. The mismanagement was attributable to Henry Hartop, who was appointed manager in 1829 and subsequently was assisted by his son, John. The administration at the ironworks was not that dissimilar to Biram's. A confused accounting system hid the true extent of the failings of the operation and its manager's incompetence. From 1845 Daniel Maude, while trying to curtail Biram, was also gathering

[46] See, for example, SA, WWM/A/152, household annual statement of account, 1845. The furniture entries include payments for cutlery, glasses, clocks and bell hanging, while the collieries contain payments for hay and the poor of the various townships.
[47] NRO, Fitzwilliam (Milton) MSS, Daniel Maude to Earl Fitzwilliam, 27 December 1848.
[48] SA, WWM/G35/31, Robert Chaloner Snr to Lord Milton, 24 November 1831.
[49] SA, WWM/G35/262, Robert Chaloner Jnr to Earl Fitzwilliam, 5 July 1851.

evidence against Hartop in an effort to convince the earl that it was in his best interests to lease the ironworks.[50]

Newman had long been sceptical of Hartop's management and voiced his concerns to the earl. Correspondence from his former partners Messrs Graham identified serious issues in his accounts to the point that the Grahams were not willing to sign a new lease on Milton Ironworks as long as he remained a partner.[51] Despite Newman's criticism, the earl appointed Hartop manager of Elsecar Ironworks. The failure of Milton Ironworks in 1848 created a perfect storm scenario as it allowed the auditor and land agent a unique opportunity to incite change. Maude wrote to the earl explaining that 'in the long run you will be the gainer by selling your minerals and giving another the fair trader's profit for manufacturing for you', advice the earl was willing to take.[52] More significantly, this decision demonstrated that Biram's hegemony over industrial concerns was far from absolute. However, any attempts to reprimand the colliery agent would require a united front on the part of the land agent and auditor coupled with careful negotiation. There is little doubt that Maude's education and training greatly aided both men in this objective. In his correspondence with Fitzwilliam, probing questions into business defects due to obvious bad practice were diplomatically peppered with praise for the colliery agent who, 'it ought not be overlooked ... had great experience'. Simultaneously, Fitzwilliam was made aware of the cost to the estate for enabling this to continue.[53] Just as Newman and Maude seemed to be leveraging control of the situation, the economy began to recover as improved infrastructural links resulted in a greater demand for coal.[54] Providentially for Biram, amidst increasing receipts, the criticisms of Newman and Maude were muted. Biram remained in his position until his premature death in 1857 at the age of fifty-three.[55]

[50] See, for example, SA, WWM/G50/4a, Daniel Maude to Earl Fitzwilliam, 25 August 1845.

[51] SA, WWM/G44/9, Messrs Graham to Earl Fitzwilliam, 1 December 1828. The partnership was subsequently dissolved and the Grahams continued to operate Milton Ironworks.

[52] SA, WWM/G50/9b, Daniel Maude to Earl Fitzwilliam, 15 April 1849. The earl subsequently re-let both ironworks to William Dawes, an ironmaster from Birmingham.

[53] SA, WWM/G50/9a, Daniel Maude to Earl Fitzwilliam, 15 April 1849.

[54] SA, WWM/T2/29a and WWM/T2/29b, Earl Fitzwilliam to Lord Milton, 26 November 1851.

[55] SA, SY337/X1/88, Wentworth burials, Holy Trinity church, 5 February 1857.

CONCLUSION

Benjamin Biram was not a bad man. He was well liked among the mining community at Wentworth and possessed an obviously scientific mind. His ingenuity resulted in the introduction of numerous devices that improved working conditions within the mining industry.[56] However, when it came to issues of administration, he was seriously lacking in the necessary skills for the role. As the third generation of his family to serve the estate, his employment, work record and retention only serve to illustrate how damaging landlord paternalism could be to the landed estate. Yet, this was an ideology successive generations of Earls Fitzwilliam actively subscribed to, recruiting from within family groupings. Although commendable, it prevented the estate from realising its full economic potential as the workforce it created was one-dimensional. The skillset consisted of those handed down by successive generations rather than any formal training and relied heavily on a good relationship with those in charge. Though not all the estate enterprises were defunct, those that required regular injections of cash to counteract losses suffered through incompetence.

The two-man management system at Wentworth was adequate during the eighteenth century when concerns were relatively small. As the nineteenth century progressed, the diversity and ever expanding economic functions required more specialised administration than occupational pluralism would allow. However, the three-man system which the 4th earl created was beset with difficulty from the outset. From its inception, the new structure was considerably weaker than its predecessor; it was beset with in-built inequalities as a consequence of differing salaries and relationships with the various earls. Under the old system, Charles Bowns retained overall authority but under the new, Newman's authority was minimised by the 4th earl dividing the role of agent and auditor. Equally, the Birams' close relationship with each landlord further eroded the land agent's power, creating tension between both agents. Undoubtedly, the arrival of Daniel Maude greatly assisted Newman and marked a turning point in the fortunes of the estate. His no-nonsense, vigilant approach was invigorating among the casual recklessness of Biram, Hartop and to a lesser degree, the 4th and 5th earls whose wealth enabled them to indulge bad investments and tolerate bad management. In dividing his interests, the 4th Earl Fitzwilliam could not have foreseen the inter-managerial conflict that would develop

---

[56] *Sheffield and Rotherham Independent*, 1 November 1856.

within the management structure on the estate. Consequently, when issues began to emerge, the family's belief system prevented them from rectifying the problem. For at Wentworth, a job – whether in the house, on the land or down the mine – was a job for life with few exceptions.

5

The Courtown Land Agents and Transnational Estate Management, 1850–1900

Rachel Murphy

INTRODUCTION

THE NATURE OF ESTATE agencies across the four nations during the nineteenth century varied depending on the size and location of the estate, and the financial situation of the landlord.[1] Large estates often included an estate office, managed by a sole agent supported by a network of sub-agents. Other estates were managed by agencies who worked for multiple landowners in a particular region, such as Hussey and Townsend, a Cork-based firm which managed eighty-eight estates in 1880.[2] On smaller estates individuals such as the farm steward may have taken on the role of agent, and Sir John Benn-Walsh managed his Cork estate himself, despite living in England.[3] In short, just as estates were not homogenous, neither were the agencies that managed them.

This chapter considers the management structure of a transnational estate during the second half of the nineteenth century, using the Courtown estate as a case study. It examines the roles of the agents, sub-agents and bailiffs employed on the estate during this period. It is hoped that the study will enable comparison with other estates within

---

[1] This chapter is based on R. Murphy, 'Chapter 5: Estate as organisation: the agency structure', in 'Place, community and organisation on the Courtown estates, 1649–1977' (unpublished PhD thesis, University College Cork, 2017), pp. 198–216. The PhD in History and Digital Humanities was funded under a Digital Arts and Humanities Postgraduate Fellowship (2011–15) under Ireland's Higher Education Authority (HEA) PRTLI Cycle 5.

[2] J. S. Donnelly Jr, 'The Kenmare estates during the nineteenth century', *Journal of the Kerry Archaeological and Historical Society*, 21 (1988), p. 33.

[3] J. S. Donnelly Jr, 'The journals of Sir John Benn-Walsh relating to the management of his Irish estates, 1823–64, part II', *Journal of the Cork Historical and Archaeological Society*, 81:231 (1975), p. 38.

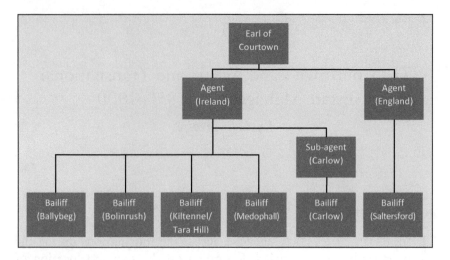

Figure 4 Structure of the Courtown Estate Administration, c. 1858.

the four nations, leading to a deeper understanding of the role of the
land agent during the Victorian period.

In the latter half of the nineteenth century the Earl of Courtown held
approximately 23,000 acres of land across Ireland and England. His
estates included 14,426 acres in Wexford, 7,395 acres in Carlow and
1,493 acres in Saltersford, Cheshire.[4] The estates consisted of distinct
locations in Ireland, namely Ballybeg, Bolinrush, Kiltennel, Medophall
and Tara Hill in County Wexford, as well as land in County Carlow,
and Saltersford in Cheshire.

Figure 4 shows the Courtown estate's administrative structure c. 1858.
There were two main agents at this time, both of whom reported to the
Earl of Courtown. One, based at the estate office near Courtown, was
responsible for the Irish estates. The second, located in Leicestershire,
managed the English estate. The head agent for the Irish estates was
supported by a sub-agent in Carlow. The agents and sub-agents were
assisted by bailiffs, individuals who lived in each distinct area of the
estate, providing the agents with local knowledge and passing on messages from them to the tenants.

The Courtown estate was small in comparison with other estates
such as the Marquess of Downshire's 120,000-acre estate or the
198,572-acre estate of the Duke of Devonshire. However, similarities

---

[4] J. Bateman, *The Great Landowners of Great Britain and Ireland* (Leicester,
1971), p. 108.

are evident between the structure that was in place in Courtown and that of the Downshire estates in Antrim, Down, King's County (Offaly) and Wicklow. W. A. Maguire, writing about duties of the Downshire head agent in the 1820s, notes that he was 'responsible, in a general way, for supervising all the estates with all their agents and subordinate personnel, in central control of a uniform system of management'.[5]

On any estate the primary duty of the agent was to collect rents twice annually, ensuring that tenants did not fall into arrears. In England, gale days, the days on which rent was due, were most frequently Lady Day (25 March) and Michaelmas (29 September). By contrast, 1 May and 1 November were more common in Ireland. Emrys Estyn Evans notes that these dates are 'old Irish . . . marking the beginning and the end of the summer grazing season when cattle were assembled and rents paid in kind'.[6] A custom generally only found in Ireland was that of the 'hanging gale' in which tenants were permitted to be six months in arrears of rent.[7] Rent was collected at the 'rent audit', which was held either at the agent's office or in a hotel. On the Courtown estate, the Saltersford estate rentals were returned on separate manuscripts, while from 1858 onwards all Irish estate rentals were compiled into printed ledgers arranged by estate. Such standardisation allowed for easier consolidation and comparison of information across estates. The agent presented the final figures to the landlord in an annual audit, thereby enabling the Earl of Courtown to review estate income and expenditure. Hussey notes that the standard payment for land agents was 'five per cent, on the rents received',[8] a sure incentive for agents to try to ensure rents were paid as efficiently as possible.

The agents were responsible for creating the tenancy arrangements and memoranda. As such, they were required to possess some legal understanding.[9] In Ireland there were three key types of tenancy arrangement in the mid-nineteenth century: leases, which could run for a fixed period or a term of lives, yearly tenancies and tenancies-at-will. The

---

[5] W. A. Maguire, *The Downshire Estates in Ireland, 1801–1845* (Oxford, 1972), p. 164.

[6] E. E. Evans, *The Personality of Ireland, Habitat, Heritage and History* (Cambridge, 2005), p. 73.

[7] Donnelly, 'Journals of Sir John Benn-Walsh, part II', p. 22.

[8] S. M. Hussey, *Reminiscences of an Irish Land Agent* (London, 1904), p. 39.

[9] C. E. Curtis, *Estate Management: A Practical Hand-Book for Landlords, Agents, and Pupils* (5th edn, London, 1901), p. 5.

agent was also charged with ensuring that tenants complied with the
conditions of their tenancy arrangements. Some agents, such as William
Steuart Trench who managed the Lansdowne estate in Kerry, have been
criticised for being too stringent in the regulations they applied to their
tenants.[10] On the Courtown estate the agents were relatively reasonable, which may have reflected the 5th earl's paternalistic approach to
landlordism. However, strict rules still applied and tenants could be
fined or even threatened with a notice to quit if they did not abide by
the conditions. Generally, these rules related to improving the estate and
increasing its earning potential. For example, sub-division was prohib-
ited. In Ireland, the system of partible inheritance, where property was
split equally between offspring, had been common prior to the Famine.[11]
On small plots of land this could have disastrous consequences, leading
to over-farming and over-population. Conacre was also forbidden. This
was land, generally used for potatoes, that was prepared by the occupier
and let on an eleven-month lease at a high rent.[12] One of the issues with
letting conacre land was that it often became exhausted. Although there
was sub-letting on the Courtown estate, the agents preferred to let land
directly to tenants and thereby control the rental that came from it.
Tenancy agreements included clauses regarding land use, to ensure that
farmers practised crop rotation. When one farmer admitted to growing
crops without permission, the agent noted that 'he had better be served
with notice to quit'.[13] The agents' rental books include many references
to individuals requesting permission to sow tawny oats or cut turf, for
instance.

If they wanted to move or emigrate, tenants were permitted to sell
their interest in their holding, but they were required to notify the agents
of their intention. In addition, the incoming tenant had to meet the
approval of the agent.[14] The agents disapproved when one tenant made
a settlement leaving his farm to his son 'without landlord's knowledge
or approval or agent's either', though it appears they agreed to this

[10] G. J. Lyne, *The Lansdowne Estate in Kerry Under W. S. Trench 1849–72*
(Dublin, 2006), p. liv.
[11] C. Ó Gráda, *Ireland Before and After the Famine: Explorations in Economic
History, 1800–1925* (Manchester, 1993), p. 181.
[12] For full definition, see J. Byrne, *Byrne's Dictionary of Irish Local History*
(Cork, 2004), p. 76.
[13] Trinity College Dublin [hereafter TCD], MS 11183/V/122, fo. 100, Patrick
Kavanagh, Knockmore, 21 June 1866.
[14] See, for example, TCD, MS 11183/V/143, fo. 19, John Byrne, Ballinamona.

subsequently.[15] On another occasion a tenant's nephew was permitted to live in his house with the caveat that 'as the nephew has been a drunkard he is only allowed to take him in on trial'.[16]

There were several routes that the agents could take if a tenant fell into arrears. First, they could give the tenant extra time to find the required money and, if there was a genuine reason for the tenant's being unable to pay, the Courtown agents were normally quite lenient. There are many examples of tenants being given extra time to pay their rent, for instance on the death of a child.[17] Generally, the agents only accepted payment of rent in full, and tenants asking to split the rent were often sent away. However, they allowed one tenant who was supporting 'nine children and his old father aged ninety-one' to split his rent.[18] The second course of action that landlord and agent could take if rents were not being paid was to offer rent reductions. On the Courtown estate, however, the 5th earl preferred to offer payment in kind, such as providing tenants with seed potatoes that they could plant, rather than reducing the rental. The third course of action was for the agent to serve ejectment proceedings. Although many ejectment proceedings were served, during the mid- to late nineteenth century only a small proportion resulted in tenant evictions.[19] An ejectment decree was the landlord's first step in recovering rent, and for this reason the number of ejectment decrees has little correlation with the number of actual evictions. Furthermore, tenants who were evicted were frequently reinstated or readmitted as caretakers.[20]

THE HEAD AGENTS: IRELAND

In 1858 Sir John-Benn Walsh remarked how satisfied he was with the land agent he had recently employed to manage his Kerry estate, describing him as

> an active, energetic, intelligent man in the prime of life, seems a good man of business, is resident in Listowel [near to the estate], is thoroughly acquainted

---

[15] TCD, MS 11183/V/132, fo. 122, John Lawlor, Knockmore.

[16] TCD, MS 11183/V/128, fo. 121, Patrick Kennedy, Tinnacarrig, 23 May 1877.

[17] TCD, MS 11183/V/136, fo. 2, John Carr, Aghnaglear, 11 May 1886.

[18] TCD, MS 11183/V/132, fo. 171, Moses Murphy, Slievedurda, 22 March 1886.

[19] B. Solow, *The Land Question and the Irish Economy, 1870–1903* (Harvard, 1971), pp. 51–7; K. O'Neill, *Family and Farm in Pre-famine Ireland: The Parish of Killashandra* (Madison, 2003), p. 37.

[20] Solow, *Land Question*, p. 54.

with the country, and is a good, practical agriculturalist. He appears very zealous and is obliging and pleasant to deal with.[21]

This description indicates some of the key qualities that landlords sought in the agents of their Irish estates. Such a broad range of skills was necessary since the duties of the land agent were extremely varied, including, according to Samuel Hussey, agent on the Kenmare estate, 'a great deal of office work, drawing up agreements with tenants, receiving rent, superintending agricultural and all landlords' improvements, sitting as magistrate and representing the landlord when the latter is absent at poor-law meetings, road sessions, and on grand juries'.[22]

During the 5th earl's lifetime, three key individuals were associated with the head agency of the Courtown estates in Ireland: James Smyth Scott, George Stopford and Frederick Turner. Scott was appointed head agent of the Courtown estate by the 4th earl in July 1858, shortly before the latter's death. Scott's predecessor, Captain Robert Owen, had abused his position of trust, embezzling the 4th earl out of an estimated £20,000–£25,000 over a period of thirty years.[23] The 5th earl took precautions to prevent this happening to him; soon after he succeeded to the title, he and Scott entered into a money bond for £10,000. The bond, which was in Scott's name and related to his position as 'agent and receiver' of the Courtown estate, would be declared void if Scott should 'well, justly, truly and honestly in every respect behave himself in said office or employment of agent'.[24]

In his 1904 publication *Reminiscences of an Irish Land Agent*, Samuel Hussey commented on the high social status of the nineteenth-century Irish land agent:

> The profession of a land agent in Ireland is on a far higher social plane than in England. In many cases the younger son or brother of the landlord is the agent for the family property; and in some instances this has worked uncommonly well. In other cases, gentlemen by birth conducted the business, or else the administration of several estates was consolidated and carried on from one office.[25]

Although Sir John Benn-Walsh was of the view that 'a gentleman of ordinary intelligence and business habits might manage a considerable

[21] Donnelly, 'Journals of Sir John Benn-Walsh, part II', p. 26.
[22] Hussey, *Reminiscences*, p. 39.
[23] TCD, MS 11183/P/59/1, 'History of the Stopfords', 2 April 1855, p. 158.
[24] TCD, MS 11183/P/6/319, money bond between Earl of Courtown and Scott, Armstrong and Cox, dated 10 January 1859.
[25] Hussey, *Reminiscences*, p. 41.

estate, paying one or two bailiffs and accountants, far more economically than through gentleman agents',[26] Reilly concludes that 'having examined the careers of over 100 agents in King's County it appears that the majority came from a landed background'.[27] The gentleman agent predominated on large Irish estates; for example, Lyne states that Trench, the agent on the Lansdowne estate in Kerry, was 'very much a gentleman agent'[28] while Maguire notes that 'in the case of the Downshire estate, it was clearly necessary that the chief agent . . . should be a gentleman'.[29] Although employing such men may have indicated a landlord's status, Maguire suggests that gentleman agents were preferred because their 'manners and habits permitted easy social intercourse between employer and agent'.[30]

Even though the Courtown estate was smaller than the Lansdowne or Downshire estates, the head agents of Lord Courtown's Irish estates always came from a solid, upper-class, establishment background. For instance, James Scott was born in Dublin in 1820 to a Church of Ireland family. His father, like Hussey's, was a barrister while his mother, Anne Knox, was granddaughter of the 8th Earl of Meath (a family with whom the Stopfords also had connections). Scott was educated at King William's College on the Isle of Man between the ages of thirteen and sixteen. In 1844 he married Janet Broughton, daughter of Hugh Broughton, formerly the Deputy Cashier of Excise in Edinburgh.[31] By 1852 Scott was tenant of Lawnsdowne Demesne on the Earl of Portarlington's Ballymorris estate, Queen's County,[32] and a county magistrate.

By the time Scott started working at the Courtown estate, he was already experienced in estate management and the workings of the Encumbered Estates Court. He had assisted the Conrahy family in selling their land in Queen's and King's Counties,[33] and helped George Young find a purchaser for his 10,000-acre estate in Donegal.[34] He had also

[26] Cited in Donnelly, 'Journals of Sir John Benn-Walsh, part II', p. 33.

[27] C. Reilly, *The Irish Land Agent, 1830–60: The Case of King's County* (Dublin, 2014), p. 38.

[28] Lyne, *Lansdowne Estate*, p. xlvi.

[29] Maguire, *Downshire Estates*, p. 191.

[30] Maguire, *Downshire Estates*, p. 191.

[31] *Dublin Evening Mail*, 18 November 1844.

[32] *The Advocate*, 21 January 1852.

[33] National Archives of Ireland, Landed Estates Court O'Brien Rental Set, vol. 5, p. 48 [Conrahy, Ballynahemey and Derrymore, Queen's County, 13 February 1851].

[34] *Dublin Daily Express*, 18 August 1856.

acted as agent for the Hammersmith Ironworks in Ballsbridge, Dublin.[35] Following his move to Wexford, Scott became established in local gentry networks, and in June 1859 he was appointed to the Commission of the Peace for County Wexford.[36] The Scott family resided at Levuka House in Courtown, and frequently engaged in dinners and entertainment at Courtown House.[37] They benefited from their connections with the Earl of Courtown, and were mentioned in the fashion and varieties section of the newspaper.[38]

A month after he had appointed James Scott agent for the Courtown estate, the 4th Earl of Courtown informed his son that he had decided to 'do away with the old-fashioned practice of allowing tenants to be always half a year in arrear of rent'.[39] This referred to the hanging gale, and the Courtown estate was unusual in removing it. While it was attractive to new tenants, as it gave them six months to grow crops and raise money for their rent payments, there was also a view that being in arrears put the tenants at a greater risk of being evicted for non-payment if the landlord so wished. According to the 5th earl, removing the hanging gale was carried out without difficulty, and 'the "back half year" paid up'.[40] It is likely that this innovation was put in place by Scott to make the estate run more efficiently. In addition, a number of tenants on the Kiltennell estate had been paying their rent to the steward, but Scott required them to pay the agency directly.[41] There is a sense that Scott and the 5th earl, both new to their roles, were eager to improve the running of the estate. From an economic perspective, the agent ideally let the land to suitable tenants at a fair rent to both landlord and tenant.[42] As leases lapsed, Scott organised the revaluation of certain holdings.

As well as managing the estate rentals, Scott was responsible for implementing a number of projects for Lord Courtown. For example, he arranged for the analysis of spring water on the estate to establish

[35] *Sanders News-letter*, 24 April 1856.

[36] *Dublin Evening Mail*, 24 June 1859.

[37] *Freeman's Journal*, 5 March 1877.

[38] For instance, the *Dublin Evening Mail*, 12 October 1860 notes that James S. Scott, Esq., JP has arrived at Courtown Harbour.

[39] TCD, MS 11183/P/59/1, 'History of the Stopfords, Part 1', 6 August 1858, p. 169.

[40] TCD, MS 11183/P/59/1, 'History of the Stopfords, Part 1', 6 August 1858, p. 169.

[41] TCD, MS 11183/V/121, fo. 254, Michael Milton, Mountalexander.

[42] Curtis, *Estate Management*, p. 3.

whether it had medicinal properties (it did not). He also organised the analysis of local soil which Lord Courtown feared was poisoning the crops, but experts advised that the Macamore soil was simply not very fertile and required mechanical turning, followed by the addition of artificial fertiliser. Other projects that were considered at this time included the development of a mill and a fertiliser business, though neither came to fruition. These examples suggest that Hussey's description of the duties of the Irish agent were, in the case of James Scott at least, fairly accurate. Certainly, he had to be able to understand agriculture, engineering and the law to such a level that he could, at a minimum, project manage initiatives in these areas.

Despite the considerable responsibilities attached to managing the Courtown estate, Scott undertook work for other estates. For example, in 1866 he advertised land for letting on the Clara Demesne, County Offaly (386 acres of demesne lands).[43] Most agents, particularly those working with multiple estates, needed a team to assist them. After leaving Trinity College Cambridge,[44] the 5th earl's youngest son, George Stopford, started working at the agency office in 1879.[45] In the following year he was joined by Scott's nephew, Frederick Turner.[46] He was the son of Scott's sister Antonia, who had married John Turner, a well-connected Welsh wine merchant. In 1881 George Stopford (then aged twenty-one) and Frederick Turner entered into partnership, establishing the firm Stopford and Turner. Initially, they took over two small agencies which Mr Scott found 'unprofitable and troublesome'.[47] In the following year Scott took Stopford and Turner into partnership with him in the Courtown agency.[48] Shortly after this he notified the earl of his intention to leave Courtown, suggesting that Stopford and Turner manage the day-to-day business, although he said they could refer to him if necessary.[49] Alarmed by this, Lord Courtown informed Scott that

[43] *Freeman's Journal*, 28 September 1866.

[44] J. Venn, *Alumni Cantabrigienses* (Cambridge, 2011), vol. 2, p. 55.

[45] TCD, MS 11183/P/59/1, 'History of the Stopfords, Part 1', 19 August 1879, p. 78.

[46] TCD, MS 11183/P/59/1, 'History of the Stopfords, Part 1', 20 July 1880, p. 81.

[47] TCD, MS 11183/P/59/1, 'History of the Stopfords, Part 1', 18 November 1881, p. 90.

[48] TCD, MS 11183/P/59/1, 'History of the Stopfords, Part 1', 24 April 1882, p. 93.

[49] TCD, MS 11183/P/59/1, 'History of the Stopfords, Part 1', 5 April 1882, p. 92; 27 November 1882, p. 95.

the agency role was to be taken from him, and he offered Stopford and Turner the agency of the Courtown estate.[50]

Thus, a year after their partnership had been established, Stopford and Turner became head agents of the Courtown estate. In the following year Lord Courtown informed the Saltersford sub-agents that Stopford and Turner would take direct responsibility for the English estate too.[51] Some of the family seemed concerned about Stopford's business acumen initially. In a letter to George Stopford, the 5th earl reprimanded his son for failing to inform a tenant that he was not permitted to sell the clay and gravel on his land: 'I think you had not spoken to Murray [the tenant] about this, so you had better see at once for some regulation being made.'[52] Elsewhere, his brother noted that he was 'careless about answering letters', though he reported that Turner was 'aware of George's defects but that he is improving and spoke highly of him'.[53] Turner, seven years Stopford's senior, was more experienced and is more visible in the records, so it is possible that he was the driving force in the business. He was also a new breed of professional land agent, which Hussey referred to when he wrote in 1904 that 'in my time the landlord was the sole judge of the agent's qualifications, but the profession has become a branch of the Engineering Surveyors' Institution'.[54] In 1890 Turner was selected as arbitrator for the landlord on the Tottenham estate, County Wexford during the Plan of Campaign.[55] He was a council member of the Irish Land Agents' Association and of the Irish Branch of the Surveyors' Institute.[56] To accommodate their growing business, Stopford and Turner established a Dublin office at 13 Anglesea Street, maintaining the local office in Gorey.[57] As well as managing the Courtown estate, they acted for others, including Lord Ardilaun (Muckross estate, County Kerry)[58] and the Leigh-Whites (Bantry estate, County Cork).

[50] TCD, MS 11183/P/59/1, 'History of the Stopfords, Part 1', 28 November 1882, p. 95; 18 December 1882, p. 96.

[51] TCD, MS 11183/P/59/1, 'History of the Stopfords, Part 1', 21 May 1883, p. 98.

[52] TCD, MS 11183/ V/38, fo. 8, John Murray, Ballinacarrig. Enclosed letter dated 12 September 1890.

[53] TCD, MS 11183/P/59/1, 'History of the Stopfords, Part 1', 26 March 1885, p. 105.

[54] Hussey, *Reminiscences*, p. 42.

[55] *Flag of Ireland*, 12 April 1890.

[56] *Dublin Daily Express*, 31 August 1894, p. 7; 23 June 1905, p. 3.

[57] *Dublin Daily Express*, 9 May 1903, p. 7.

[58] *Dublin Daily Express*, 24 April 1915, p. 4 and referenced in J. M. Ryan, 'Deer forests, game shooting and landed estates in the South West of Ireland, 1840–1970'

THE HEAD AGENTS: ENGLAND

In 1858 the agents for the Saltersford estate were Edward Fisher and Son of Market Harborough, whose firm mainly managed estates in Leicestershire and Northamptonshire. They can be viewed as head agents since they reported directly to the Earl of Courtown, and had no involvement with James Scott. Given the small size of the English estate at just 1,500 acres, the nature and complexity of the work they under-took was much less than that of Scott, and later Stopford and Turner, so in this sense they were the lesser of the two agencies. David Spring suggests that, in contrast with the Irish land agent, English land agents shared similar social origins to their Scottish counterparts. He describes them as 'the sons of practical men, often familiar from youth with the varied business of land management'.[59] This was certainly true of Fisher and Son. Their land agency firm had been established in 1830 by Edward Fisher's father, and had been greatly involved in enclosure awards and valuations. After leaving school, Edward Fisher joined his father's firm, and the professional expertise he acquired there was wide-ranging. As well as managing the estates of Sir Geoffrey Palmer and Mr George Payne, he was mineral agent for the Ecclesiastical Commissioners, a member of the Iron and Steel Institute and Royal Agricultural Society, and a Fellow of the Surveyors' Institute.[60] Fisher was a man of standing in public and religious spheres, with an interest in politics, writing to Lord Courtown: 'I hope your Lordship's neighbourhood is free from the spirit which seems so prevalent in Ireland for it must indeed be a most serious time for resident landowners.'[61] The Fisher papers include direct correspondence between the Earl of Courtown and the Saltersford agents. Other than the Saltersford estate, most of their clients were landholders in Leicestershire and Northamptonshire.

Given Fisher's distance from Saltersford (100 miles), he had to rely on the assistance of others in the area including local clergy and solicitors. As on the Irish estates, rents were paid twice annually. To pay their dues the tenants generally met the agent in Macclesfield – either in Bate Hall (formerly owned by the Earl of Courtown), or in one of the

(PhD thesis, University College Cork, 2001), available at <https://cora.ucc.ie/bit stream/handle/10468/1035/RyanJM_PhD2001.pdf> (last accessed 18 July 2014); *Dublin Daily Express*, 9 May 1903, p.7.

[59] D. Spring, *The English Landed Estate in the Nineteenth Century: Its Administration* (Baltimore, 1963), p. 100.

[60] *Leicester Chronicle and Leicestershire Mercury*, 9 March 1901.

[61] TCD, MS 11183/P/58/39, Mr Fisher to Lord Courtown, 1866.

other inns or hotels. The agent then remitted the rental income to Lord
Courtown's bank in London, informing the earl and his solicitors. Lord
Courtown met Mr Fisher at least once a year, often in the spring when
he first arrived in London for the Season. Given his infrequent visits to
Saltersford, the 5th earl relied on Fisher's advice regarding the tenants
and the land.

The transfer of the agency of the Saltersford estate to Stopford and
Turner in 1882 was relatively short-lived. In 1896 Stopford and Turner
informed Lord Courtown that they wished to give up the Saltersford
agency as they could not do justice to it.[62] They informed the tenants:

> We have with Lord Courtown's approval appointed Messrs. Turner and Son,
> auctioneers etc., Macclesfield, sub-agents of above Estate. We shall thank
> you in future to pay your rent to them, also that they have now the sole
> management of the Estate under our supervision, be good enough to address
> all communications you may have to make to them.[63]

Turner and Son were local auctioneers based at 10–12 Church Street,
Macclesfield. This firm remained sub-agent for the Courtown estate
until it was sold, Turner's son taking over the business following his
father's death c. 1910.[64]

OTHER ROLES ON THE ESTATES

While the head agents in Ireland managed the Wexford estates directly,
for most of the second half of the nineteenth century a sub-agent was
responsible for the Carlow estates. The main duties of the sub-agents
consisted of organising local administrative affairs, such as collecting the
tenants' rents and poor rates. The sub-agent for the Carlow estate was
the Honourable Edward Sydney Stopford, younger brother of the 5th
Earl of Courtown. He had been appointed to the role in 1854 by their
father, the 4th earl. Edward Stopford continued in his role as sub-agent
until a year or so before his death in April 1895, as evidenced by a
letter dated April 1894 to his nephew George Stopford which included a
'draft for the rent collected with poor rates and list'.[65] The estate papers
provide very little information about the Hon. Edward Stopford's relationship with the Carlow tenants, though one farmer mentioned 'the

[62] TCD, MS 11183/P/59/3/2, 'History of the Stopfords, Part 2', p. 162, 11
October 1896.

[63] TCD, MS 11183/P/58/1/276, Stopford and Turner [n.d.].

[64] *Manchester Courier and Lancashire General Advertiser*, 4 January 1910.

[65] TCD, MS 11183/V/136, fo. 32.

friendly feelings that always existed between the late Hon. Mr Stopford, Borris, and my father'.[66] The sub-agent was expected to keep a close eye on what was happening on the estate, and one of the formal rental books includes a list of tenants compiled by Edward Stopford detailing who was unable to pay their rent and why.[67] As well as the core duty of collecting rents, the sub-agent informed the head agent of any issues or queries. For instance, when a tenant wanted to build a house on his land, the sub-agent informed the agents, who wrote to him explaining that the tenant was permitted to do so under the terms of his lease.[68] Following Edward Stopford's death Stopford and Turner, the main agents of the Courtown estates, took over the Carlow management.

Each of the six smaller estates that together made up the Courtown estate had a bailiff or rent-warner who supported the agent or sub-agent. This was the case in both Ireland and England. These individuals resided locally, and were usually medium-sized tenant farmers. Though the precise duties of the bailiff varied from estate to estate, and even from location to location within one estate, essentially theirs was a role of messenger and go-between. Describing the role of the bailiff on Sir Henry Barron's estate in Waterford, a local solicitor noted:

> it was his duty to give notice to the tenants when the rent fell due, to collect the small arrears from them, and also to pay, himself, or see that the tenants paid, the county cess due in respect to their several holdings.[69]

This seems also to have been the case on the Courtown estate. In addition, the Courtown bailiffs were required to supply information about tenants to the sub-agent or head agent. For example, the Courtown head agents asked the Carlow bailiff to identify tenants who were sub-letting their land.[70] On some estates bailiffs were accused of coercing tenants into voting for the landlord or threatening them.[71] For example, the bailiff reporting to Richard Stacpoole, agent of an estate in County Clare, was reported to have told a tenant that if he objected to taking

[66] TCD, MS 11183/V/136, fo. 132, Francis Doyle, Lissalican to Stopford and Turner, 19 November 1897.

[67] TCD, MS 11183/V/132, fo. 95.

[68] TCD, MS 11183/V/126, fo. 84, John Purcell, Ballyknockcrumpin.

[69] *Waterford Chronicle*, 28 November 1862.

[70] For example, in a letter dated 13 March 1906 the Carlow bailiff informed Stopford and Turner that Eliza Maher of Ballyblake rented a small amount of land to John Griffin; TCD MS 11183/V/139, fo. 33.

[71] For instance, 'The representation of Kilkenny', *Freeman's Journal*, 12 November 1868.

a lease, he 'would make an example of him for the rest'.[72] In addition he was responsible for presenting tenants with notices to quit.[73] It is hardly surprising, then, that in some cases bailiffs were threatened or boycotted. More frequently they were treated with caution by the rest of the community because, as one article suggested, should a tenant farmer transgress any estate regulations then 'the spies who are always about him convey the information *"to the office"*'.[74] From the perspective of agent and landlord, the bailiff occupied a position of trust, and as such had to be well selected. Analysis of the bailiffs on the Courtown estates does not show any homogeneity in terms of size of farm or religious beliefs. In three cases the role of bailiff was passed down from father to son, which suggests that family loyalty may have been a factor. The amount of remuneration received for this role is not evident from the manuscript sources.

There is a certain amount of confusion around the use of the word 'bailiff'. Within the Courtown estate it was used to refer to a local individual who conveyed messages from the agent or sub-agent to the tenants. However, the term 'bailiff' can have different meanings including 'an officer who executes writs and processes, distrains, and arrests', 'the agent of the lord of a manor, who collects his rents; the steward of a landholder, who manages his estate' and 'one who superintends the husbandry of a farm for its owner or tenant'.[75] As a result, the researcher must rely on context to determine exactly which role is being referred to, and it seems there was sometimes some overlap. Furthermore, in the case of the Courtown estate the words 'bailiff' and 'rent-warner' were used synonymously, and indeed rent-warning was one of the primary duties of the bailiff.[76] The term 'rent-warner' was fairly widely used in Ireland in the nineteenth century, and was the title of a play by T. O'Connor.[77] Richard Stacpoole described his bailiff's duties as 'to warn tenants of the rent day, and [send] messages', and he noted that the bailiff 'never negotiated any lettings with the tenants'.[78] On the

---

[72] *Freeman's Journal*, 2 February 1882.

[73] *Freeman's Journal*, 2 February 1882.

[74] 'How the Irish land system breeds disaffection', *Fraser's Magazine for Town and Country*, 77 (January–June 1868), p. 261.

[75] 'Bailiff, n.', *OED Online*, June 2017, available at <http://www.oed.com.ucc.idm.oclc.org/view/Entry/14701> (last accessed 20 November 2017).

[76] TCD, MS 11183/V/148.

[77] T. O'Connor, *The Rent Warner: An Irish Drama, in Five Acts* (Limerick, 1883).

[78] *Freeman's Journal*, 2 February 1882.

other hand, a contemporary newspaper described a rent-warner as an 'under agent',[79] and in the 1901 census William Denby, a bailiff on Lord Courtown's estate at Medophall,[80] described himself as a 'rent-warner and sub-agent'.[81] In the 1911 census he described himself as 'bailiff and steward'.[82] Living on the Donovan estate at Ballymore, it is likely he worked there in some capacity which may explain the dual roles, but it also suggests that the role of the bailiff or rent-warner varied from estate to estate, and the terminology used to describe this role was somewhat interchangeable and location-dependent. On the English estate, there is some evidence of individuals who may have discharged a similar role, though this is never explicitly stated.[83]

CONCLUSION

Every landed estate was unique, but it is possible to make some generalisations about their overall administrative structure. The typical model on a fairly large, dispersed estate such as Courtown was to have a head agent, supported by one or more sub-agents, who were in turn supported by a local network of individuals who were, in Ireland, often described as bailiffs or rent-warners. In the case of the Courtown estate, the head agents of the Irish estate from 1850 to 1900 came from an upper-class, establishment background while Fisher and Son, the agents for the English estate, were recognised for their considerable experience in land agency business from the early nineteenth century. Professional experience and social position were more important than family ties. Family members did, however, play key roles in estate administration, the 5th earl's brother being the Carlow sub-agent while his son was a partner in the head agency. Managing an estate from a distance was challenging, as evidenced by Stopford and Turner's comment that they could not do the Saltersford estate justice from their base in Ireland. Although the acreage of Saltersford was small, and there were only ever seventeen or fewer holdings, local knowledge was very important, and

[79] *Cork Examiner*, 27 January 1860.

[80] TCD, MS 11183/V/140, list of bailiffs on inside cover.

[81] William Denby, 1901 census, available at <http://www.census.nationalarchives. ie/reels/nai001273096/> (last accessed 20 November 2017).

[82] William Denby, 1911 census, available at <http://www.census.nationalarchives. ie/reels/nai003560691/> (last accessed 20 November 2017).

[83] For instance, Ashton Latham was tasked with finding out which tenants had paid tithes; see Northampton Record Office, FS48/3/79, Ashton Latham to Edward Fisher, 31 August 1847.

without this it was hard to manage. To run a large, dispersed estate effectively it was generally necessary to have a network that included representatives in each locale.

6

Peter Fairbairn:
Highland Factor and Caribbean Plantation
Manager, 1792–1822

Finlay McKichan

INTRODUCTION

A CLASS OF PROFESSIONAL land agents appeared later in Scotland
than in England. Their role was to make recommendations based
on rational study of the options and use of systematic methods to
increase productivity. An early example of this new breed of men in the
Highlands was Peter Fairbairn, who in 1792 was appointed chief factor
of the Seaforth estates. These consisted of the island of Lewis, Lochalsh,
Kintail and Glenshiel in Wester Ross and scattered lands in Easter Ross.
He was based at the family seat, Brahan Castle near Dingwall, where he
acted also as secretary to the proprietor, Francis Humberston Mackenzie
of Seaforth. Seaforth had been profoundly deaf from childhood and
Fairbairn developed an ability to support and work effectively with his
employer.[1] What other expertise did he bring? He was not a Highlander
nor a Gaelic speaker. However, proprietors often thought that, if a
factor was not native, he would be less vulnerable to local rivalries, and
thus his authority would be increased.[2] Fairbairn was born in 1762 at
Smailholm, Roxburghshire, where runrig lands had been divided by
1740 and let to one sixth of the original number of tenants. It seems
likely that Peter's father John Fairbairn (born 1714) was one of these
new tenants. One of John's other sons, Andrew, became a tenant farmer
on the Seaforth estate.[3]

---

[1] F. McKichan, 'Lord Seaforth (1754–1815): the lifestyle of a Highland proprietor and clan chief', *Northern Scotland*, 5:1 (2014), pp. 50–74; see pp. 51–3.

[2] A. Tindley, '"They sow the wind, they reap the whirlwind": estate management
in the post-clearance Highlands, c. 1815–c. 1900', *Northern Scotland*, 3 (2012), pp.
66–85, especially p. 68.

[3] D. Alston, entries on Peter Fairbairn at <http://www.spanglefish.com/slavesan-
dhighlanders> (last accessed 29 November 2016) and <http://www.person/ances-
try.co.uk/tree> (last accessed 2 January 2016); *Statistical Account of Scotland*, 3,

Peter, therefore, came to Ross-shire with a knowledge of the improved
agriculture of south-east Scotland. In the spring of 1794 Seaforth purchased the small estate of Moy, near Brahan. Fairbairn commented,
'I would wish to see a rental and survey of the lands, which would
show what may rationally be expected from improvements, and in
what manner it could be laid out most advantageously in commodious
farms.'[4] At about the same time, he recommended that the unimproved
farm of Dunglust, also near Brahan, should be enclosed and the existing
tenants removed to 'make an excellent farm fully equal to the stock of
most tenants'. He demonstrated that he had no particular sympathy
for Highland small tenants by suggesting that the Dunglust people 'will
never become better and have an unpleasant appearance'.[5] He argued
that the estate should 'put a proper face upon it by inclosing and other
improvements', after which its true value could be established and a
good rent secured. He was 'fully persuaded it is the best and most
economical of any that can be followed'.[6] The use of the language of
improvement and concepts such as 'rational and 'economical' marked
the new style of factor, seeking to make recommendations based on
evidence.

A NEW BROOM

Fairbairn succeeded as chief factor George Gillanders, who had been
agent for successive proprietors of the Seaforth estate since 1761, as
factor of Lewis based in Stornoway until his son replaced him in that
position in 1775.[7] From 1765 he had a joint commission for all the
Seaforth estates with Dr John Mackenzie, Seaforth's commissioner,[8] but
till 1775 he was not often on the mainland and he clearly took orders
from Mackenzie.[9] By 1780 George was the chief factor.[10] After the
appointment of Fairbairn in 1792 George and Alexander were retained

pp. 217–18, Parish of Smailholm, Roxburghshire, <http://stataccscot.edina.ac.uk/
link/1791-9/Roxburgh/Smailholm> (last accessed 3 January 2016).
   [4] National Records of Scotland [hereafter NRS], GD46/17/3, P. Fairbairn to
F. H. Mackenzie, 30 March 1794.
   [5] NRS, GD46/17/3, P. Fairbairn to F. H. Mackenzie, 1 March 1794.
   [6] NRS, GD46/17/3, P. Fairbairn to F. H. Mackenzie, 30 March 1794.
   [7] NRS, GD427/215/1, Dr J. Mackenzie to G. Gillanders, 7 January 1775.
   [8] NRS, GD427/141, scroll factory by Kenneth Mackenzie of Seaforth, 1765.
   [9] For example, NRS, GD427/215/1, Dr J. Mackenzie to G. Gillanders, Stornoway,
January 1773.
   [10] NRS, GD427/305/5, Earl of Seaforth to G. Gillanders, 1 February 1780.

for the time being in a subordinate capacity, presumably because of their detailed knowledge of the lands and tenants. However, as George complained, 'our powers are much curtailed and circumscribed'.[11] One respect in which Fairbairn brought new skills was in accounting. When in 1793 Seaforth wanted to check George's accounts, even George accepted that this should be delayed until Fairbairn was free to assist him.[12] He was tasked with sorting out the estate's accounting system, and in this showed a highly developed work ethic. In March 1794 he was 'busy with the arrangement of the [Home] farm accounts to enter them in order and make out a proper state – the duty is really arduous ... tho' I bestow from fourteen to sixteen hours of the twenty four day'; however, this was 'most necessary groundwork for the future'.[13] His conscientiousness is illustrated by a comment that 'all papers any way relating to the Lewis I carry with me in case they may be useful'.[14] The difference between his accounting methods and those of his predecessors was starkly illustrated after Alexander Gillanders died suddenly in Stornoway on 4 August 1794.[15] His boxes of papers were sent to Fairbairn, who immediately began a detailed audit and, through Seaforth, asked for what appeared to be missing items. George was incandescent. He wrote to Seaforth on 23 August that he

> Never suspected your prying beyond what was needful. Had there been none but yourself I would have been happy you had seen into every paper my son was in possession of ... I am sure you would avoid every dispute that might shock the feelings of the poor disconsolate widow, and am sure there won't be the least shadow of dispute twixt us in spite of officiousness and malice.[16]

It was not surprising that Gillanders responded with what Fairbairn claimed to be 'rudeness and indelicacy' to this request. Fairbairn had acted with very indelicate speed. However, although George asserted the accuracy of Alexander's intromissions, he wished to have a friend of his involved in checking them.[17] This incident illustrates that Seaforth's old

[11] NRS, GD46/17/3, G. Gillanders to F. H. Mackenzie, 8 February 1794.
[12] NRS, GD46/17/3, G. Gillanders to F. H. Mackenzie, 2 October 1793.
[13] NRS, GD46/17/3, P. Fairbairn to Mrs M. Mackenzie, 23 March 1794.
[14] NRS, GD46/17/13, P. Fairbairn to F. H. Mackenzie, 18 August 1795.
[15] *Sun*, British Library Burney Collection 17th and 18th Century Newspapers, 22 August 1794.
[16] NRS, GD46/17/3, G. Gillanders to F. H. Seaforth, 23 August 1794.
[17] NRS, GD46/17/3, G. Gillanders to F. H. Mackenzie, 18 August 1794, 23 August 1794.

and new advisors had different attitudes to accuracy in accounting and precision in record keeping.

Fairbairn's accounting skills were also valuable in surveys of the estate's potential. In 1792 he carried out a survey in Kintail. An illustration of the traditional estate manager's reaction to Fairbairn is given in a letter by Archibald Macrae, who held a tack or lease of a large farm in Kintail and was sub-factor there. He reported on Fairbairn's methods to George Gillanders with some incredulity that

> He [Fairbairn] was prepared with a blank book ruled in columns in the manner of an account book, for the names of the farms, the several tacksmen or possessors, the number of people on each farm, the number of their cattle, the quantity of seed corn sown and average returns. He questioned the people also on the distempers affecting their cattle and those who had not a sufficiency of hill grass.[18]

This was rational management in action, and not at all what had been practised by George and Alexander Gillanders. They held large farming tenancies in several parishes in Lewis, and paid as much attention to their own business interests as to Seaforth's concerns. In the parish of Lochs, for example, they held three tenancies in 1783 totalling a rent of £77, which represented 20 per cent of the rental of the parish, and they seem to have set their own rents low.[19] Fairbairn tenanted one farm as part of his salary package, but spent most of his time on Seaforth's service and saw it as his duty to rationally promote his employer's interests. He was a professional manager in a sense which the Gillanders, father and son, were not. This was a surprising appointment by a proprietor whose attitudes were in many ways conservative. Improving factors were not new in the Highlands. Between 1762 and his death in 1765 William Lorimer, factor of the Grant estates in Strathspey, was the driving force behind the conversion of shielings to cultivation by improving tenants. Unlike Fairbairn, he was a graduate (of Aberdeen University) and studied improvement by reading texts and by correspondence with and visits to improving landowners. However, his changes seem to have been premature and, by concentrating on arable, interrupted the existing cattle trade. They were partially reversed after his death.[20] In the 1790s

---

[18] NRS, GD427/212/12, A. Macrae, Ardintoul to G. Gillanders, 22 October 1792.
[19] NRS, GD427/14/8, rental of Lewis crop, 1783.
[20] A. Ross, 'Improvement on the Grant estates in Strathspey in the later eighteenth century: theory, practice, and failure?', in R. W. Hoyle (ed.), *Custom, Improvement and the Landscape in Early Modern Britain* (Farnham, 2011), pp. 289–312, especially pp. 291–5, 304–5.

major estates were still being managed by traditional factors. Notably, the factor of the Sutherland estate, subsequently known for ruthless improvement, was through the 1790s till 1802 John Fraser. He was 'trained in the old ways [and] positively resisted the new and disruptive ideas of improvement and clearance'.[21]

Like most of the new breed of professional Highland factors, the result of Fairbairn's rational study was to recommend sheep farming. He made the following proposal a year after his appointment:

> I understand some of the Glenshiel people begin cordially to relish sheep farming and hope they will all come into it with little difficulty . . . Geanies' shepherd cannot be forward before Saturday or Sunday next [Donald Macleod of Geanies – a proprietor and sheep farmer in Easter Ross], and there is a necessity for him to visit Glenshiel . . . I trust matters can be so brought about as to introduce sheep farming, secure a handsome augmentation [of rent] and continue your tenants.[22]

Seaforth had made it a condition that the existing small tenants should be retained. The problem was that introducing sheep farming on an economic scale was incompatible with continuing existing tenants. Unlike many clan chiefs, he retained what was by then coming to be regarded as an old-fashioned wish to protect his small tenants. Why, therefore, did he employ an agent with such views? He had inherited large debts with the estate in 1783 and in the following decade had increased them by extravagant living and an unwillingness to reduce the number of joint holdings, let to large-scale sheep graziers or sell land.[23] He badly needed to increase his income and he seems to have hoped that Fairbairn would assist him in doing so. By the early 1790s, although he still wished to protect his small tenants, he believed that 'lasting improvements in agriculture can only be expected from men of much larger funds than can possibly be attracted to a small highland farm'.[24] He liked to think of himself in the fashionable role of agricultural improver. Two of his proposers for election to the Royal Society in 1794 were leading

---

[21] E. Richards, *A History of the Highland Clearances: Agrarian Transformation and the Evictions, 1746–1886* (London, 1982), pp. 288–9; R. J. Adam (ed.), *Papers on Sutherland Estate Management 1802–1816* (Edinburgh, 1972), vol. 1, pp. xii–xiv, xxix.

[22] NRS, GD46/17/3, P. Fairbairn to F. H. Mackenzie, 23 October 1793.

[23] McKichan, 'Lifestyle of a Highland proprietor and clan chief', pp. 53–8.

[24] Mitchell Library, Mackenzie Miscellanea, 591706,-711,-837, 'Humble hints for Doctor Walker's use so far as relates to Ross-shire'. The author is indebted to Dr A. MacCoinnich for this reference.

improvers, Arthur Young and Sir John Sinclair.[25] By 1799 he was one
of five vice presidents of the Highland Society of Scotland, an important
part of whose mission was to encourage agricultural improvement.[26]
Eric Richards describes Seaforth's factors as being 'mesmerised' and
'conflicted' by his inconsistent and contradictory policies.[27]

How did Fairbairn's attributes and role compare with those of land
agents outside the Highlands? William Keir managed the Buccleuch
estates in south-west Scotland from 1772 to 1810. He had the advantage
in laying out new farms of being a skilled surveyor, which Fairbairn
was not. Archibald Macrae reported that on his visit to Kintail in 1792,
'Mr Fairbairn in his book sketched a plan of the intended village at
Plock of Lochalsh [Plockton]. I understand Seaforth wanted to have it
more particular, and Mr Fairbairn goes this day to Plock to complete
his survey.'[28] Keir was well read in the works of Adam Smith and
other Scottish Enlightenment writers and able to compose theoretical
justifications, such as in a report on the estate's sheep farms in 1791.[29]
Fairbairn was no theoretician, nor is there any evidence of his reading
Enlightenment texts. However, his use of concepts such as 'rational'
and 'economic' show that he had imbibed ideas derived from political
economy.

Most Irish agents appear to have been in the lower ranks of the
gentry and some combined an agency with commerce.[30] As has been
shown, Fairbairn was probably from the ranks of tenant farmers
(certainly no higher) and was virtually a full-time land agent. While
Terence Dooley has argued that by the nineteenth century Irish agents
enjoyed a high degree of autonomy because so many proprietors were

[25] Royal Society Library, EC/1794/05, election certificate of Francis Humberstone
Mackenzie, 26 June 1794.

[26] *Whitehall Evening Post*, 17 January 1799.

[27] E. Richards, *The Highland Estate Factor in the Age of the Clearances* (Laxay,
2016), pp. 56, 58. For details of Seaforth's inconsistent policies, see F. McKichan,
'Lord Seaforth and Highland estate management in the first phase of clearance
(1783–1815)', *Scottish Historical Review*, 221 (2007), pp. 50–68.

[28] NRS, GD427/212/12, Macrae, Ardintoul to G. Gillanders, 22 October 1792.

[29] B. Bonnyman, *The Third Duke of Buccleuch and Adam Smith: Estate
Management and Improvement in Enlightenment Scotland* (Edinburgh, 2013), pp.
8, 84–5, 128–31, 185–6.

[30] R. Richey, 'The eighteenth-century estate agent and his correspondence,
County Down: a case study', in R. J. Morris and L. Kennedy (eds), *Ireland and
Scotland: Order and Disorder, 1600–2000* (Edinburgh, 2005), pp. 35–44, especially
pp. 35–40.

absentees,[31] Rosemary Richey suggests that in the eighteenth century, although the Irish land agent had a high social status, major decisions were made by the proprietor.[32] Fairbairn was in a similar position, but he was not necessarily subservient. For example, in 1795 he criticised Seaforth's limited investment of cash in his joint fishing venture at Loch Roag with Bailie McIvor of Stornoway. He wrote with remarkable candour that 'the want of a sufficient supply of cash now would frustrate the establishment and the advantages expected from it ... the Bailie embarked in this business in full confidence of you being a partner'. At the same time he criticised what he considered his master's excessive expenditure on building new churches and schools on Lewis. He recommended a pause 'to get the buildings in hand finished and settled and ease a little the great yearly expense you have been at in that island'.[33] This was not the language of a particularly humble servant. He often complained that Seaforth, absent from Brahan for much of the year, was keeping him waiting for directions.[34] It was not novel for a factor to criticise his employer. In 1772, at a time of famine in the Central Highlands, James Ross, the chamberlain of the Gordon estates, wrote to the Duke of Gordon that 'the distress of the poor ... calls loud for compassion and assistance – instead of the expense of some carousing expected on the Marquis and Lady Madelina's birthday'. He argued that some oatmeal should be given to the poor instead of offering it at near market price.[35]

Fairbairn's advice, however apparently economically rational, was not always taken. For example, at the 1801 set of Glenshiel, he proposed that if the existing tenants did not offer enough (the advisers hoped for the rent to rise by 100 per cent), this would 'give good reasons to hold the country out to strangers', in other words large-scale sheep graziers. All that Seaforth would allow was that the holdings should be consolidated into small farms to run sheep held by combinations of existing tenants (which resulted in a 47 per cent rental increase).[36] Eric Richards points out that, as the new breed of Highland factor had to mediate such tensions between commercial aspirations and traditions of paternalism,

[31] T. Dooley, *The Big Houses and Landed Estates of Ireland: A Research Guide* (Dublin, 2007), pp. 18–19.

[32] Richey, 'Eighteenth-century estate agent', p. 44.

[33] NRS, GD46/17/15, P. Fairbairn to F. H. Mackenzie, 1 December 1795.

[34] For example, NRS, GD46/17/3, P. Fairbairn to F. H. Mackenzie, 8 May 1794.

[35] D. Taylor, *The Wild Black Region: Badenoch 1750–1800* (Edinburgh, 2016), p. 150.

[36] McKichan, 'Lord Seaforth and Highland estate management', pp. 53–4.

this did not make for popularity with the tenantry or always with the employer.[37] Notwithstanding, Seaforth very much valued Fairbairn's services. He later wrote that at this period 'as my secretary, book-keeper and chamberlain, his habits were perfect clockwork, his diligence indefatigable and neither I nor anyone in my confidence had the slightest suspicion of his honesty'.[38]

While Seaforth's word was always decisive, Fairbairn was sometimes at the centre of the decision-making process and influenced the outcome. To try to solve his pressing financial problems, Seaforth (ennobled in 1797) became Governor of Barbados in November 1800.[39] About six weeks before he set sail for Barbados, Colin Mackenzie, his Edinburgh law agent and man of business, wrote: 'I wish to God a sale could be effected in one or other of these quarters . . . [Lochalsh, Kintail or Ussie (near Brahan)] for without it I see nothing to be looked for but difficulty and vexation.'[40] In the event, Lochalsh was sold to Hugh Innes for £38,000. Seaforth made the terms of sale a few days before he left London on 10 February for his transatlantic voyage.[41] However, Innes was to pay for Lochalsh in instalments, with the first of £17,000 being paid within four months and the next instalment not till January 1802.[42] This was insufficient to solve the immediate issue, which was a serious cash-flow problem. When he left Britain Seaforth faced demands which were between £8,000 and £9,000 greater than likely incomings.[43] Mackenzie commented on 'the poignant feelings to which your situation gave rise at the time of your sailing'.[44] Seaforth, therefore, was aware while still in London that further lands needed to be sold. Fairbairn was involved in the negotiations with Innes and tried to interest him in Kildun (near Brahan).[45] Innes was not receptive, and a sale of land so near Brahan Castle was unacceptable to Seaforth. What was achieved was the purchase by Innes in April 1801 (a month after Fairbairn also sailed

[37] Richards, *Highland Estate Factor*, pp. 63–5.

[38] NRS, GD46/17/37/32, Lord Seaforth to Inglis, Ellis and Co., 9 February 1811.

[39] *London Gazette*, 29 November 1800.

[40] NRS, GD46/17/14, C. Mackenzie to Lord Seaforth, 26 December 1800.

[41] NRS, GD46/17/19/111, C. Mackenzie to V. Gibbs, 21 April 1801.

[42] NRS, GD46/17/19/363, 'State of Lord Seaforth's affairs made up to 15 Oct. 1801'. Innes took sasine on 19 February 1802; NRS, Register of Sasines, Ross-shire Abridgements, No. 695, 1781–1868.

[43] NRS, GD46/17/19/107–8, C. Mackenzie, report to Vicary Gibbs, 21 April 1801.

[44] NRS, GD46/17/20, C. Mackenzie to Lord Seaforth, 11 June 1801.

[45] NRS, GD46/17/19/435, P. Fairbairn to Lord Seaforth [n.d. but clearly late January or early February 1801].

for Barbados) of three Kintail farms adjoining Lochalsh for £7,200. This was the first part of the ancient Mackenzie patrimony of Kintail to be sold. The attraction was that the purchase price was expected to be paid very soon.[46] Fairbairn claimed the credit for advising it. He wrote that 'finding the sale of any part of the Brahan estate both improper and impracticable, I advised the sale of Fadoch, Killelan and Corriedoine, being the north side of Glen Elchaig, which I expected Innes to grasp at'.[47] Fairbairn's advice was followed and Innes took the bait.

THE HIGHLAND FACTOR IN THE CARIBBEAN

In a further effort to solve his pressing financial problems Seaforth made an agreement in January 1801 with partners to invest in uncultivated land in Berbice, Guyana, to grow cotton.[48] In 1801 Seaforth's major sources of home income were the net rental of Lewis and Kintail (£4,000) and home pay and regimental off reckonings (about £2,600); however, interest payments on debts were expected to total £5,162 and annuities payable £1,436 (totalling about the same as his home income). His Barbados salary of £3,000 he wished to be topped up by £1,000 from home funds to support his family and for entertaining expenses.[49] The Berbice speculation was vital to supplement his income and, more importantly, to offer any prospect of reducing his debts without further land sales. If successful, it would effectively have subsidised his small tenants in Ross-shire.[50] He was encouraged to invest in Berbice by the success there of other Highland proprietors, perhaps particularly that of his neighbour in Easter Ross, James Fraser of Belladrum, and the Baillies of Dochfour, near Inverness, and Bristol.[51] However, Caribbean plantations were hazardous enterprises, with success being threatened by weather conditions, market prices and mortality or unrest among the

[46] NRS, GD46/17/19/95,108–13, C. Mackenzie to V. Gibbs, 21 April 1801; Register of Sasines, Ross-shire Abridgements, No. 696, 1 February 1802.

[47] NRS, GD46/17/19/208–9, P. Fairbairn to Lord Seaforth, 6 June 1801.

[48] NRS, GD46/17/19/552, copy agreement, Lord Seaforth et al. re purchase of land belonging to the Berbice Company, 2 January 1801.

[49] NRS, GD46/17/19/363–6, 'State of Lord Seaforth's affairs made up to 15 Oct. 1801'.

[50] Richards, *Highland Estate Factor*, p. 59.

[51] D. Alston, '"Very rapid and splendid fortunes"? Highland Scots in Berbice (Guyana) in the early nineteenth century', *Transactions of the Gaelic Society of Inverness*, 63 (2006), pp. 208–36, especially pp. 212–13; D. J. Hamilton, *Scotland, the Caribbean and the Atlantic World, 1750–1820* (Manchester, 2005), pp. 92, 199.

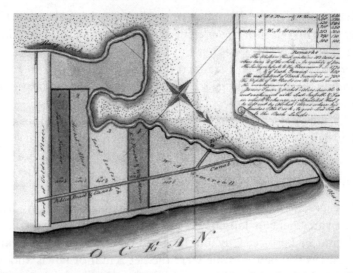

Figure 5 Berbice: west coast lots, 1803, property of Lord Seaforth. National Records of Scotland, GD46/17/19, lots A and B.

enslaved black labour force. Seaforth understood the risk he was taking and wrote to his closest friend that 'such a scene of probable wealth was opened to me that I was tempted to . . . try my fate'.[52]

Guyana has been described as 'the last Caribbean frontier' and as 'the edge of the British world'.[53] It was to become by the 1830s second only to Jamaica in the British Caribbean in the production of sugar, but in 1801 had only recently (1796) been conquered from the Dutch.[54] Berbice, one of the Guyana colonies, was a narrow territory stretching inland along each side of the Berbice River (see Figure 5). The Dutch had tended to settle well up the river for security and because cultivation was easier. The coastal lands, which had to be reclaimed from the sea by dikes and polder canals, were more expensive to work, but potentially more fertile. Plantations there were developed in the course of the first decade of the nineteenth century by British capital, with Berbice becoming especially committed to cotton.[55] Lots were drawn among Seaforth's partners and he became

[52] British Library [hereafter BL], Add. MS 42071,vol. 2, fos. 285–7, Lord Seaforth to C. F. Greville, 21 March 1801.

[53] K. Candlin, *The Last Caribbean Frontier, 1795–1815* (Basingstoke, 2012), pp. 26–9, 45.

[54] N. Draper, 'The rise of a new planter class? Some countercurrents from British Guiana and Trinidad, 1807–33', *Atlantic Studies: Global Currents*, 9:1 (2012), pp. 65–83, especially pp. 67–8.

[55] D. Alston, '"The habits of these creatures in clinging one to the other": enslaved

major partner in two plantations west of the Berbice River, which were in due course named Brahan and Kintail. He also acquired a third planta- tion on the East Sea Coast, named Seawell. His friend the Inverness-shire landowner Edward Satchwell Fraser of Reelig became a minor partner in these plantations.[56] Seawell was intended not for cultivation but for resale. Land speculation was, therefore, added to the already hazardous planta- tion business. A further layer of risk was added by the uncertain title to the land purchases created by the ambiguous sovereignty of Berbice. Although occupied by Britain, the colony was not formally annexed till 1814. Meantime, Dutch law continued to apply and the governor through whom the purchase had to be registered in Berbice was Dutch. Furthermore, the purchase was made from Dutch proprietors resident in Holland, which was currently, as 'The Batavian Republic', under French control and there- fore an enemy state. A British statute required government permission to acquire landed property from parties resident in enemy countries, which permission the partners did not have.[57] Seaforth was taking an enormous commercial risk, and there is no evidence of its being seriously costed. His share of the purchase price was £10,000, approximately twice the annual rental of the Ross-shire estates.[58]

In view of the satisfaction Fairbairn had given hitherto, it is perhaps not surprising that he was appointed the plantation attorney to be responsible for the 'care, management, sale or disposal, cultivation and improvement' of the Berbice estates.[59] He was to 'transmit clear and articulate accounts of his management, outlays and receipts'. It was also envisaged that he would act as Seaforth's personal secretary in Barbados. He was to have for five years the substantial salary of £500 and one sixth of the 'whole free profits'. If he was still alive after the five years (despite the perils of yellow fever and malaria), he would be given a sixth part of the concern.[60] Fairbairn sailed for Barbados in

Africans, Scots and the plantations of Guyana', in T. M. Devine (ed.), *Recovering Scotland's Slavery Past: The Caribbean Connection* (Edinburgh, 2015), pp. 99–123, especially p. 102.

[56] NRS, GD46/17/19/585–8, division of lands in Berbice, 28 December 1801, 31 December 1801; GD46/17/19/568, valuation between Lord Seaforth and E. S. Fraser, 28 December 1801.

[57] NRS, GD46/17/19/371–3, Lord Seaforth to E. S. Fraser, 16 October 1801.

[58] NRS, GD46/17/21, C. Mackenzie to Lord Seaforth, 29 March 1802.

[59] NRS, GD46/17/11, letter of attorney, Lord Seaforth to Peter Fairbairn, 31 July 1801.

[60] NRS, GD46/17/11, contract and agreement between Lord Seaforth, Col. Alexander Mackenzie and Peter Fairbairn, 1801, re Berbice, 23 February 1801.

March 1801, leaving behind on Moy Farm in Ross-shire his wife and children, and was not to return until 1819. He reached Berbice in early 1802 and appointed the first of the under-managers who would provide the daily supervision of the plantations.[61] Barry Higman has argued that a successful plantation attorney needed to have prior experience in supervisory roles on plantations and practical experience of plantation cultivation.[62] Fairbairn did not fit this template. Scots were heavily involved in plantations in Berbice and other parts of Guyana at this period.[63] Henry Gibbs Dalton, an early historian of Guyana, wrote that, although they plunged as readily as other Europeans into 'the vortex of dissapation', Scots 'exemplified the well known caution and parsimony of their race and came to fill some of the highest situations'.[64] However, Fraser of Reelig had serious doubts about Fairbairn's suitability. He cautioned, 'I believe Fairbairn will prove a most faithful servant and associate in the concern, but you know experience in planting is not attained soon.'[65] Seaforth presumably preferred to deal with a trusted employee with whom he had developed effective working methods.

What were the circumstances in which Fairbairn managed the plantations? In October 1801 Britain signed preliminary articles of peace with the French Republic (the Peace of Amiens), and it soon became clear that Guyana would be returned to Dutch sovereignty. This had 'an electric effect' on British planters already operating in Berbice.[66] Although it was only occupied by Dutch forces for ten months before war resumed and British control was restored, the land market in the colony was seriously damaged.[67] Fairbairn lamented that Seawell, 'had the peace not taken place ... would have sold readily and well'.[68] The second instalment on the purchase price, of £2,262, was due in May 1802 and had been expected to be paid from the sale price of Seawell. Because of delays in registration, possession of the lands was not achieved until the

---

[61] NRS, GD46/17/11, P. Fairbairn to Lord Seaforth [n.d. but early 1802].

[62] B. W. Higman, *Plantation Jamaica 1750–1850: Capital and Control in a Plantation Economy* (Kingston, Jamaica, 2005), pp. 92–3.

[63] Analysed most recently in Alston, 'Enslaved Africans', pp. 101–9.

[64] H. G. Dalton, *The History of British Guiana* (2 vols, London, 1854–5), vol. 1, pp. 306–7.

[65] NRS, GD46/17/20/73, 98, E. S. Fraser to Lord Seaforth, 13 May 1801, 7 June 1801.

[66] NRS, GD46/17/20/206–7, P. Fairbairn to Lord Seaforth, 28 November 1801.

[67] Mitchell Library, Mackenzie Miscellanea, Dr Caddell to Lord Seaforth, 13 May 1802.

[68] NRS, GD46/17/19/581–2, P. Fairbairn to Lord Seaforth, 24 December 1801.

summer of 1802. This was followed by delays in surveying caused by wet weather.[69] In consequence, the first cotton crop, on Brahan, was not harvested until late 1803 or early 1804. The third instalment, of £1,867, was due in May 1803 and was supposed to be paid from the first crop, which did not come till over six months later.[70] Kintail was not got into cultivation until late 1804. The purchase instalments had to be raised instead by further borrowing on the security of the Ross-shire estates. By 1805 not only had the Berbice concern increased rather than reduced the British debt, but also it was itself almost £4,000 in debt.[71]

Delay in building revenue caused another problem. Guyana planters' prospects of profit depended on increasing the area under cultivation as rapidly as possible. This required an increasing force of enslaved labourers. Purchase of slaves was made on credit, with payment depending on the success of the next crop.[72] Seaforth's financial problems did not encourage generous credit terms. Accordingly, Fairbairn regularly complained that he was unable to buy as many slaves as he needed.[73] The shortage of slaves was not helped by the 1805 Order in Council limiting the import of slaves to conquered colonies like Berbice to 3 per cent annually of the existing force to replace casualties.[74] British policy makers were very uncertain in whose hands Guyana would end up, and wished to limit the extension of cultivation.[75] Fairbairn protested that 'the lands are our own . . . and consequently no power can prevent us cultivating when we please', and hoped that ways could be found to evade or minimise the effects of the order.[76] However, it effectively ended any hope of the sale of Seawell.

Alternately wet and dry seasons (contrary to the experience of 1799–1800, on which Seaforth had based his expectations) diminished the value of the cotton crop as well as increasing the cost of provisions to feed the slaves. There were almost ten years of disastrous weather, either too dry or too wet. In 1806 Fairbairn complained that 'the rains

---

[69] NRS, GD46/17/21, C. Mackenzie to Lord Seaforth, 29 March 1802, 28 October 1802; P. Fairbairn, 'General state of Berbice concern', 1 July 1802.

[70] NRS, GD46/17/26, P. Fairbairn to Lord Seaforth, 18 January 1804.

[71] NRS, GD46/17/26, C. Mackenzie to Lord Seaforth, 26 April 1805.

[72] Alston, 'Highland Scots in Berbice', p. 216.

[73] For example, NRS, GD46/17/25/5, P. Fairbairn to Lord Seaforth, 17 January 1805.

[74] NRS, GD46/17/25/284–6, Order in Council, 15 August 1805.

[75] D. B. Ryden, *West Indian Slavery and British Abolition, 1783–1807* (Cambridge, 2009), p. 276.

[76] NRS, GD46/17/27, P. Fairbairn to Lord Seaforth, 20 November 1805.

exceed anything previously experienced . . . we must have a dry season to succeed'.[77] Colin Mackenzie reported seven months later that 'the Berbice accounts will this year only just balance, if that'.[78] By 1810 Fairbairn was becoming desperate and wrote to Lady Seaforth that 'bad season succeeded bad season . . . Let the crop be what it may, the expense must go on – the negroes must be fed, clothed, etc.'[79] To make matters worse, cotton prices were falling due to economic depression caused by American competition and French blockade, which impeded sales in Europe. By 1811 the balance due by the Seaforth plantations to the selling agents Inglis, Ellis and Co. had reached £7,387.[80] In 1812 they were refusing to act for Seaforth and were pressing for payment of the debt.[81]

Clearly, Fairbairn cannot be blamed for the effects of these problems. How successfully did the skills and qualities he demonstrated as a Ross-shire factor transfer to his duties as a Caribbean plantation attorney? As has been seen, in Ross-shire he had been regarded as a conscientious and accurate accountant and absolutely honest. When, in 1811, ten years after the purchase, the Berbice plantations were still not making money and Fairbairn was unwilling to supply accounts, Seaforth began to doubt his probity and application. He complained that 'while I stayed in the West Indies [until 1806] he gave me satisfaction, but since I left the country I have not been able to extract the slightest resemblance of an account from him'. He was aware of 'the enervating effects of the climate' and that Fairbairn had often been ill. He contemplated removing him from his position, and even considered sailing to Berbice to assess his performance.[82] Inglis, Ellis and Co. were much less inclined to doubt his honesty and pointed out that many Berbice concerns were suffering from the poor seasons.[83] Fairbairn now bought the Ross plantation in Berbice at the same time as he was complaining that he had 'met with disappointment only . . . I have been yearly sunk deeper in trouble and difficulty.'[84] Colin Mackenzie's view was that 'though I feel it difficult to relinquish the confidence with which Fairbairn's character

[77] NRS, GD46/17/24/368–70, P. Fairbairn to Lord Seaforth, 6 March 1806.
[78] NRS, GD46/17/24/81, C. Mackenzie to Lord Seaforth, 3 October 1806.
[79] NRS, GD46/17/35/249, P. Fairbairn to Lady Seaforth, 1 February 1810.
[80] NRS, GD46/17/37, T. Coutts to Lord Seaforth, 19 March 1811.
[81] NRS, GD46/17/37/237, C. Mackenzie to Lord Seaforth, 27 April 1812; GD46/17/37/285, J. Gladstone to Lord Seaforth, 6 May 1812.
[82] NRS, GD46/17/37/32, Lord Seaforth to Inglis, Ellis and Co., 9 February 1811.
[83] NRS, GD46/17/37/27, John Inglis to Lord Seaforth, 11 February 1811.
[84] NRS, GD46/17/37/52, P. Fairbairn to Lord Seaforth, 8 February 1811.

and conduct impressed me in this country, I own there is so much room most improperly left by him for suspicion to grow up'.[85]

In the event Fairbairn remained in office and in 1812 a full report was obtained from James Baillie Fraser, son of Seaforth's friend and partner Edward Satchwell Fraser. J. B. Fraser had a decade's experience as a planter in Berbice and had known Fairbairn well. He asserted that 'no man living is more scrupulously correct in the money transactions that relate to that community'. His view was that Fairbairn's probity and accounting skills did transfer to Berbice. Nevertheless, he saw Fairbairn's failure to send accounts as 'the chief charge' against him and 'culpable in the extreme'. He could only explain this by 'the continual series of uninterrupted misfortunes which has marked . . . the few late years, [and] has made it a most unpleasant task to write frequently or circumstantially'.[86] However, as early as January 1804 Colin Mackenzie had found it necessary to press Fairbairn for regular transmission of accounts and to reassure Lady Seaforth about his integrity.[87] In early 1805 Fairbairn claimed that 'all the books, papers, etc. have been kept in ample detail', and excused his failure to send accounts on the unconvincing grounds that he wanted to carry out an appraisement of the plantations first.[88] It was not till the end of August 1805 that he eventually sent (reasonably accurate) accounts to Colin Mackenzie.[89] Perhaps these failures were the result of the heat and Fairbairn's periodic bouts of fever. He wrote in 1805 that 'I have had another spell of sickness, but have got over it. I am much weakened, but shall soon get round.'[90] Unlike some of his under-managers and many other white people in Guyana, he always did 'get round' and survive. However, the consequence of his failure to send accounts and the nature of his reports undoubtedly created suspicion. He could not resist offering unrealistic hopes for the future. In 1806, after reporting that 'the second crop was inconsiderable, which leaves the total far below the estimate', he managed to claim that 'our prospects look charmingly and I have no doubt will give a great crop to relieve us of all embarrassments'.[91] As Colin Mackenzie put it in 1811,

[85] NRS, GD46/17/37/188–9, C. Mackenzie to Lord Seaforth, 28 April 1811.
[86] NRS, GD46/17/36, J. B. Fraser to Lord Seaforth, 14 December 1812. Quotations from J. B. Fraser in the following pages are from this document.
[87] NRS, GD46/17/26, C. Mackenzie to Lady Seaforth, 23 January 1804.
[88] NRS, GD46/17/27, P. Fairbairn to Lord Seaforth, 4 February 1805.
[89] NRS, GD46/17/27, C. Mackenzie to Lord Seaforth, 27 December 1805.
[90] NRS, GD46/17/27, P. Fairbairn to Lord Seaforth, 17 December 1805.
[91] NRS, GD46/17/24/446, P. Fairbairn to C. Mackenzie, 22 September 1806.

his letters were 'only gay as to the future'.[92] Suspicion was increased by his purchase of the Ross plantation and the fear that he was doing this with misappropriated funds. J. B. Fraser was sure this was not the case. Fairbairn, he was convinced, never had such a large sum of Seaforth's money at his disposal. He had bought the Ross plantation as a speculation on his own account with borrowed money, and 'has I believe been sorely disappointed'.[93]

Seaforth's remark about the enervating effects of the climate implies a belief that Fairbairn did not display the energy and devotion to duty in Berbice which he had done in Ross-shire. However, Fraser argued that 'Mr Fairbairn's attention to his business, his steady personal attention and labour . . . has the interests of the concerns deeply at heart.' He did make a fundamental criticism that 'Mr Fairbairn was much more at home in conducting the indoor share of the concern than the executive agricultural part – that his zeal and integrity as a man and capacity as a man of business far exceeded his skill and activity as a planter'. According to Fraser, a major problem was that 'his want of local experience sometimes subjected him to a more expensive scale of execution in his plans than otherwise might have been the case', especially at first. He was guilty of improvement schemes 'which have been very expensive, in various ways, and the crop has seldom paid the current outlay'. In particular, he attempted to cultivate more land than was possible with his own force of enslaved labourers. How far is this fair? Fairbairn was very conscious that the business model required a rapid start and regular expansion to pay the purchase instalments. When he did get possession, after the initial delays, he was understandably keen to move forward as quickly and extensively as possible. On Brahan an impolder (a reclamation) of 'almost the whole lot' was made,[94] which Fraser believed extended cultivation too far and into indifferent land. On Kintail Fairbairn also decided 'to make impolder of larger extent than we once reckoned on'.[95] In this case it seems to have been justified. Fraser thought its cotton land fine, and it was given a canal which both drained a wide area and was used to ship out the crop.

Fairbairn's determination to develop cultivation quickly does seem to have caused him to buy slaves earlier than necessary and consequently waste money. In December 1801, at least six months before they could

[92] NRS, GD46/17/36, C. Mackenzie to Lord Seaforth, 12 June 1811.
[93] NRS, GD46/17/36, J. B. Fraser to Lord Seaforth, 14 December 1812.
[94] NRS, GD46/17/21, P. Fairbairn to Lord Seaforth, 29 May 1802.
[95] NRS, GD46/17/21, P. Fairbairn to Lord Seaforth, 1 May 1802.

be used, he had already bought twenty enslaved labourers at the considerable price of £1,741. These were newly arrived slaves and he argued this enabled them to be 'seasoned' (acclimatised) and that they had been hired out since January. By May a further thirty-three had been bought, thirteen of whom were skilled and already seasoned. These could only be bought for ready money, and he was already complaining that 'the grand difficulty is the payment'.[96] However, when he was taken to see six seasoned slaves, he 'could not resist making the purchase' at a cost of £571.[97] Thus, at the beginning of July, with operations only just starting, fifty-three slaves had been purchased.[98] However, he was not alone. Fraser conceded that 'had a few only suffered, blame might have attached to the manager, but . . . the misery is general'. Because of bumper crops in Guyana in 1799 and 1800, combined with a high price for cotton, there was, as Fraser put it, 'a general trend for expensive cultivation, a want of economy in justifying improvement'.

No evidence has been found of a long-term estimate of the costs of and likely income from the Berbice plantations. However, in December 1801 Fairbairn did produce a detailed estimate for the first year.[99] By far the greatest expense was to be slave purchase – £1,741 for the twenty already acquired and an estimated £1,500 for a further twenty and £200 for two drivers in May 1802 (an estimated total of forty-two). As has been seen, the number actually purchased by July 1802 was fifty-three, confirming extravagance in slave purchase. In addition, he expected to spend £440 on hiring enslaved labourers. The other major expense was impoldering, estimated to cost £583 by contracting out to Hector Mackenzie, a Ross-shire man who owned a slave gang in Berbice. Purchase of provisions for the slaves was estimated at £348. Total expenses for the first year were expected to be £5,263. Fairbairn hoped that the first crop would raise between £1,200 and £1,300 about the end of 1802. In the event, due to delays for which he was not responsible, the first crop was not harvested until a year later.

Fraser claimed that plantation managers who tried to expand cultivation beyond the capabilities of the slave force they could afford had to resort to 'the almost ruinous expense of hiring negroes'. It would appear that Fairbairn was guilty of this. In a paper on Berbice written by Seaforth in 1801, he had argued that renting slaves from other owners was bad

[96] NRS, GD46/17/21, P. Fairbairn to Lord Seaforth, 29 May 1802.
[97] NRS, GD46/17/21, P. Fairbairn to Lord Seaforth, 21 June 1802.
[98] NRS, GD46/17/21, 'General state of Berbice concern', 1 July 1802.
[99] NRS, GD46/17/19/580, 'P. F. Berbice, Plan of Cultivation etc., 24 Dec. 1801'.

practice. The hirer did not have the same interest in their welfare.[100] However, in 1802, as soon as he started operations, Fairbairn used a task gang (i.e. hired slaves) to impolder.[101] Digging the polder canals in the sea clay was regarded as the most arduous work for slaves, and he could have claimed he was saving Seaforth's own slaves from this.[102] However, he justified it as a substitute for slaves whom he had not the resources to purchase. In 1805 he wrote to Seaforth that 'I should have immediately twenty new negroes, but the credits yet deter me' (very limited credit was available). He had hired twelve slaves for the season for Kintail 'who will greatly assist the labour' and ten for Brahan, 'the cultivation of the estate being more extensive than they [the existing slaves] could manage'. However, he rejected claims that he was extravagant. He argued that 'I have conducted this concern, not only with economy, but I may say with rigid economy.'[103] The nature of the concern was that it should continue to expand its production, but to attempt this was made more expensive by the poor seasons and delays.[104]

The other great error which Fraser believed Fairbairn guilty of was 'omitting to establish a sufficient proportion of plantain walk for supporting the negroes, thus relying on purchase'. The Guyana colonies were unusual in having plantain grounds under direct estate supervision, as opposed to giving slaves their own plots.[105] In particularly dry seasons in 1803 and 1804, plantain was not available locally and American flour had to be imported at high cost.[106] The governor of Berbice reported in 1804 that 'the late dry weather has reduced the inhabitants to the utmost distress for want of provisions for their negroes'.[107] An Act of the Court of Policy (the local assembly) in 1806 alleged that coastal planters had relied on plantain purchases rather than allocate fertile

[100] BL, Add. MS 42071, vol. 2, fo. 299, 'Guiana-from Lord Seaforth'.

[101] NRS, GD46/17/21, P. Fairbairn to Lord Seaforth, 'Memorandums, Berbice' [n.d. but summer 1802].

[102] R. B. Sheridan, 'The condition of the slaves on the sugar plantations of Sir John Gladstone in the colony of Demerara, 1812–49', *New West Indian Guide*, 76:3–4 (2002), pp. 243–69, especially pp. 245, 266.

[103] NRS, GD46/17/27, P. Fairbairn to Lord Seaforth, 17 January 1805 (emphasis in original).

[104] NRS, GD46/17/26, P. Fairbairn to Lord Seaforth, 8 December 1804.

[105] J. R. Ward, *British West Indian Slavery,1754–1834: The Process of Amelioration* (Oxford, 1988), p. 114.

[106] A. O. Thompson, *Unprofitable Servants: Crown Slaves in Berbice, Guyana, 1803–1831* (Kingston, Jamaica, 2002), p. 61.

[107] The National Archives, CO112/1, fo. 7, Van Batterburg to Secretary of State, 26 June 1804.

land for provision grounds.[108] Is it fair to say that Fairbairn fell into this trap? From the outset he was conscious of the importance of plantains. One reason why he chose Brahan to cultivate first was that he thought it would provide good plantain grounds, which could be immediately planted on the new impolder, and in a year or so he hoped would supply also Kintail.[109] By April 1803 dry weather was causing him much expense and trouble in purchasing, but the new plantains at Brahan were growing luxuriously and he was still optimistic for the future.[110] However, by early 1804 the plantains were so stunted that he was obliged to feed the slaves on American flour. What appeared to be good plantain land at Kintail was too hard to dig.[111] In July 1804 American flour (described by Fairbairn as 'the principal branch of expense') was still being used, but at last rain had come. He expected soon to have the concern's own provisions.[112]

There continued to be periodic failures in the plantain crop. In 1809 he laid out a large new walk on Kintail, which soon nearly supplied its own slaves and he expected within six months would also supply Brahan (whose plantains had been destroyed by rain). Ironically, the hopes for Kintail were dashed by a succeeding very dry spell. In February 1810 he was becoming desperate, was now having to buy in plantains from the more distant Demerara River and was afraid even that expensive source might dry up.[113] Unfortunately, when he at last in 1812 had a surplus of provisions he could not sell them.[114] Without comparative figures for plantain cultivation on other Guyana plantations, it is difficult to be certain that Fairbairn allocated enough ground to plantains. But he certainly devoted constant attention to the issue. In 1804 he assured Seaforth that this 'requires the first attention', and this it seems to have been given.[115] The decade of unfavourable weather probably explains his continued difficulty in provision supply.

[108] A. O. Thompson, *A Documentary History of Slavery in Berbice, 1796–1804* (Georgetown, Barbados, 2002), p. 75.

[109] NRS, GD46/17/21, P. Fairbairn to Lord Seaforth, 1 May 1802.

[110] NRS, GD46/17/24/125,128, P. Fairbairn, 'Particulars of the Berbice Concerns', 24 April 1803.

[111] NRS, GD46/17/26, P. Fairbairn to Lord Seaforth, 18 January 1804.

[112] NRS, GD46/17/26, P. Fairbairn to Lady Seaforth, 12 July 1804.

[113] NRS, GD46/17/35/51, P. Fairbairn to Lord Seaforth, 20 April 1809; GD46/17/35/86, P. Fairbairn to Lord Seaforth, 29 July 1809; GD46/17/35/247, P. Fairbairn to Lord Seaforth, 15 February 1810; GD46/17/35/249, P. Fairbairn to Lady Seaforth, 1 February 1810.

[114] NRS, GD46/17/37/331, P. Fairbairn to Lord Seaforth, 4 June 1812.

[115] NRS, GD46/17/26, P. Fairbairn to Lord Seaforth, 18 January 1804.

J. B. Fraser had himself come home in 1812 after his father had concluded that 'Berbice is a poison' and had given up. Another Scottish planter who failed in Berbice was William Macpherson. He had borrowed to buy a half share in the Rising Sun plantation, and was quite unable to meet the first payment, due in 1812. He returned to Britain in early 1813, having transferred the land and slaves to his creditor as full payment of the debt.[116] It was possible to make money from cotton in Guyana, as demonstrated by Joseph Porter. When he died in 1815 (the same year as Seaforth), he was one of the dozen wealthiest Britons to die that year.[117] However, by 1813 Seaforth had given up hope and was keen to 'get rid as quickly as possible upon the best terms I can of my West Indies Estates'.[118] Nevertheless, it seems clear that no sales in Berbice were concluded during his lifetime.[119]

One of J. B. Fraser's most direct criticisms of Fairbairn was of his treatment of his family, who were left to work the Moy farm unsupported by him. Fraser put this down to 'the general laxity of manners prevalent in these colonies' and, perhaps snobbishly, described him as 'not a man of the most refined habits and sentiments'.[120] David Alston has shown that, like many plantation managers hitherto, Fairbairn took an enslaved African woman, Charmion, as a concubine. In the decade after 1811 they had five children.[121] William Macpherson also had a black concubine, by whom he had three children.[122] This practice was now becoming less acceptable. Christer Petley points out that 'attitudes to interracial sexual relationships changed ... and colonists became more hesitant about mixed-race liaisons'.[123] This may have contributed to the increasing suspicion with which Fairbairn was regarded at home.

---

[116] S. Foster, *A Private Empire* (Miller's Point, NSW, 2011), pp. 159–60, 165–6.

[117] Draper, 'Rise of a new planter class?', p. 71.

[118] NRS, GD46/17/41, Lord Seaforth to Sir A. Mackenzie of Avoch, 30 May 1813.

[119] NRS, GD46/1/143, C. Mackenzie, 22 July 1815 and Wm Mackenzie, 24 July 1815 to Lady Hood Mackenzie on the proposed sale of Berbice plantations, still apparently in Seaforth hands.

[120] NRS, GD46/17/36, J. B. Fraser to Lord Seaforth, 14 December 1812.

[121] D. Alston, 'A forgotten diaspora: the children of enslaved and "free coloured" women and Highland Scots in Guyana before emancipation', *Northern Scotland*, 6:1 (2015), pp. 49–69, especially pp. 60–1.

[122] Foster, *Private Empire*, pp. 141–3, 161–2.

[123] C. Petley, 'Rethinking the fall of the planter class', *Atlantic Studies: Global Currents*, 9:1 (2012), pp. 1–17 (quote at p. 12).

CONCLUSION

From time to time Peter Fairbairn promised to return to Scotland,[124] but he did not do so until 1819. Coming home involved facing up to debts on the Moy farm, and it may be that until 1819, as he claimed, he really could not afford to.[125] By then, however, he owned not only the Ross plantation but also part of Brahan, Seawell and Kintail.[126] The Seaforth advisors were sceptical about his intentions. Patrick Cockburn, the estate's Edinburgh accountant, commented that 'Mr Peter Fairbairn's intentions and his performance seem to be very different things.'[127] However, when Cockburn was persuaded of Fairbairn's bona fides, he soon accepted various bills and the produce of Moy in payment of the debts. He wrote to J. A. Stewart Mackenzie, husband of Lord Seaforth's daughter and heir Mary, that it 'must give your lady much satisfaction to find unfavourable impressions removed agt. an old servant who had once enjoyed the confidence of her father'.[128] Lady Seaforth, the dowager, commented that 'he is a very systematic person and was for many years of the greatest use to us'.[129]

In 1820 Fairbairn returned to Berbice, and he died there at Plantation Ross in 1822. The *Demerara Chronicle* in its obituary referred to him as 'the Hon. Peter Fairburn, late member of Courts of Policy and Justice'.[130] That he survived until his death as a planter and was highly regarded in the community should be taken into account in judging his performance as a plantation attorney. Fairbairn's longevity in that climate is remarkable and fully justified E. S. Fraser's comment in 1802 that his 'health seems to agree with Guiana'.[131] J. B. Fraser wrote of him in 1812 that 'he is neither too tenacious of his own opinion nor averse from seeking

[124] For example, NRS, GD46/17/32/196, P. Fairbairn to Lord Seaforth, 24 September 1810.
[125] For example, NRS, GD46/17/45, P. Fairbairn to C. Mackenzie, 16 January 1816.
[126] NRS, GD46/17/52, J. A. Stewart Mackenzie to Pat. Cockburn, 17 June 1819; P. Cockburn to P. Fairbairn, 29 October 1819; Alston, <http://www.spanglefish.com/slavesandhighlanders>.
[127] NRS, GD46/17/52, P. Cockburn to J. A. Stewart Mackenzie, 10 September 1819.
[128] NRS, GD46/17/53, P. Cockburn to J. A. Stewart Mackenzie, 29 October 1819.
[129] NRS, GD46/17/52, copy letter Lady Seaforth to P. Cockburn, 28 October 1819.
[130] Alston, 'Highland Scots in Berbice', pp. 222, 234, n. 58.
[131] NRS, GD46/17/21, E. S. Fraser to Lord Seaforth, 28 July 1802.

advice and frequently solicits it from his more experienced neighbours'.[132] It seems likely that he had overcome his inexperience and was able to take advantage of improved market and weather conditions. In early 1816 he wrote to Colin Mackenzie that 'I should have been induced to sell off and quit the colony, but now the aspect is greatly changed for the better both in crops and markets.'[133] This suggests that he may have started switching from cotton to sugar cultivation. In 1815 there was a price rise in sugar, which accelerated the trend to sugar in Berbice.[134] It should be remembered that many of the reasons for the failure of the Seaforth plantations, arguably the most important ones, had been factors outside Fairbairn's control and unwise decisions made by others (especially Lord Seaforth).

[132] NRS, GD46/17/36, J. B. Fraser to Lord Seaforth, 14 December 1812.
[133] NRS, GD46/17/45, P. Fairbairn to C. Mackenzie, 16 January 1816.
[134] Alston, 'Enslaved Africans', p. 114.

PART III

Challenges and Catastrophe: The Land Agent under Fire

7

The Tenant Right Agitation of 1849–50: Crisis and Confrontation on the Londonderry Estates in County Down

Anne Casement

INTRODUCTION

IN THE AUTUMN OF 1846, as the effects of the widespread attack of the fungus *Phytophthora infestans* on the potato crop in Ulster began to be felt, the Londonderry family of Mount Stewart, County Down owned or were co-lessees of several significant properties in Ulster. These comprised the Ballylawn estate near Manorcunningham on the eastern shore of Lough Swilly in County Donegal, an estate of some 7,000 statute acres founded on land acquired by a Scottish ancestor following the Plantation of Ulster. This was managed in conjunction with approximately 2,200 acres west of Muff (now Eglinton) in County Londonderry, and some property in Londonderry city itself acquired through a subsequent marriage into the Cowan family. In 1744 the Stewart family purchased the manors of Comber and Newtownards on the shores of Strangford Lough in County Down, which by 1848 had been significantly enlarged by the acquisition of adjoining townlands, together with the Florida estate near Killinchy, to comprise an estate of some 23,000 statute acres. In 1786 the family bought a half-share in the 23,000 statute acre Salters' portion at Magherafelt in County Londonderry.

These estates were the property of Charles Stewart, 3rd Marquess of Londonderry (see Figure 6), who had inherited them in 1822 from his half-brother Robert Stewart, Lord Castlereagh and subsequently 2nd Marquess of Londonderry, who as Foreign Secretary had played a pivotal role at the Congress of Vienna. Charles himself had gained a fine reputation during the Napoleonic and Peninsular Wars as a bold and fearless leader of men. He also enjoyed some success as a diplomat, culminating in his appointment as Ambassador to Austria, in which capacity he, too, attended the Congress of Vienna.

In 1819 Charles Stewart had married secondly Frances Anne née

Figure 6 Charles Stewart, Marquess of Londonderry.
Image courtesy of the National Portrait Gallery,
London.

Vane-Tempest, the only child of the wealthy British nobleman Sir Henry
Vane-Tempest and his Irish wife Anne Catherine McDonnell, who was
Countess of Antrim in her own right. Upon her father's death in 1813,
Frances Anne inherited a 12,000-acre estate and sizeable colliery interests in County Durham, and upon the death of her mother in 1834,
around 10,000 acres of the Antrim estate in County Antrim. In 1823
Charles relinquished his ambassadorship to Austria and applied himself
with vigour to the management of his own estates in Ulster and his
wife's estates and colliery interests in County Durham. He embarked on
a highly ambitious and risky scheme to develop the potential and profitability of the collieries, and was to become one of the leading colliery
owners of the day. He and his wife were renowned for their extravagant
lifestyle and love of pomp and public display. Although the couple spent
the bulk of their time in England, their interest and involvement in the
management of their Ulster estates is clearly evident from the agents'
correspondence.

The Londonderry estates in England and Ulster were managed entirely
separately by a team of agents. The Ulster estates were managed by
agents under the overall supervision of John Andrews, who personally
administered the County Down estate from the Londonderry estate
office in Newtownards. His Derry and Donegal estates were managed
by John Lanktree, who also had responsibility for Lady Londonderry's

estate in County Antrim, and was based from 1848 in the Londonderry estate office in Carnlough. The Salters' estate was managed by Andrew Spotswood on behalf of Lord Londonderry and his co-lessee Sir Robert Bateson of Belvoir Park, County Down.

John Andrews was the eldest son of a prosperous Presbyterian family of millers, linen bleachers and drapers from Comber, County Down. He commenced his working life in the family business, taking special responsibility for the orders and correspondence, but was also deeply involved in the management of the 500-acre Andrews family farm at Carnasure on the outskirts of Comber. He and two of his brothers were passionate advocates of improved farming practices and were active members of the Chemico-Agricultural Society, established in 1846. Since 1833 the family farm had been divided into a large and small farm, each being thoroughly rained and managed on the rotational basis, including the cultivation of green crops for animal feed. The small farm, at 17 acres, was much the same size as an average holding in County Down, and was intended to demonstrate how the principles of close-cropping could be applied on such a farm, utilising only simple techniques and implements.[1]

There is a popular and widely held theory that upon his second marriage Charles Stewart became one of the wealthiest men in Britain and that this income was available to be spent on his Irish property.[2] An annual income from his wife's estates of as much as £175,000 has been quoted by one local commentator but a figure of between £35,500 and £50,500 at about the time of his marriage is more accurate.[3]

Under the terms of the marriage settlement, Charles was obliged to provide for his wife's mother, aunt and children of the marriage; in addition, great stress was laid on the need to apply his future wife's income to the maintenance of the equipment of the collieries and the renewal of existing leases. The paternal estates in Derry and Donegal, which he inherited in 1821, and those in Down, which he inherited in 1822 on

---

[1] A. L. Casement, 'The management of landed estates in Ulster in the mid-nineteenth century with special reference to the career of John Andrews as agent to the 3rd and 4th Marquesses of Londonderry from 1828 to 1863' (unpublished PhD thesis, Queen's University of Belfast, 2002), ch. 3.

[2] T. McCavery, 'The famine in County Down', in C. Kinealy and T. Parkhill (eds), *The Famine in Ulster: The Regional Impact* (Belfast, 1997), pp. 99–128, especially p. 101.

[3] T. McCavery, *Newtown: A History of Newtownards* (Belfast, 1994), p. 130; R. W. Sturgess, 'The Londonderry Trust, 1819–54', *Archaeologia Aeliana*, 5th series, 10 (1982), pp. 179–92, especially p. 180.

the death of Lord Castlereagh, were excluded from this arrangement.[4] It has been estimated that the settlement only provided resources for Lord Londonderry to bring the collieries into good working order, to look after family dependents and to spend £14,000 on his social life. Little or nothing was available to pay off the Vane-Tempest debts, to support his political patronage or to acquire a London residence and renovate his wife's family home at Wynyard Park.[5]

Frances Anne's mineral wealth was precarious and required a great outlay of capital before it could be fully exploited. The only good security that could be offered for this purpose was the modest income from her farms in Durham (£10,500 in the 1820s), and after 1834 in Antrim (between £1,500 and £2,300 in the 1830s), and the already heavily mortgaged equipment of the collieries.[6] By contrast, Lord Londonderry's inheritance comprised chiefly freehold property.

Lord Londonderry's financial position in Durham forced him to rely heavily on his Irish income to meet his personal expenditure. From late 1834 onwards he received a monthly allowance of £600 from the income of his Irish estates. The stress laid on meeting these payments, promptly and in full, is quite evident from his correspondence with John Andrews. Likewise, the terms of the marriage settlement and the tremendous demands placed upon Durham income demonstrate that English funds would not have been available for Irish purposes. By contrast, the two largest mortgages secured on the Down estates appear to have been negotiated for use in England, and Irish rentals are known to have played a part in financing the development of Seaham harbour. Andrews on one occasion had cause to remind Lord Londonderry of the many times during his career that he had been obliged to provide accommodation bills as security for loans advanced by the marquess in English transactions.[7]

CRISIS ON THE LONDONDERRY ESTATES

The numerous sales of landed property which took place under the aegis of the Encumbered Estates Court are testimony to the critical blow dealt to the finances of Irish estates by the repeated failure of the potato crop in the 1840s. The Londonderry estates were no exception in facing

[4] Sturgess, 'Londonderry Trust', pp. 180–1.
[5] Sturgess, 'Londonderry Trust', p. 182.
[6] Sturgess, 'Londonderry Trust', pp. 180–2.
[7] Casement, 'Management of landed estates in Ulster', ch. 2.

extreme financial difficulties during this period. However, the critical moment occurred not after the almost total loss of the potato harvest in 1846 but in 1850, and was the result not only of the subsequent severe attacks of blight in 1848 and 1850 but also of several other factors, not all directly related to the repeated failure of the potato crop. When crisis point was finally reached in late 1850, it was brought about primarily by the activities of the Tenant League and not *Phytophthora infestans*. No documented account of the crucial influence of the activities of the League on the financial viability of Irish estates has been noted, but a study of the Andrews letters reveals that, on the Londonderry estates for certain, they produced a management crisis unparalleled in the career of an agent of twenty-two years' standing, which was not amenable to solution by conventional methods.

As a result of the severe attacks of blight in 1846, 1848 and 1850, the circumstances of the tenantry at large had been seriously reduced. Many of the best tenants had been forced to draw on their savings to pay their rent, and others who formerly paid promptly were now unable to do so.[8] The failure of the potato crop had two profound effects on the financial viability of the tenantry: it resulted in the need to replace the potato in their diet with grain, which previously would have been sold, and in the loss of income from the sale of a pig, which, fattened on potatoes, formerly contributed to the rent.[9] In addition, during 1849 the price of every agricultural commodity declined significantly. In the sharp depression following the repeal of the Corn Laws, when yields were reduced by poor weather, wheat fell to its lowest average price for seventy years. The value of barley and oats also dropped, although less severely, and livestock prices fell quite sharply.[10] The price of butter also deteriorated between 1846 and 1850.[11] Andrews summarised the situation thus:

> Since 1845, when the first potato blight struck us, our course has unquestionably been retrograde. The reduced prices consequent upon free trade have certainly aggravated the difficulties of the farmer, but the loss of the potato, and of that which the potato produced – on which the tenantry generally

[8] Public Record Office of Northern Ireland [hereafter PRONI], Londonderry papers, D/Lo/C 158 (159), 26 April 1851. Unless otherwise stated, all correspondence is between John Andrews and Lord Londonderry.

[9] PRONI, D/Lo/C 158 (77), 5 June 1850.

[10] J. D. Chambers and G. E. Mingay, *The Agricultural Revolution 1750–1880* (London, 1966), pp. 178–9.

[11] J. S. Donnelly Jr, *The Land and the People of Nineteenth-Century Cork* (London, 1975), p. 80.

depended for a half a year's rent, has been the deadly blow. When I have
urged, that during protection we had prices of grain occasionally as low as
they are yet, I have been answered – but then we had the potato.[12]

As in previous times of difficulty there were calls for a reduction of rents,
the attack being led by the newspaper editors who numbered many of the
tenant class among their readership, the priests in the Roman Catholic
districts and Presbyterian ministers in the North.[13] When Charles Gavan
Duffy re-established the *Nation* newspaper in September 1849 he was
impelled, by his own crusading public spirit and by the need to foster cir-
culation, to find a substitute for the moribund repeal agitation. The land
question was the answer. As 1850 began, Presbyterian tenants in Ulster
were well advanced into a campaign to obtain legislative endorsement
of the Ulster custom.[14] Farmers were alarmed at the fall in agricultural
prices and poor crop yields, and many held long leases with fixed rents
which were becoming increasingly difficult to pay. They were also faced
with a decline in the value of their land as a result of the famine, which
depreciated the value of their interest in their holdings. Naturally, this
was a worry most of all to Ulster farmers, and goes a long way to
explain their willingness to join the agitation. Adding to their concern
was the failure of Sharman Crawford's 1847 bill to legalise the right
for them to sell their holdings. There was also talk that land reform
legislation might be passed that would explicitly deny the legality of the
Ulster custom.[15] Prior to the famine, labourers comprised the bulk of the
agricultural community, but the effect of the famine was to transform
this situation into one where tenant farmers were in the majority.[16] This
change in the composition of the agricultural community must also have
contributed to the popularity of the tenant-right campaign. An important series of tenant-right meetings were held throughout Ulster in early
1850, including one in Newtownards on 19 January.[17] Although there
was no evidence to suggest there was a conspiracy to refuse payment of
rent, Andrews believed many were not making as strenuous an effort as

[12] PRONI, D/Lo/C 158 (58), 20 January 1850.
[13] PRONI, D/Lo/C 158 (58), 20 January 1850.
[14] R. V. Comerford, 'Churchmen, tenants, and independent opposition, 1850–56',
in W. E. Vaughan (ed.), *A New History of Ireland. Vol. V: Ireland under the Union,
I (1801–70)* (Oxford, 1989), pp. 396–414, especially p. 399.
[15] S. Clark, *Social Origins of the Irish Land War* (Princeton, 1979), p. 213.
[16] Clark, *Social Origins*, p. 152.
[17] G. Hall, 'The significance of town commissions in Ulster in the nineteenth
century' (offprint in the possession of W. Maguire, n.d.), p. 13; PRONI, D/Lo/C
158 (58), 20 January 1850.

they might to pay their rents, in the hope that the agitation would result in a reduction. The agitators did, nonetheless, conduct a widespread and highly successful campaign of intimidation, by means of arson attacks and the distribution of threatening notices, to ensure that no new tenant could be found to occupy a farm from which the previous tenant had been evicted.[18] As Andrews wrote:

> I could have set the deserted Kilmood farm to three persons, but they have all been frightened by threatening letters, one of which, threatening myself, has been brought to me. Of course, I disregard it, but country people have a terror of the incendiary and the assassin. I have therefore been obliged, for this year, to make arrangements for having it cultivated on your Lordship's account, and I am sending Campbell tomorrow to value all the buildings, that, if any burning shall take place, I may adopt measures for having the amount levied from the townland.[19]

The use of intimidation to prevent another tenant taking on the farm of a tenant who had been evicted was well established. According to one witness before a House of Commons committee in 1824, the usual target of agrarian crime was 'the property of the landlord who distrained or ejected a tenant, or the property of the tenant who had succeeded the former tenant'.[20]

TENANT RIGHT: THE IMPACT AND RESPONSES TO THE CRISIS ON THE LONDONDERRY ESTATES

The effects of the agitation, coupled with the agricultural crisis, were to have another major and unforeseen consequence, namely the loss of the value of tenant right which was to prove of great detriment both to the financial circumstances of the tenants themselves and to the rental income and management policy of the Londonderry estates.[21] As a result of the successful campaign of intimidation an evicted tenant was no longer able to find a purchaser for his farm, and his tenant right thus became effectively worthless. Similarly, any tenant in financial difficulties, and threatened with the prospect of eviction, would be unable to gain relief by obtaining a loan, as the only security which he possessed,

[18] PRONI, D/Lo/C 158 (58), 20 January 1850; (60), 10 February 1850; (62), 18 February 1850; (63), 21 February 1850; (71), 3 March 1850.
[19] PRONI, D/Lo/C 158 (60), 10 February 1850.
[20] *First Report from the Select Committee on Districts of Ireland under the Insurrection Act* [372], HC 1824, viii, 8.
[21] PRONI, D/Lo/C 158 (80), 18 July 1850.

namely his tenant right, would be of no value should he default on his loan.

Although there was little consensus as to its meaning and interpretation, tenant right, or the Ulster Custom, was habitually referred to in terms of the '3Fs': free sale, fair rents and fixity of tenure, whereby a tenant enjoyed a reasonable expectation of security of tenure so long as the rent was paid, and was permitted to sell the right to occupy his holding to another tenant acceptable to the landlord. The custom was most fully developed in the centre of Ulster and along its north-eastern seaboard, and weaker on the periphery. Its value was highest in Down and Antrim. It was particularly valuable on the Londonderry estates as Lord Londonderry granted this privilege 'in its entirety', and it was understood that a life-lease might be considered to be a perpetuity as long as the rent was paid, and improvements made at the tenant's own expense would not be taken into account in rent calculations. As Andrews noted:

> No tenant for life could be expected to account for the enormous outlay which would attend the construction of farm steadings and execution of draining and other extensive improvements on small farms. Under the belief that they are doing it for themselves and their children, the tenantry, who have confidence in their landlords, are advancing and will advance.[22]

It might thus be assumed that in Ulster tenant right was generally perceived as a right of occupancy, and an entitlement to be compensated for improvements made.

This loss in the value of tenant right had four major consequences. It resulted first in the accumulation of arrears, as tenants were no longer able to obtain loans on the security of tenant right, and landlords could no longer rely on the sale of tenant right as a means of realising the arrears of a defaulting tenant.[23] Second, it made other creditors, such as shopkeepers, press tenants to repay their debts, for instance by means of the civil-bill court or by forcing a farmer to sign a bill of sale for property on his farm or for his interest in the farm.[24] As Andrews acknowledged, other creditors had come in with decrees and executions 'intercepting monies that were for the office'.[25] Third, it removed the means by which an evicted tenant, upon the sale of his farm, could

---

[22] PRONI, D/Lo/C 512 (1), 5 January 1846; Casement, 'Management of landed estates in Ulster', ch. 9.
[23] PRONI, D/Lo/C 158 (80), 18 July 1850; (104), 29 November 1850.
[24] PRONI, D/Lo/C 158 (80), 18 July 1850; Clark, *Social Origins*, pp. 130–1.
[25] PRONI, D/Lo/C 158 (96), 20 October 1850.

obtain a sum to re-establish himself elsewhere; and fourth, it led to a strong disinclination to use eviction to remove destitute tenants:

> In such cases the resort to evictions, unless the sale of tenant right shall in some shape again become available, will produce an extent of suffering, and excite the public mind, and call forth a burst of censure, which it will be difficult to withstand; unless, as has been done by many landlords in such cases, means should be supplied to aid in the emigration of the evicted tenants, or in their settlement elsewhere.[26]

The tenant-right agitation thus significantly added to the arrears and reduced the income of an estate as it caused the claims of creditors to take precedence over the payment of rent, destroyed the creditworthiness of the tenants, the ability to collect arrears upon eviction and the means of replacing a bad tenant with a better one. It also resulted in tenants delaying payment of their rent in the hope of a reduction.

Vaughan is of the opinion that landlords and tenants could not effectively bargain with each other because the existing relationship between landlord and tenant lacked that reciprocity of pressures that exists when one party's ability to hurt the other is limited by the damage it inflicts on itself.[27] Such a reciprocity of pressure did, however, result from the collective action by tenants to prevent a new tenant occupying the farm of a tenant who had been evicted. The freedom of action of the tenants was governed by their ability to suffer the loss of the value of their tenant right and the goodwill of their landlord, whilst that of the landlord was governed by the ability to withstand a considerable diminution in rental income and the inefficient management of his estate. The ability of such action to circumscribe and curtail the freedom of action of an agent managing a landed estate was succinctly summarised by Andrews:

> What to do as to the eviction of some, who ought to be turned out, I know not. It is positively the fact that tenants cannot now be found for farms. I should meet the burnings without hesitation, if I could find tenants, but the panic, and present feeling that the hopes of agriculture are gone, intimidate those who might be able to enter upon farms, and too few have capital to do so, and nothing would so much gratify the disaffected as to see farms lying waste and untenanted ... And it is my feeling that in the worst cases, if a year's rent could be obtained within the year, it would be safer to defer the extreme measure of eviction.[28]

---

[26] PRONI, D/Lo/C 158 (104), 29 November 1850.
[27] W. E. Vaughan, *Landlord and Tenants in Mid-Victorian Ireland* (Oxford, 1994), p. 208.
[28] PRONI, D/Lo/C 158 (109), 18 December 1850.

To support his view, Andrews cited the difficulties encountered by other major local landowners:

> We may evict, but under the panic of this crisis purchasers for farms cannot be found, and these landlords who are now doing so are obliged to improve the farms they take, and cannot then find eligible tenants to take them at remunerative rents. Lord Dufferin is forced to make large sacrifices in this way; and Lord Downshire, I learn, is getting many farms upon his hands.[29]

Clutching at straws, he was forced to hope for an upturn in agricultural fortunes and a speedy end to the agitation, for,

> If confidence should again be restored, and even modified sale of tenant right be reestablished, means would be supplied for discharge of arrears, and affording some provision for the dispossessed tenants, and all our difficulties would become manageable.[30]

What other counsel might Andrews have offered? Lord Londonderry, when threatening those tenants in arrears who had voted for the tenant-right candidate in the 1852 election, declared he was 'not afraid of setting his lands to Scotchmen or letting them lie waste'.[31] The planting of Scotsmen on the Down estates would surely have been met by extreme intimidation and widespread civil disorder. Farms lying waste and untenanted would, as Andrews noted, only give heart to the agitators, and the loss of income so sustained would exacerbate an already critical economic situation. Although it might be feasible for the estate to cultivate a few farms 'in hand', it was impossible for them to do so on a significant scale.

Furthermore, in addition to creating a crisis on an individual estate, such collective action, if maintained and escalated, had the potential to bring about change on a national scale, as was to be demonstrated in the Land War. Vaughan in his discussion of the reasons why there was no mass movement against landlordism before 1879, stresses the difficulties of organising something analogous to a trade union among a tenantry that prior to that time had no corporate traditions, institutions or leadership. Moreover, he believes that the separate, individual nature of farms and the freedom of farmers to determine policy on their own holdings only discouraged a sense of collective identity.[32]

Had the tenants been better organised and led, and had the Tenant

---

[29] PRONI, D/Lo/C 158 (57), 10 January 1850.
[30] PRONI, D/Lo/C 158 (104), 29 November 1850.
[31] PRONI, D/654/N5/2.
[32] Vaughan, *Landlord and Tenants*, pp. 202–4.

League not decided to concentrate on a parliamentary solution to the land question, the 1850 tenant-right agitation might have resulted in the establishment of a more balanced and dynamic partnership between landlord and tenant. As it was, by December 1850 Andrews was able to conclude that 'The Tenant League is making its impotency apparent.'[33]

The loss of value of tenant right had another significant effect on the financial management of the Down estates. Whilst it retained its value, Andrews had been in the habit of taking promissory bills from tenants whom he thought capable of redeeming them within a short period, and getting them discounted on his own credit:

> I admit freely and at once, that my reliance on the value of tenant right led me to give aid to the tenants, and to exercise forbearance, and to involve myself seriously, all of which the failure of tenant right and the altered circumstances of the times have proved to have been short-sighted and injudicious.[34]

The practice of taking tenants bills ceased altogether in July 1850 as the tenants were failing to honour bills taken in 1849, Andrews therefore becoming liable for the amount owed.[35] Its discontinuation increased further the financial difficulties of the Down estates. By late 1850, mounting arrears exacerbated an already critical financial situation, and resulted in the income of the Down estates being insufficient to meet the calls made upon it. As Andrews noted in October 1850:

> Till within the last year I was enabled to hold my ground and to make good all payments and remittances to your Lordship. The change of circumstances [i.e. the failure of tenant right and falling agricultural returns] has interposed an unexpected barrier.[36]

The rental of the Down estates in 1845 was £21,667. The total annual charges were £11,733, including interest of £5,348 on mortgages under the trust deed or charges to the trustees, mortgages to other private borrowers and private bonds; other charges such as annuity payments (£1,915) and Lord Castlereagh's annual allowance of £3,000; salaries of the agent, bailiffs, clergy and schoolmasters; office and estate expenses; Crown and chief rents and poor rate.[37] By 1850 the rental had increased hardly at all (£21,861), but the total annual charges had increased to £13,167. The amount of interest due under

[33] PRONI, D/Lo/C 158 (109), 18 December 1850.
[34] PRONI, D/Lo/C 158 (96), 20 October 1850.
[35] PRONI, D/Lo/C 158 (60), 10 February 1850; (133), 25 September 1851.
[36] PRONI, D/Lo/C 158 (96), 20 October 1850.
[37] PRONI, D/Lo/C 158 (164) [n.d.].

the trust deed and on loans from the accumulating fund, mortgages to private borrowers and private bonds had risen to £6,357.[38] This increase was due to a rise in interest on old loans and interest on new loans, for example a loan towards the cost of rebuilding Mount Stewart; to which was to be added payment of an interest charge of £830 formerly levied on the Derry and Donegal estates.[39] The poor rate payments had also increased dramatically from £350 in 1845 to £900 in 1850.[40] Andrews was fully aware of the dangerous financial position the estate now found itself in: 'Your Lordship will see how deeply these [charges] cut into the surplus, even if times were good; and rents secure; and how formidable the whole becomes when the very reverse is the case.'[41]

Maguire notes that at the prevailing rate of 5 per cent for Irish borrowings, an Irish landowner could with safety encumber his property to as much as eight times its gross annual rental, equivalent to an interest charge of two fifths (40 per cent). Whether the encumbrance was dangerous or not depended to some extent on how much of it was made up of non-productive debt such as family charges, as distinct from productive kinds such as the purchase of land.[42] On estates sampled by Vaughan, the amount of rent spent on interest payments ranged from zero to 39 per cent between 1850 and 1880, with an average figure of 17 per cent. The 1850 interest payment on the Down estates of £6,357 plus £830 (£7,187) represented roughly 33 per cent of the gross rental and, if annuity payments of £1,915 (£9,102) are also included, this figure rises to roughly 41 per cent of the gross rental.

In 1850 the small surplus income of the Derry and Donegal estates (ranging from £518 to £894 between 1835 and 1849) was eliminated by the granting of an abatement of rent.[43] The Down surplus alone (£9,956 is the figure stated) was thus expected to meet items such as the shortfall of £1,350 between the income and expenditure of Mount Stewart house, gardens and demesne, subscriptions and interest on bank loans, together with outstanding bills for the decoration and furnishing of Mount Stewart and the cost of a distribution of manure to the

[38] PRONI, D/Lo/C 158 (126), 13 August 1850.
[39] PRONI, D/Lo/C 158 (109), 18 December 1850.
[40] PRONI, D/Lo/C 158 (164) and (126), 3 August 1850.
[41] PRONI, D/Lo/C 158 (102), 7 November 1850.
[42] W. A. Maguire, *The Downshire Estates in Ireland 1801–1845* (Oxford, 1972), p. 84.
[43] PRONI, D/654/H2/7, Agent's Order Book, pp. 74, 165.

tenantry.[44] There was also the question of Lord Londonderry's annual allowance of £7,200 and living expenses whilst in Ireland. As Andrews acknowledged:

> With Derry funds withdrawn, and £830 of Derry charges added to Down burthens, it would not be possible for me, even if times were as good as before 1845, to keep up remittances of £600 monthly, even if no other orders for payments were addressed to me . . . From November 1849 to November 1850 payments of all kinds in your Lordship's account . . . amounted to upwards of £7200.[45]

Until October 1849 Lord Londonderry had been 'shielded from every inconvenience'.[46] However, for some months of 1850 his allowance was not paid at all or only in part.[47] Andrews, deprived of the ability to meet his obligations to Lord Londonderry and the estate creditors by taking bills from the tenants, had no alternative but to adopt coercive measures against those tenants whom he felt able but reluctant to pay. He had already served many ejectment notices and notices to quit, and had the bailiffs at work conveying notes to the best tenants, and stringent messages to the great body, but counselled Lord Londonderry that 'the condition of the tenantry at large has been seriously deteriorated since 1845, and that no power, which can be brought into operation, could realise hastily and summarily the rents and arrears now due'.[48]

Prior to the first attack of potato blight in 1845, Andrews had succeeded in bringing the arrear 'into small bounds'.[49] At the settlement of September 1846 Andrews reported that the arrear of rent due the previous November was £1,381, but when the 1849 rents became due it had reached £4,296 and by November 1850 the arrear was £12,658.[50] The major portion of the arrear thus comprised the rents of 1849, due for

---

[44] PRONI, D/654/H2/7, Agent's Order Book, p. 165; PRONI, D/Lo/C 158 (109), 18 December 1850.

[45] PRONI, D/Lo/C 158 (109), 18 December 1850. By Derry, Andrews surely implies Derry and Donegal as on another occasion he writes 'which with the reduction occasioned by the withdrawal of the Derry and Donegal surplus, leaving the Down estate subject to £830 of Derry and Donegal interest, would very greatly bring down the available surplus from Newtownards office'; D/Lo/C 158 (98), 3 November 1850.

[46] PRONI, D/Lo/C 158 (122), 20 June 1851.

[47] PRONI, D/Lo/C 158 (60), 10 February 1850; (77), 5 June 1850.

[48] PRONI, D/Lo/C 158 (77), 5 June 1850; (102), 7 November 1850.

[49] PRONI, D/Lo/C 158 (80), 18 July 1850.

[50] PRONI, D/Lo/C 512 (29), 4 August 1847; D/Lo/C 158 (113), 7 April 1851; D/Lo/C 158 (113), 7 April 1851. By March 1851 the arrear had been reduced to £7,996; D/Lo/C 158 (113), 7 April 1851.

payment whilst the tenant-right campaign was in full swing. As Andrews explained in two letters written on the same day in December 1850:

> Our now frightful arrear is the accumulation of those five years [since 1845], greatly aggravated during the last by the destruction of the credit of the tenantry, mainly resulting from the wicked proceedings of the Tenant League agitators, in consequence of which monies on their way to the office, were in many cases intercepted by decrees at the suit of creditors being satisfied to prevent incarceration.[51]

Lord Londonderry, incensed by Andrews's inability to meet his monthly allowance and the support given by his tenantry to the activities and demands of the Tenant League, in autumn 1850 ordered a campaign of strong and vigorous coercive measures to collect the outstanding arrears.[52] Lord Londonderry viewed matters differently to Andrews, attributing the accumulation of arrears to poor management on Andrews's part, and castigating him for his hopeful views, indulgencies, softness and mistaken leniency, and courting popularity.[53] By January 1851 Andrews was 'quite sure that such an amount of coercion, as I have used, was never attempted on any County Down estate before. The number of processes issued for the session exceeded any precedent.'[54] Such measures assisted the recovery of £9,000 of rent and arrears in the last three months of 1850.[55] Lord Londonderry believed that yet more stringent measures would realise larger receipts, a view with which Andrews did not concur, citing the opinion of a Scottish agent, respected by Lord Londonderry, Lord Eglinton's Commissioner, Mr Gairdner, that under present circumstances 'considerate leniency, aid and encouragement are advisable and necessary, and that a different course would only have the effect of reducing men in a desperate state to a condition of greater desperation and despondency'.[56] Lord Londonderry, unconvinced, decided

---

[51] PRONI, D/Lo/C 158 (108), 18 December 1850.

[52] PRONI, D/Lo/C 158 (108), 18 December 1850; D/Lo/C 161 (2), 14 January 1852.

[53] PRONI, D/Lo/C 158 (118), 29 May 1851.

[54] PRONI, D/Lo/C 158 (145), 12 January 1851.

[55] PRONI, D/Lo/C 158 (203), 7 January 1852.

[56] PRONI, D/Lo/C 158 (145), 12 January 1851. The Eglinton Castle estate on the outskirts of Irvine in Ayrshire had considerable mining and other industrial interests, which may have connected it to the Londonderry estates. Lord Londonderry had also attended the Eglinton tournament of 1839. Some of the most respected agents were Scotsmen, from farming families, and Scottish agriculturists were much favoured. In the early 1800s Robert, 1st Marquess of Londonderry had employed a dynamic Scot named Greenfield who had completely transformed the farming enterprise

in late 1850 to 'bring in the heavy brigade' in the shape of Robert Kelly, his Belfast solicitor.[57] Despite this escalation of pressure, no more money was collected in last three months of 1851 than in the same three months of 1850, notwithstanding the fact that in autumn 1850 Andrews was acting alone, whereas by late 1851 Lord Londonderry had assumed a leading role in estate management, Mr Kelly was in post, abatements had been granted and coercive measures were at full stretch.[58]

Kelly attempted to explain this apparent lack of success by suggesting that the returns of 1850 and 1851 should be compared not against each other but against those of 1846–9; and concluded that if similar pressure had been brought to bear during these years, there would have been no arrear on the estate.[59] This is surely too simplistic and naive a response. The fear, uncertainty and suffering of 1846–7 directed policy on the best estates to the alleviation of hardship and aid of the farmer. For Lord Londonderry to have implemented a campaign of extreme coercion, when neighbouring landlords were offering abatements of rent and drainage loans and implementing relief measures on their estates, would have flown in the face of his paternalistic principles and destroyed his reputation with the electorate and nation as 'the best landlord in Ireland'.[60] There would also undoubtedly have been widespread civil disobedience. Furthermore, the repeated attacks of potato blight in 1846, 1848 and 1850 reduced or wiped out the savings of the tenants, and prevented the fattening of a pig which made a significant chapter to the rent. Not until 1850 was the cultivation of green crops significantly extended and pork beginning to be produced without potatoes.[61] Andrews had his own view of the events of recent years:

> I greatly question if almost any agent has received, during the years of pressure, so much in actual cash, without abatements and allowances, as I have done ... During the disastrous year of 1849 beset as I was by all the obstacles and annoyances arising from the agitations of the Presbyterian

at Mount Stewart by introducing many new techniques. Under his direction the farming enterprise at Mount Stewart prospered, encompassing the keeping of dairy cows, beef fatteners, veal calves and sheep including Merinos. Non-Conformists were at the time ineligible to take degrees at English universities, and many gentlemen such as Andrews thus spent time at Scottish universities, so clearly there was much cross-fertilisation between the two locations.

[57] PRONI, D/Lo/C 161 (1), 1 January 1851.
[58] PRONI, D/Lo/C 161 (2), 14 January 1852.
[59] PRONI, D/Lo/C 161 (2), 14 January 1852.
[60] PRONI, D/Lo/C 111 (6), 22 September 1849.
[61] PRONI, D/Lo/C 158 (109), 18 December 1850.

ministers and Tenant League, I got in, without discount or allowance of any
kind, six sevenths of the full rental. During the current year, commencing
1st October last, I am not without the hope that nearly a full year's rental
will be received.[62]

He also offered a reasoned explanation for the unexceptional returns
of late 1851. An unseasonal scarcity of water for the flax mills had
prevented many tenants getting their flax cleaned. Blight destroyed more
of the potato crop in 1851 than in any year since 1846, wheat prices
were very low and receipts had fallen off dramatically in December due
to the disappointment felt by the tenantry at the terms of the abatements
offered by Lord Londonderry, and to a feeling that, as the abatement
was to remain in force until 1 February, payment was not expected
before then.[63] A Great Baronial Tenant Right Meeting was also held in
Newtownards in October 1851.[64]

With hindsight, Andrews considered that had he been able to anticipate the loss of value of tenant right and the reluctance of the tenantry to
replace the potato with other green crops, despite the repeated failures
of this crop, it might have been more beneficial to have granted abatements and allowances at an earlier stage of the crisis. Fear of diminishing
the income of the estate, heavily burdened as it was by fixed payments,
made him reluctant to do so.[65]

Agricultural fortunes began to recover in late 1852.[66] This, coupled
with continued pressure on the tenants, enabled Kelly to inform Lord
Londonderry that the amount of money collected by the office in a single
day had exceeded that collected on any one day for some years; and he
anticipated that there would be a considerable reduction in the arrear by
the end of the year.[67] As Andrews candidly acknowledged:

Your Lordship may rest assured that there is every disposition to make the
most of the favourable change in the state of the agricultural interest which
has enabled us to effect what we have already accomplished. It is very far
from my wish to press any view of exculpation of myself even to the extent
which I consider fair, but I cannot refrain from submitting to your Lordship
that during the famine years, when the arrear on the Down Estates was

[62] PRONI, D/Lo/C 158 (122), 20 June 1851.
[63] PRONI, D/Lo/C 158 (168), 7 December 1851; (174), 7 January 1852; (132),
15 September 1851; (135), 14 October 1851; (168), 7 December 1851.
[64] PRONI, D/Lo/C 158 (137), 29 October 1851.
[65] PRONI, D/Lo/C 158 (80), 18 July 1850; (102), 7 November 1850; (159), 26
April 1851.
[66] PRONI, D/Lo/C 161 (14), 3 December 1852.
[67] PRONI, D/Lo/C 161 (16), 19 December 1852.

accumulating, the greater part of Ireland was going to ruin, and that, even had the consequence of inflicting ruin upon the tenantry been disregarded, no power could have effected what gradually improving circumstances have rendered practicable.[68]

By the following November he was able to reassure Lord Londonderry that

The receipts of October have been large. They are greatly in advance of those of October last year, though there was then the stimulus of reductions for prompt payment; and in this I hope your Lordship will recognize the anxiety of the tenants to meet your Lordship's wishes, which I feel confident will, on the year, be satisfied by receipts considerably exceeding those of former years.[69]

Events on the Londonderry estates in Down in the early 1850s thus illustrate Vaughan's finding that although agents and landlords could influence the pattern of arrears and receipts on their estates, fluctuations in the value of agricultural output determined the size and incidence of arrears and receipts. When considering his twelve sample estates as whole, a clear pattern emerged: arrears were high in the late 1840s and early 1850s, in the early 1860s and in the late 1870s. Between these crises were periods of recovery, the most dramatic being in the mid-1850s and mid-1860s.[70] Nonetheless, circumstances on the Londonderry estates demonstrate that previously unremarked external forces – albeit linked to agricultural fortunes, such as the tenant-right campaign – were also capable of substantially increasing arrears.

CONCLUSION

For twenty-two years a frank and genuinely cordial relationship existed between Lord Londonderry and his agent. However, in late 1850 the marquess's annoyance with Andrews's inability to meet promptly the payment of his monthly allowance and to provide sufficient funds for other expenses incurred by him, and Andrews's reaction to his employer's imputation that he had undertaken certain financial transactions with a view to personal gain, resulted in a quarrel between the two men of such seriousness that Andrews became convinced that Lord Londonderry intended to replace him.[71]

[68] PRONI, D/Lo/C 158 (231), 16 January 1853.
[69] PRONI, D/Lo/C 158 (263), 1 November 1853.
[70] Vaughan, *Landlord and Tenants*, p. 115.
[71] PRONI, D/Lo/C 158 (102), 7 November 1850; (119), 27 May 1851; (120), 10 June 1851.

There is evidence to suggest that Lord Londonderry was subject to special financial pressures at this time. In June 1850 Andrews commented, 'I shall do all I can to ward off difficulty, but I deeply lament that I cannot render your Lordship the satisfaction you desire, and which the state of your English finances renders so peculiarly necessary.'[72] In early 1849 the Bank of England had raised interest rates to 8.5 per cent, and production stopped in many mills and manufactories.[73] Also colliery profits were more volatile under conditions of free trade; for example, after 1844 the lowest profit in a working year was recorded in 1852 (£4,106), and the highest (£60,561) was achieved a mere two years later in 1854.[74] Lord Londonderry was also in all probability in poor health at the time of the dispute. In early 1851 he undertook an unexpected three-month tour of Europe, apparently for medical reasons.[75] Three years later, aged seventy-six, he died from the effects of pneumonia. Evidence that his faculties and judgement may have been impaired could be adduced from the observation that he repeatedly misunderstood facts stated to him by Andrews.[76]

There were few of his acquaintance with whom Lord Londonderry did not fall out at some point or other.[77] In the run-up to the 1852 election, he disputed first with his son and then with his nephew, David Ker. There had been a complete breakdown in relations between himself and John Andrews's predecessor, John Cleland, and in 1841 he quarrelled violently with the very able agent and colliery manager in Durham, John Buddle.[78] He subsequently reconciled his differences with Buddle, in cognisance of the latter's obvious capabilities and the difficulty of securing a more able replacement. His quarrel with Andrews arose at a time when the difficulties of the preceding five years had stretched the agent's management and financial skills and equipoise to their limit:

> I may truly say that since the unhappy decline of Irish agricultural prosperity, which commenced in 1845, and attained its climax in the autumn of 1849

[72] PRONI, D/Lo/C 158 (77), 5 June 1850.
[73] PRONI, D/Lo/C 158 (78), 25 October 1849.
[74] Sturgess, 'Londonderry Trust', p. 99.
[75] PRONI, D/Lo/C 158 (159), 26 April 1851.
[76] PRONI, D/Lo/C 158 (157), 12 February 1851; (159), 26 April 1851; (122), 20 June 1851.
[77] G. Worsley, 'Wynyard Park, County Durham – 1', *Country Life*, 28 August 1986, pp. 614–17, especially p. 615.
[78] PRONI, MIC/570/17 (136), copy letters to Emily, Viscountess Castlereagh, 10 January 1828; A. Heesom, personal communication, 1999.

my efforts in your Lordship's service have been attended with unmitigated difficulty and embarrassment, and that tranquility and enjoyment have been strangers to my mind. The pressure of care arising from the impossibility of realizing your Lordship's expectations and from the inability to arrest the downward progress of the tenantry, of the cause and mode of relieving which, as I regarded them, I always failed to communicate to your Lordship, and the contemplation of my serious involvements created an incubus which for the last two years has proved intolerably oppressive.[79]

Lord Londonderry's assertions of financial irregularity on Andrews's part centred on his belief that the latter had been motivated to offer loans to himself and the tenants by the prospect of charging interest on such transactions, accusations that Andrews was able to entirely refute.[80] The Unitarian beliefs of the Andrews family placed great emphasis on ethical behaviour. It is perhaps not unrealistic to suggest, therefore, that Lord Londonderry's allegation that Andrews was guilty of malpractice was pivotal in his decision to mount a strong defence of his actions. He also sought a proper security for the sums loaned by him to Lord Londonderry:[81]

I unhesitatingly appeal to your Lordship, could I have acted otherwise than I did, when there were imputations affecting my character, and even my veracity, accompanied with a refusal to recognize claims which are in my own view so just and of such importance to my family. Your Lordship made it my duty to act as I have done, and if I had not done so, my self respect and my position in society would have been sacrificed. Your Lordship made it also my duty to myself to look to my own protection in a pecuniary point of view.[82]

A scheme for the repayment of the sums owed was agreed in the second half of 1851 with Lord Londonderry's cousin, John Vandeleur Stewart, acting as arbiter. Andrews remained in post, but for some months the marquess assumed almost all responsibility for the management of the Down estates. To assist him in his task of administration, he insisted that all surplus cash from the receipts of the estates be remitted directly to him, and that he should be responsible for making the fixed payments.[83] To be better informed about the condition of the estate and its tenants, from August 1851 to 1852 he ordered the keeping of an

---

[79] PRONI, D/Lo/C 158 (121), 15 June 1851.
[80] PRONI, D/Lo/C 158 (127), 30 July 1851.
[81] PRONI, D/Lo/C 158 (119), 27 May 1851.
[82] PRONI, D/Lo/C 158 (120), 10 June 1851.
[83] PRONI, D/Lo/C 158 (170), 17 November 1851.

Agent's Order Book in which his instructions and details of their imple-
mentation were recorded, together with reports on estate matters and
his views thereon.[84] The letters written by Andrews in late 1851 reveal
that the dispute resulted in a marked change in the relationship between
employer and agent: his former frank and full discussion of events was
replaced by little more than a monthly statement of account, verified by
the sub-agent Robert Kelly, and a discussion thereof.

It is apparent from the tone of the Andrews correspondence from
February 1852 onwards that harmony reigned again between landlord
and agent, brought about in all probability by the difficulties presented
by the 1852 election, when Lord Londonderry was to rely heavily on
Andrews's judgement of the political situation in Down and expertise as
a political manager, and Andrews rose wholeheartedly to the challenges
offered by the contest.[85]

[84] PRONI, D/654/N5/2.
[85] PRONI, D/Lo/C 166 (23), 7 February 1852.

8

Frustrations and Fears:
The Impact of the Rebecca Riots on the Land
Agent in Carmarthenshire, 1843

Lowri Ann Rees

INTRODUCTION

Thomas Herbert Cooke's time as land agent on the Middleton Hall estate in south-west Wales is well documented in a series of letters dating from 1841 to 1847, now held at the National Library of Wales. This is a rare collection, and one which presents unique insights. Being personal in nature, these letters reveal information that would not have been preserved in estate records. In this sense, they are a valuable resource to the historian. Cooke's letters, written to his mother and brother in his native Northamptonshire, list the duties undertaken by the land agent. However, they also give a real sense of his various frustrations and fears, many of which stem from the difficult relationship with his employer, Edward Abadam. The letters are also revealing of the attitude of a newcomer to the local area, with Cooke critical of the use of the Welsh language in church, agricultural practices of the tenantry and poor quality of the land he was expected to manage. Whilst he appears as a rather melancholic character, pessimistic and critical, his tendency to worry was completely justified during the summer of 1843, when he witnessed at first hand the Rebecca Riots. This chapter will introduce Cooke and his employer before discussing how the letters chart the activities of Rebecca and her daughters in the immediate vicinity of the estate. It will reveal how the land agent and his employer became targets of Rebecca's wrath, highlighting the potentially difficult position estate middlemen held within society.

'HE KNOWS BUT LITTLE OR NOTHING OF BUSINESS': DIFFICULT TIMES AT MIDDLETON HALL

Born on 28 January 1798 and baptised at Paulerspury, Northamptonshire, Thomas Herbert Cooke was the eldest son of a prosperous yeoman farmer, Thomas Cooke, and his wife Charlotte née Kirby. On his father's death in 1822, Cooke inherited the family estate, which included land in the parishes of Silverstone and Whittlebury. However, according to the terms of his father's will, provisions had to be made for Cooke's six sisters, leaving the heir with very little money in order to sustain the estate. In September 1830 Cooke set sail for Halifax, Nova Scotia, presumably in search of employment opportunities. Ultimately, this sojourn proved unsuccessful and he returned to England. His early experiences of financial difficulties and challenges give context to the often fretful tone of his letters.[1]

It was in August 1841 that the forty-three-year-old Cooke arrived in Carmarthenshire to take up the post of land agent on the Middleton Hall estate on a wage of £200 a year. His employer was the ailing Edward Hamlin Adams (1777–1842), an attorney from Jamaica who had grown rich 'by questionable commercial practices during the Napoleonic wars'.[2] Cooke was informed that his new employer was a stockbroker who had generated most of his fortune in the years during the Napoleonic Wars by 'speculating in the funds'.[3] Adams had purchased the estate in 1825 following the death of the previous owner, the Scottish former East India Company servant, Sir William Paxton (c. 1744–1824). Following a lucrative career in India, where Paxton rose to become Master of the Calcutta Mint, he purchased the Middleton Hall estate on his retirement and commenced an ambitious scheme of improvement. Between 1793 and 1795 a neo-classical mansion designed by the architect Samuel Pepys Cockerell was built high on top of a hill above the original house, commanding impressive views towards the Tywi Valley. The landscape surrounding the parkland was improved in the picturesque style, celebrated in travel writing, and captured in a series of watercolour prints by the artist and land surveyor Thomas Horner in 1815.[4] Middleton Hall was therefore an estate that had grown

---

[1] R. J. Colyer, 'The land agent in nineteenth-century Wales', *Welsh History Review*, 8:4 (1977), pp. 401–25, especially p. 410; the author is most grateful to Martin Cooke for sharing additional information about his ancestors.

[2] According to his great-granddaughter, the author Violet Paget; P. Gunn, *Vernon Lee, Violet Paget, 1856–1935* (London, 1964), p. 16.

[3] National Library of Wales [hereafter NLW], MS 21209 C, Thomas Herbert Cooke to his mother, 6 November 1841.

[4] P. K. Crimmin, 'Samuel Pepys Cockerell: his work in west Wales, 1793–1810', *Carmarthenshire Historian*, 4 (1967), pp. 7–21; S. Fox, '"The Fidelity of a Mirror": the late eighteenth and early nineteenth century landscape at Middleton Hall' (unpublished MA thesis, University of Wales Trinity Saint David, 2014).

and seen extensive building and renovation, but was in a state of decline by the time of Cooke's arrival.

Cooke's first impression of Middleton Hall and Paxton's parkland was favourable:

> The scenery of the Park and neighbourhood, more bold and picturesque than you can well imagine, in fact there is such endless diversity of hill & vale, wood & water, walks, shrubberies & waterfalls, that I may truly say I never saw in any country, any scene to equal it.[5]

However, on inspecting the wider estate Cooke soon realised that his duties would be considerable. Having seen a farm that was greatly neglected, having been uncultivated for four years, he declared: 'I do not want to go nearer it, for it cuts a most wretched appearance, as you may well suppose, its spontaneous produce having this year been sold for a very small sum.'[6] Further evidence gleaned from these letters confirms that the estate was in decline by the time Cooke took up his post.[7]

The relationship between landlord and land agent at Middleton Hall was strained, particularly between Cooke and his employer's eldest son and heir, Edward Abadam (1809–75), whom Cooke principally dealt with following the death of Edward Hamlin Adams a year after Cooke's appointment.[8] Through Cooke's letters we learn more about the nature of this relationship. Cooke's initial impression of Abadam's 'somewhat extraordinary character'[9] is most descriptive:

> He knows but little or nothing of business – detests farming, – is meanly suspicious of every living creature – is an infidel, and frequently a scoffer at all

---

[5] NLW, MS 21209 C, Cooke to his mother, 1 September 1841.

[6] NLW, MS 21209 C, Cooke to his mother, 7 September 1841.

[7] For more analysis of Cooke's comments on the management of the Middleton Hall estate, including agricultural improvement and farming methods, see Colyer, 'Land agent in nineteenth-century Wales'.

[8] Edward Abadam had changed his surname for personal reasons. He adopted the prefix 'Ab' to the Adams name by legal deed, as it was believed the family name had originally been 'Ab Adam'. In his will, Abadam explained he had changed his name by deed poll on 9 October 1851; NLW, D. M. C. Charles Box 1, will and codicil of Edward Abadam [n.d.]. In the family history, Abadam wrote: 'Now, February 1860, having proved our noble descent through Lord Abadam and the long use of that name in our own Family I have resumed and sign it Edw. Abadam 14th July 1836'; Carmarthenshire Record Office [hereafter CRO], Morris of Bryn Myrddin Collection, MS 121, family history of the Abadam family, copy made for Conrade Abadam, Middleton Hall, from his father, Edward Abadam, 14 July 1865.

[9] NLW, MS 21209 C, Cooke to his mother, 8 May 1842.

religion, – *is fickle*, and *capricious* in the extreme, and exceedingly irritable, – he is all smiles and sunshine, one day, and perhaps in a few hours after, will be just the reverse . . . he has *invariably* treated me with respect – but if he ever treats me, as I have seen him treat others, I would leave him, even if I and all my family were driven to a workhouse the very next day. He is certainly the most difficult subject you can well imagine or that I ever had to deal with.[10]

Cooke saw Abadam as erratic and unreliable, this very fact reinforced when Abadam left the estate for London, promising to be back within a fortnight, but not reappearing until a month later. Cooke bitterly remarked when Abadam had gone how he had left 'every matter and thing in the most unsettled state that can well be imagined; he loves to have his own hand in every little matter, seldom suffering me to act without first consulting him, even in our day affairs'.[11] Abadam's constant demands on his time greatly upset Cooke; this is evident in the frequent complaints he made in his letters:

Mr Adams himself is so very *tedious*, in transacting business; *dwelling hours without end*, on *the most trivial matters*, never seeming so well satisfied, or pleased, as when he has got me in the Office (tied to the table leg as I am apt to think it) and hindering me from going about my most important matters of business. This being one of his many strange peculiarities.[12]

It appeared that Abadam wished Cooke to work round the hours he kept, hours which were most irregular. Abadam would usually rise at around one or two in the afternoon, before eating breakfast at two or three. The hours up until five or six were spent writing or visiting Middleton Hall.[13] He would arrive back late to a spoilt dinner at his residence at Clearbrook at around ten at night. Cooke and Abadam would then stay up late working, sometimes until three in the morning. On Cooke's departure, Abadam would not retire to bed; instead he stayed up drinking coffee and smoking cigars until dawn, going to bed between the hours of five and seven. On some occasions, he would stay up to see at what time his employees arrived for work in the morning. Cooke explained that whilst his master stayed up until the early hours of the morning, he had the luxury of sleeping on until midday. Cooke was expected to stay up late but also rise early to keep the estate accounts,

---

[10] NLW, MS 21209 C, Cooke to his mother, 8 May 1842 (emphasis in original).

[11] NLW, MS 21209 C, Cooke to his mother, 1 April 1844.

[12] NLW, MS 21209 C, Cooke to his mother, 23 July 1842 (emphasis in original).

[13] At this time Abadam was resident at Clearbrook Cottage, a sizeable house built on the outskirts of the park.

farm 400 acres of land and undertake a myriad of other duties expected of him. Cooke proclaimed:

> I have often heard it remarked, that it is better to wear out, than to rust out, but as this life is but short, it is surely the duty of every *rational being* to avoid *both extremes*, and think of something beyond the cares and troubles of this world, or the inordinate cravings of worldly minded persons whose sole God is Mammon, and who care *little* for any one thing, beyond the gratifications, which are to be bought with money.[14]

Cooke felt that his master's constant interference only served to slow him down and was glad of the opportunity to carry on with his work in peace when Abadam was absent from the estate. Cooke was obviously under considerable pressure and deeply unhappy, even though he himself claimed he did not have time to be downcast, working up to fourteen or fifteen hours a day.[15] However, it must be remembered that these letters only convey Cooke's perspective and that equivalent letters written by Abadam would invariably present a different account.

Whilst the relationship between landlord and agent was strained, during the summer of 1843 an opportunity arose for Cooke and Abadam to unite in the face of an external threat, and Cooke's severe views of his employer to soften, for a while at least.

THE MIDDLE MAN: CAUGHT BETWEEN PATRIARCH AND PROTESTORS

The first recorded appearance by Rebecca and her daughters is in 1839, when a band of men destroyed the tollgate at Efailwen, on the border between Carmarthenshire and Pembrokeshire. Rioting reached its peak during the summer of 1843, coinciding with Cooke's letters. The protestors, reacting to socio-economic problems, including a decrease in agricultural profit, increase in rents and failing harvests, were protesting against the payment of tolls to the Turnpike Trusts and their unfair regulation. Men would disguise themselves in women's clothing and under cover of night descend upon the tollgates, destroying them before disappearing into the night. The name Rebecca probably derives from Genesis 24: 60, whereby Rebecca's children are urged to 'possess the gates of those who hate them'. The idea of the rioters led by the figurehead of the mythical Rebecca has direct parallels with

---

[14] NLW, MS 21209 C, Cooke to his mother, 16 June 1844 (emphasis in original).
[15] NLW, MS 21209 C, Cooke to his mother, 8 May 1842.

other contemporary rural protest movements in Britain and Ireland, such as the Swing Riots and Luddites in England, and the Rockites in Ireland, led by the figure of Captain Rock.[16] During the summer of 1843 the activities of Rebecca and her daughters intensified, with the rioters turning their sights towards private property, including that of the landed gentry.[17]

Rebecca is first referenced in Cooke's letters when he writes to his mother on 28 May 1843 of the destruction of a tollgate at the end of the nearby market town of Carmarthen. This was notable as he had been at Carmarthen himself only that day.[18] In his following letter, almost two months later, he related to his mother that 'I have but little news to communicate, at all likely to interest you, as there is nothing at all stirring here but "Rebecca".'[19] Cooke explained how by then the rioters had turned their attention towards Middleton Hall, and more specifically, towards him. On the previous Tuesday night, a band of rioters had visited the mansion demanding to see the butler. In the meantime the butler had fled the mansion, cowering amongst some nearby bushes for two hours whilst the rioters taunted the only female servant in the house. However, the rioters remained outside the hall and left without causing any physical harm to the property or its inhabitants. The following evening a threatening letter arrived, signed by 'Rachael

[16] A. Randall, *Riotous Assemblies: Popular Protest in Hanoverian England* (Oxford, 2006); C. J. Griffin, *The Rural War: Captain Swing and the Politics of Protest* (Manchester, 2012); J. S. Donnelly Jr, *Captain Rock: The Irish Agrarian Rebellion of 1821–24* (Cork, 2009).

[17] For more on Rebecca attacks on gentry land and property, see L. A. Rees, 'Paternalism and rural protest: the Rebecca Riots and the landed interest of south-west Wales', *Agricultural History Review*, 59:1 (2011), pp. 36–60. For more on the Rebecca Riots, see Rh. E. Jones, *Petticoat Heroes: Gender, Culture and Popular Protest in the Rebecca Riots* (Cardiff, 2015); D. J. V. Jones, *Rebecca's Children: A Study of Rural Society, Crime and Protest* (Cardiff, 1989); D. Williams, *The Rebecca Riots: A Study in Agrarian Discontent* (Cardiff, 1955).

[18] Conrad Davies highlights how Cooke does not explain to his mother who Rebecca was, suggesting that there may be a few letters missing from the collection. It is, however, possible that his mother was already aware of the activities of Rebecca and her daughters, as news of the riots were widely reported in the press, including *The Times*. One of their reporters, Thomas Campbell Foster, was sent to south-west Wales to report the latest news of the disturbances; C. Davies, 'The Rebecca Riots: letters from the front', *The Carmarthenshire Antiquary*, 40 (2004), pp. 88–103, especially pp. 91, 103; NLW, MS 21209 C, Cooke to his mother, 28 May 1843.

[19] NLW, MS 21209 C, Cooke to his mother, 23 July 1843.

and Paul for Rebecca'.[20] In this letter Cooke was referred to as 'the fat steward' and the bailiff as 'the old Bum'.[21] It seems that Cooke had ordered the bailiff to collect rent from those who were finding it difficult to pay, an act which inflamed the rioters. Although no violence ensued on that evening, three days later every window in the bailiff's house was smashed. Whilst Cooke's property was spared, on the very same night, to intimidate the agent, a gun was fired and a horn blown outside one of the windows. The band of thirty or forty men dressed in white proceeded to destroy the Porthyrhyd tollgates and break the windows of the tollhouse. Cooke commented that the village looked 'as tho' it had been taken by an enemy'. The rioters then moved on to destroy the tollhouse at the nearby village of Llanarthney. The leader of this group was a tall, broad man dressed in women's clothing, riding side-saddle. Following this attack, Cooke lamented in a letter to his mother: 'It is difficult to guess where all this will end – the country is in a state of all but open rebellion the country people frightened out of their senses.'[22]

Soon after this incident, Cooke himself had a close encounter with the rioters, which he described in eerie detail in one of his letters to his mother. At the start of this letter Cooke assured his mother that the rioters would not harm him as a perfect opportunity had been presented to them. On his way home at midnight after transacting business with Abadam, Cooke ran into a group of about forty rioters. They stood motionless and silent in the narrow lane, armed with guns and long poles, all dressed in white, their faces concealed by veils. Cooke was forced to direct his horse with great difficulty through the silent crowd. He remarked that 'Several of them were so near me, that I could have struck them with my stick, but I thought it more prudent to thrash my horse instead of them, and was glad to get off so cheaply.'[23]

By this time, more threatening letters had been sent to Edward Abadam. As reported in *The Times*, these letters promised an attack on the Middleton Hall mansion and Abadam's other properties.[24] Soon after Cooke himself received a threatening letter notifying him that he should leave Wales, pledging that if he declined he would never again know peace or happiness. The letter addressed him, 'Imp what

---

[20] There were instances of threatening letters signed by the mythical right-hand men and women of the leader, Rebecca.

[21] NLW, MS 21209 C, Cooke to his mother, 23 July 1843.

[22] NLW, MS 21209 C, Cooke to his mother, 23 July 1843.

[23] NLW, MS 21209 C, Cooke to his mother, 6 August 1843.

[24] *The Times*, 25 July 1843.

do you want here', and accused him of advising Abadam to maintain
a high level of rent. Cooke later commented how he and other land
agents who enforced the payments of such high rents were naturally
disliked, but that he had to carry out his employer's orders, no matter
how unfair they seemed.[25] He referred to a land agent employed on an
unnamed estate, some seven miles away from Middleton Hall, whose
nearly completed new home was partly destroyed by the rioters. In light
of this attack, Cooke feared that his turn would be next, but vowed to
give Rebecca and her daughters a fight: 'If ever they burst in the door of
my house I will surely send some of them to "kingdom come".'[26] As a
protection measure Cooke regularly laid three loaded pistols next to his
bed, along with a brace of swords and a dagger. He had even instructed
his wife and sons to load and fire the pistols in an emergency. It is clear
that how the land agent was seen to be undertaking his role had an
impact on perceptions, and subsequently, the behaviour of the rioters.

Whilst Cooke the agent proved a convenient scapegoat, the landlord
Edward Abadam's position during the riots was more complex. He was
invited to a meeting held by the local tenants and labourers to draw
up a petition addressed to the Queen, against the New Poor Law, high
taxes, rents and tithes. Abadam was invited to the meeting on the basis
that he was generally a popular figure amongst the tenantry, holding
radical opinions and refusing to pay tithes. In 1835 Abadam printed
a pamphlet (a version in English and another in Welsh) entitled 'A
Few Words addressed to the Electors of Carmarthenshire by a Loyal
Reformer, an Advocate for the Ballot, and a Friend to the Dissenter and
the Farmer'.[27] Amongst the main issues Abadam raised in this pamphlet
was the importance of the secret ballot, the coming of which would
be, in his words, 'a blessing'. He called the Conservatives 'destroy-
ers', believing only the secret ballot would free the masses from the
tyranny of the Anglican, Conservative landlord. Abadam encouraged
the tenants to stand up for their rights and oppose the oppression of the
landed interest. He referred to the corrupt boroughs which had sprung
from an unjust system that was governed by a small proportion of

[25] NLW, MS 21209 C, Cooke to his mother, 27 November 1843.

[26] NLW, MS 21209 C, Cooke to his mother, 24 August 1843.

[27] CRO, Morris of Bryn Myrddin Collection, MS 142, printed address 'A Few
Words addressed to the Electors of Carmarthenshire by a Loyal Reformer, an
Advocate for the Ballot, and a Friend to the Dissenter and the Farmer' (Bath, 1835);
MS 119, printed address 'Anerchiad at Etholwyr Sir Gaerfyrddin yn Pleidio y Tugel,
gan Ddiwygiwr Teyrngarol, a Chyfaill i'r Ymneillduwr a'r Ffarmwr, sef Edward
Abadam' (Carmarthen, 1835).

influential men. He also urged tenants to stand firm and refuse to take up leases where landlords coerced their tenants to vote as directed.[28] Cooke explained how Abadam was 'more popular among them [the tenantry] than I can well describe: the mob actually *wanted* to take the horses from his carriage, and to draw him into the town of Llandibie [sic] last week'.[29]

It could be argued that the protestors saw in Abadam a rare example of a landlord who was sympathetic to their plight. Whilst a trustee of the Kidwelly Trust and the Three Commotts Trust, Abadam persevered in convincing the Kidwelly Trust to lower their tolls.[30] In his role as chairman in 1843 Abadam vowed that the Three Commotts would remove ten bars and side gates.[31]

For all his apparent tolerance and seemingly liberal attitude, Abadam was, however, a firm believer in the landowner's rights.[32] He therefore declined the invitation to the meeting, realising that if he lent his support to the petition he would eventually be expected to reduce his rents. In addition, as a magistrate, his role was to uphold law and order locally. To be seen supporting the cause of the rioters in any way could be potentially damaging to his reputation. Indeed, a circular sent out by the government in 1830 warned magistrates of the consequences of taking sides with the rioters.[33]

David J. V. Jones explains how even the most dutiful tenants could be driven to protest and acts of violence due to the actions of an unfair landlord, explaining how Abadam, 'a natural ally of the people in the politics of protest, also allowed his fiery temper to destroy a promising relationship with his tenantry'.[34] A demonstration of this 'fiery temper' was seen on 22 August 1843, when Abadam, along with another magistrate, attended a meeting in Porthyrhyd, in the presence of around 150 of what Cooke called 'Rebeccaites'. Notices ordering people to attend this meeting had been circulated in the local chapels the previous Sunday. Abadam, having also received one of these notices, refused to risk attending the meeting unarmed, therefore he, Cooke and the

---

[28] CRO, Morris of Bryn Myrddin Collection, MS 142; MS 119.

[29] NLW, MS 21209 C, Cooke to his mother, 3 September 1843 (emphasis in original).

[30] Jones, *Rebecca's Children*, p. 306.

[31] Jones, *Rebecca's Children*, p. 229; *The Times*, 8 August 1843, 9 September 1843; *Carmarthen Journal*, 11 August 1843.

[32] Jones, *Rebecca's Children*, p. 306.

[33] Jones, *Rebecca's Children*, p. 196.

[34] Jones, *Rebecca's Children*, p. 98.

butler were present 'armed to the teeth . . . our pockets literally cramed [sic] with hostile weapons'.[35] Abadam had received a petition from his tenants demanding that he give them no less than a third return on their rents. Cooke explained that although some of the rents were quite low, overall they were 'shamefully high'.[36] In the years 1816, 1822 and 1843 the main criticism of landlords in Wales was that they refused to reduce their rents. Consequently, this caused serious economic stress for farmers for a number of years. However, permanent rent reductions were not financially viable for landlords. Between 1793 and 1843 in Carmarthenshire, Pembrokeshire and Cardiganshire there was an increase in rents of more than 100 per cent. As a result of revaluation, the rents on the Golden Grove, Crosswood and Nanteos estates increased two- and threefold during the years of war.[37] It seems that in late 1845 Abadam's rents were between 30 and 40 per cent higher than those of Lord Cawdor, landlord of the Stackpole Court estate in Pembrokeshire.[38] Abadam desired Cooke to value the whole estate in order to identify the rents that were too high, but although Cooke believed Abadam was not ready to lower his rents, he also believed his employer would be forced to as long as agricultural prices continued to remain so low. Cooke explained how Rebecca and her followers pledged to refuse to pay tithes or rents, ordering that no one was to take up recently vacated farms, nor answer to any English stewards. Cooke wearily commented:

> I am wondering when all this is to end, Mr A. threatens to become an absentee, which I am not surprised at, for it is by no means pleasant not to be able to sleep in peace and safety. It is a new state of things to us.[39]

The number of absentee landlords was growing, especially considering the threats Rebecca posed to landowners. Abadam made it clear that he believed he was making a great sacrifice by remaining resident within the county in the face of such hostility. However, those landlords who remained on their estates were aware they were amongst the minority.[40] Cooke found it hard to believe he deserved the wrath of Rebecca, explaining that:

---

[35] NLW, MS 21209 C, Cooke to his mother, 24 August 1843.
[36] NLW, MS 21209 C, Cooke to his mother, 24 August 1843.
[37] Jones, *Rebecca's Children*, p. 61.
[38] NLW, MS 21209 C, Cooke to his mother, 12 October 1845.
[39] NLW, MS 21209 C, Cooke to his mother, 24 August 1843.
[40] Jones, *Rebecca's Children*, p. 69.

Whatever authority I have been invested with, I have always exercised in the mildest possible manner, so much so that Mr A. has acknowledged that he has no fault to find with me except that I am 'too good natured' which Rebecca says in one of her Letters to me, that 'I grind the poor to enrich myself' which is a regular lie. Thus I am like the old man in the fable, I please neither side.[41]

The impending attack on Middleton Hall soon arrived. On his return home from a Quarter Sessions meeting on the night of 12 September 1843, Abadam saw a fire blazing in the distance in the direction of Middleton Hall. On his arrival, he found two large hayricks had been set ablaze at a nearby farmyard. Abadam found the woods surrounding Middleton Hall teeming with men and his family cowering in fear within the mansion. It appeared that the attackers had removed the plugs from the nearby fish ponds in order to hinder any attempts at extinguishing the fires. Whilst collecting his valuable papers together, he sent a message to Carmarthen seeking immediate military protection.[42] However, the Vice Lieutenant of Carmarthenshire, Colonel George Rice Trevor, reported that the cavalry had been nearly fifteen miles away in Llanelli during the day and there were no available carriages to transport the infantry. Colonel Trevor relayed to the Home Office that he was therefore 'compelled to withhold assistance'.[43] The press reported that the haystacks containing about 60 tons of hay could have reached upward of £200, a substantial loss to the landlord.[44] Four days later they were still smouldering. The Home Office, in response to George Rice Trevor's letter, stated that such an attack warranted the offer of a reward by the government for the detection of the perpetrators, and the granting of the Queen's pardon to any accomplices.[45] The *Carmarthen Journal* speculated on the motive for this attack, claiming:

We cannot conceive what can be the cause of Rebecca's enmity against Mr. Adams, as he has done more than almost any other gentleman in the county to redress the turnpike gate grievances; and also to remove all other causes of distress, which press on the farmers.[46]

[41] NLW, MS 21209 C, Cooke to his mother, 3 September 1843.
[42] *The Welshman*, 15 September 1843.
[43] The National Archives [hereafter TNA], Home Office Letters and Papers [hereafter HO], 45/454, George Rice Trevor to the Home Office, 13 September 1843.
[44] *Carmarthen Journal*, 15 September 1843.
[45] TNA, HO, 41/418, Home Office to George Rice Trevor, 16 September 1843.
[46] *Carmarthen Journal*, 15 September 1843.

The *Carmarthen Journal* was notoriously sympathetic towards
the interests of the gentry, and as David J. V. Jones explains, was
'the mouthpiece' of the landed elite and 'the voice of High-Church
Toryism'.[47] The article continues praising Abadam, explaining how
he had always brought employment to the area, but due to the recent
troubles had been compelled to discharge several workmen.[48] It seems
the attack on Abadam's property stood as retaliation for his deeds
as magistrate, dealing with Rebeccaites in court harshly, and for his
continual refusal to lower the rents. This attack may also have been a
response to one particular case. William Lewis, lessee of the Kidwelly
Trust between 1841 and 1842, had set up an unauthorised series of
gates at Porthyrhyd, where there were already two gates. The case
was brought before magistrates (one of whom may very well have
been Edward Abadam), but Lewis was only given a small fine for
this wrongdoing. He was punished so leniently because most of the
magistrates present were trustees of the Kidwelly Trust.[49] There was,
however, considerable sympathy for Abadam. In the aftermath of the
burning of the hay ricks, 'a retired farmer' writing to the editor of
the *Swansea Journal* claimed that he believed Edward Abadam had
suffered 'more than his share of ill-treatment and abuse'.[50] The writer
defended Abadam, stating how he was one of the best landlords in
the country and an upstanding magistrate. According to him, Abadam
had been unjustly attacked 'because he went all the *right way* with
the people, and halted when they went wrong'.[51] The nonconformist
periodical Y *Diwygiwr* (The Reformer) also drew attention to the arson
attacks at Middleton Hall. Whilst the editor, the Independent minister
David Rees of Llanelli, had urged the people to 'Agitate! Agitate!
Agitate!', adopting Daniel O'Connell's famous motto, he explained
how he had advocated peaceful methods of protest, rather than com-
mitting, what he described as, cowardly and violent acts by night.[52] The
denominational and church periodical *Yr Haul* (The Sun) also drew
attention to the burning of the hayricks at Middleton Hall, commenting
that the destruction at the hands of the rioters worsened with each
passing day.[53] Although these two periodicals were at opposite ends of

[47] Jones, *Rebecca's Children*, pp. 83, 85.
[48] *Carmarthen Journal*, 15 September 1843.
[49] Davies, 'Rebecca Riots', p. 92.
[50] *Swansea Journal*, 20 September 1843.
[51] *Swansea Journal*, 20 September 1843 (emphasis in original).
[52] Y *Diwygiwr*, October 1843.
[53] *Yr Haul*, October 1843.

the political and religious spectrum, they agreed that such attacks on private property were unacceptable.

After the burning of the hayricks at Middleton Hall, further threats from Rebecca were treated with great seriousness. Such a threat loomed only the following day, on 13 September, when news of an impending attack reached Cooke. Abadam summoned protection, and soldiers were duly stationed at Cooke's house. However, news of the arrival of the troops spread, therefore the rioters kept their distance. No further attack materialised, even after the troops left. Abadam, however, was furious when George Rice Trevor, as Colonel Commandant of the troops, amongst other officers, perceiving no immediate threat, ordered the detachment to be sent back to Carmarthen. According to Cooke, Abadam:

> had a small quarrel with the Officers for so abruptly removing soldiers, and leaving M. Hall & the country around so completely exposed to these marauders. He says a magistrate is not sufficiently protected in the execution of his duty, appears disgusted with what he calls the neglect of the Government in not putting down these outrageous doings, has packed off all his plate and his Title Deeds to a place of greater security and (I believe) is going off to France in course of a day or two quite disgusted.[54]

The first hint of activities subsiding is found in a letter dated 28 September 1843, following an intense meeting chaired by Abadam. Around 150 tenants congregated for the meeting, which lasted at least an hour and a half. Abadam's temper was frayed and he used 'most intemperate language', according to Cooke.[55] He was sure that those who had set fire to his hayricks were present at the meeting and they would receive their punishment in this world and the next. However, he agreed that he would look into reducing his rents. Abadam then proceeded to read two anonymous letters received on that day, both signed 'Rebecca'. One letter demanded that Abadam dismiss Cooke from his post as land agent and replace him with Mr Glanville, the butler. The letter writer stated 'that if he (the Butler) were to be put in the place of the thick headed Cooke he (the Butler) would be like Lot in Sodom and that no more of Mr Adams' property should be burnt'.[56]

Abadam believed the writer of this letter also to be present, and shouted in what Cooke believed was a voice that could be heard a

---

[54] NLW, MS 21209 C, Cooke to his mother, 16 September 1843.

[55] NLW, MS 21209 C, Cooke to his mother, 28 September 1843.

[56] NLW, MS 21209 C, Cooke to his mother, 28 September 1843. A reference to Genesis 19: 1–29.

quarter of a mile away, that Cooke 'suited him' and he would never
be forced to get rid of him. He assured the crowd that he had not been
advised by Cooke to turn away Welsh tenants and only let farms to
English tenants, these being 'cursed lies' that had been 'invented by the
parties themselves to serve their own base ends'.[57] He emphasised how
Middleton Hall was his property and that he would run it only as he
deemed fit, refusing to be told how to do so by any man or band of men.
Furthermore, he was disgusted that he was forced to remove himself, his
wife and children from the estate in order to protect them from his own
tenants, and this before he had finished building his late father's tomb at
the local parish church in Llanarthney. He emphasised that it was they,
the tenants, who had forced him to resort to absenteeism, claiming they
were only punishing themselves, since Abadam would not be present to
invest his money locally, but assured them that he would continue to
collect his rent when it was due. After warning the congregated masses
of the consequences of martial law, Abadam dismissed the assembled
crowd, who departed in stunned silence. Cooke suggested that perhaps
Abadam's outburst had created some impact, since the crowd left peace-
fully and no disturbances had occurred in the locality since. The following day Abadam and his family left Middleton Hall for France.

Later, on 24 October 1843 Cooke wrote that disturbances were by
then seldom, although policemen and soldiers were still placed in the
villages.[58] Cooke later commented that whilst plenty of land remained
to be let, none were willing to take up these leases due to Rebecca's
threats. Tenants were reluctant to come forward to take land where the
previous tenants had been turned out or left on account of the rent being
too high.[59] Even in late December, Cooke claimed that Wales was still
a place of great unrest, believing that the country was turning more like
Ireland with each passing day.[60]

Cooke's last reference to Rebecca appears in a letter dated 16 June
1844 where he mentioned that although Rebecca had been quiet of late,

[57] NLW, MS 21209 C, Cooke to his mother, 28 September 1843.

[58] NLW, MS 21209 C, Cooke to his mother, 24 October 1843.

[59] Cooke's letters also refer to instances of Rebecca and her daughters redressing
moral crimes, reinforcing the argument that the movement was more than just a
protest against the tolls and high rents, but was also a method of community justice,
following the *ceffyl pren* (wooden horse) tradition in Wales, and Skimmington in
England; NLW, MS 21209 C, Cooke to his mother, 27 November 1843.

[60] This was a common comparison in the press and amongst contemporaries,
with Ireland used as a benchmark to measure the severity of unrest; NLW, MS
21209 C, Cooke to his mother, 21 December 1843.

a letter was left at Clearbrook a few weeks prior threatening Abadam as he had once again allowed Constable Evan Thomas, who had taken an active part in suppressing the riots, to take a vacant cottage.[61] Cooke left Middleton Hall three years later in 1847 to take up a more lucrative (and happy) appointment as land agent to Lord Fitzhardinge at Berkeley Castle, Gloucestershire, where he stayed until his death in 1851.

CONCLUSION

Cooke's letters can be used as a lens through which to view the impact of the Rebecca Riots on one estate and locality. The nature of the threats and attacks on property can be assessed, along with the reaction of landlord and agent. It is revealing how external influences affected the nature of the relationship between employer and employee, with Abadam publicly defending Cooke in the face of demands to remove him, suggesting Abadam was aware of the importance of presenting a united front. Insight is gleaned into the emotional history of the land agent during a time of stress and strain. Cooke was a land agent who was working during a particularly challenging time, and under difficult conditions. This also included a particularly fraught relationship with his employer, who himself came from a non-traditional background.

There are many parallels between the Rebecca Riots and other instances of rural protest in Scotland, Ireland and England. Despite differing grievances and methods of protest, a common factor, captured in Cooke's letters, is the sense of fear experienced by the landed interest and their employees. Concern for their property and personal safety was at the forefront of their minds during such tumultuous periods of rural unrest.

[61] NLW, MS 21209 C, Cooke to his mother, 16 June 1844.

9

The Evolution of the Irish Land Agent:
The Management of the Blundell Estate in the
Eighteenth Century

Ciarán Reilly

INTRODUCTION

IN 1786 A SOMEWHAT despondent John Hatch requested to be relieved of his duties as agent of the Blundell estate in King's County (Offaly), insisting that the town of Edenderry was 'dwindling into ruin'. In particular, Hatch, who had replaced his father Henry as agent, highlighted that both hardship and poverty were endemic at Edenderry and in general there was not much he could do to overturn circumstances.[1] It was not, as we shall see below, the first, or indeed the last time that Hatch indicated his wish to be relieved of the agency duties. Faced with the unenviable task of managing an Irish landed estate in decline, Hatch was just one of five agents appointed to the Blundell estate during the eighteenth century.[2] It was a position in which he remained until his death in 1797, at which time irregularities were found with his management of the estate.[3] However, this was a frequent occurrence and was something which befell many eighteenth-century landed estates (and indeed later). The reason for such dilatory (and perhaps dishonest) practice was believed to have stemmed from the fact that the nature of the agents' duties was imprecise and that the role lacked any professionalism. This chapter examines the management of the 14,000-acre Blundell estate during the period 1700–80 and in particular the career of father and son combination, Henry and John Hatch, agents between them for over fifty years. Their agency of the Blundell estate offers an insight

---

[1] Public Record Office of Northern Ireland [hereafter PRONI], Blundell papers, MIC/17, John Hatch to Miss Blundell, 20 June 1783.
[2] These men included Nathaniel Taylor, the first 'agent' of the Blundell estate; Thomas Meredith; Joseph Misset; and the Hatches, Henry and his son John.
[3] See C. Reilly, *Edenderry, County Offaly and the Downshire Estate 1790–1800* (Dublin, 2007), pp. 28–9.

into the evolution and the complexities of the land agency business in eighteenth-century Ireland.[4]

In May 1705 Francis Blundell appointed Nathaniel Taylor of Edenderry as:

> my true and lawful attorney for me and in my name and to my own proper use . . . to receive all such rents yearly or half-yearly payments . . . and to do and act all such things for procuring the said rents as to him shall seem met.[5]

Taylor's credentials for the position appear to have been based solely on the fact that he was a reliable and successful farmer, and that his ancestors had come to Ireland with the first of the Blundells in the early seventeenth century.[6] The Blundell estate at Coolestown, or Edenderry as it came to be known, was typical of many landed estates in Ireland in the eighteenth century, in that an absentee proprietor left the property in the sole care of land agents who themselves were largely absentee.[7] The town of Edenderry was granted to Sir Henry Colley (sometimes Cowley) in 1562 after the plantation of Laois and Offaly, six years previous. By the early eighteenth century the estate had passed through marriage to the Blundell family, of whom Montague was created Baron and Viscount of Edenderry in 1720.[8] Edenderry had suffered considerably

[4] A number of studies deal specifically with the role of the eighteenth-century land agent including D. Dickson, *Old World Colony: Cork and South Munster, 1630–1830* (Cork, 2006); T. Barnard, *A New Anatomy of Ireland: The Irish Protestants 1649–1770* (London, 2003); M. Dowling, *Tenant Right and Agrarian Society in Ulster 1600–1870* (Dublin, 1999); M. L. Legg, *The Diary of Nicholas Peacock, 1740–1751: The Worlds of a County Limerick Farmer and Agent* (Dublin, 2005); R. Richey, 'The eighteenth-century estate agent and his correspondence, County Down: a case study', in R. J. Morris and L. Kennedy (eds), *Ireland and Scotland: Order and Disorder, 1600–2000* (Edinburgh, 2005), pp. 35–45; E. Hughes, 'The eighteenth-century estate agent', in H. A. Cronne, T. W. Moody and D. B. Quinn (eds), *Essays in British and Irish History in Honour of James Eadie Todd* (London, 1949), pp. 185–200.

[5] PRONI, Blundell papers, MIC/17, Francis Blundell to Nathaniel Taylor, 11 May 1705.

[6] The date of their arrival in Edenderry is uncertain, but they were certainly in residence after the Williamite Wars of the 1690s; see Edenderry Historical Society, *Carved in Stone* (Naas, 2010), p. 116.

[7] The Blundell estate in King's County was a fragmented unit which, in addition to the town of Edenderry, comprised the townlands of Monasteroris, Glann, Ardenderry, Coneyboro, Kishawanna and Ballymorane.

[8] Lady Sarah Blundell was the only daughter and heiress of Sir William Colley, grandson of Henry Colley. Her son, Sir Francis Blundell, was created baronet in 1620. His son, also Francis, married in December 1675 Anne Ingoldsbury, with whom he had seven sons and two daughters, namely George, Henry, Charles, Francis,

during the religious and political turmoil of the seventeenth century, which had greatly hindered its development.[9] During the Williamite Wars of 1689–91, it was claimed that Protestants at Edenderry 'had been plundered and necessitated to fly out of the country'. As a result, according to a government source, it was seen as essential to secure 'the passes from Rapparees' which would provide safe passage from Edenderry to Dublin. The remaining part of the town of Edenderry was to be garrisoned by a detachment of the standing army as there 'was a considerable fort newly raised there which would be of great advantage should any further attempts be made by the enemy'.[10] This new-found stability was reflected in the fact that by 1700 a sizeable community of the Society of Friends had resettled in Edenderry where they promoted a variety of industry.

The presence of this enterprising community meant that the Blundells now looked with renewed interest towards their King's County property. Just how great that renewed attention was is debatable, for as Lord Blundell confessed in 1721, he 'might have had a better rent roll if I had not been so inactive'.[11] And while Taylor had considerable success in raising the estate rental by turning the town's parks into small plots so that 'it can accommodate the people better', the appointment process of future agents ultimately stymied effective management.[12] Little thought was given to the credentials necessary for the management of land and people. Indeed, it was not until the mid-nineteenth century that such

William, Winwood, Montague, Anne and Sarah. Montague Blundell subsequently died without male issue in 1756. The estate was then administered by his daughters, one of whom, Mary, married in 1733 William Trumbull of Easthampstead Park, Berkshire. Their daughter, Mary, Baroness Sandys, married in 1786 Arthur Hill (later second Marquess of Downshire, 1793–1801), and so the estate passed out of the family's hands.

[9] For example, in June 1643 Colonel Preston and Colonel Monke marched through the Midlands and captured the castles of Croghan, Edenderry (Blundell) and Kinnefad and also 'prepared to lay siege to Castlejordan, a castle well manned and fortified commanding a large district of the adjacent country and belonging to Sir John Gifford, an officer in the English Army'. When the news of these attacks reached James Butler (1610–88), the Duke of Ormonde, he immediately dismissed Parliament, marched to Edenderry and retook the castles, causing considerable destruction in the process.

[10] T. Abbott, 'Quakerism in the Edenderry area 1673–1831', *Offaly Heritage*, 2 (2004), pp. 40–56.

[11] Quoted in T. Barnard, 'The world of goods and County Offaly in the early eighteenth century', in W. Nolan and T. O'Neill (eds), *Offaly: History and Society* (Dublin, 1998), pp. 371–92 (quote at p. 373).

[12] Barnard, 'World of goods and county Offaly', p. 373.

thoughts became commonplace amongst Irish landlords.

Land agents were an integral part of Irish estate life. As Constantia Maxwell has argued, the eighteenth-century land agent consisted of 'more than a glorified bailiff; he was a much more responsible officer, the landlord's man of business'.[13] However, the contemporary opinion of Irish land agents was that they did little to improve the life of the inhabitants of estates. As Toby Barnard argues, 'agencies were desired on account of legitimate and illicit rewards' and thus attracted men of unscrupulous character.[14] Likewise, analysing the role of land agents in South Munster, David Dickson questions whether the potential for fraud resulted in many agents being dishonest and whether under-remuneration for the duties also added to the embezzlement of a land-lord.[15] As a result, many relationships, he argues, between agent and landlord often ended in bitterness given the 'imprecise responsibilities of agents and their unclear codes of conduct'.[16] This was certainly the case with Joseph Misset, who was relieved of his duties at the Blundell estate in 1745.

EVOLUTION OF THE LAND AGENCY BUSINESS

The Irish land agency business was slow to evolve and while in England agents were essential players in the day-to-day management of the landed estate over several hundred years, in Ireland the evolution in some respects is difficult to trace. In Ireland land agents operated on landed estates from the end of the Cromwellian wars of the mid-seventeenth century in many different guises (in some instances they officiated in medieval times) when landowners left their estates for business or on extended leave. However, their duties were ill-defined and as a result the position had fallen into disrepute.[17] Although writing about the situation in England, the advice of Edward Laurence in 1727 warning land-owners about absenteeism was equally applicable to Ireland. Laurence urged caution where landowners 'have already suffered the knavery and

---

[13] C. Maxwell, *Town and Country under the Georges* (Dundalk, 1949), p. 115. For the role of the eighteenth-century land agent, see Barnard, *New Anatomy of Ireland*, pp. 208–38.

[14] Barnard, *New Anatomy of Ireland*, p. 210.

[15] Dickson, *Old World Colony*, p. 560.

[16] Dickson, *Old World Colony*, p. 560.

[17] J. S. Donnelly Jr, *The Land and the People of Nineteenth-Century Cork* (London, 1975), p. 173.

unfaithfulness of their stewards'.[18] As a result, it was hardly surprising that some landlords were reluctant to part with what they saw as strictly private functions, while others decided to keep the role 'in house' and appointed younger sons or family members.

Throughout the eighteenth century the terms of an agent's employment remained simple and at best he was only expected to visit the estate once or twice yearly, perhaps sending prior word of the date of his arrival. In most cases these men were referred to as 'attorney', the term 'agent' not being widely used until at least the 1750s.[19] By the end of the century the term 'agent' had become the preferred choice, perhaps because many disliked being referred to as the landlord's 'acting man' or as the duties became more defined. It is also likely that the term 'steward' came to refer to the 'subordinate estate officials', who although competent and experienced, were not educated or part of the minor gentry.[20] Moreover, the willingness or availability to pay an agent's salary, regularly 5 per cent of the rental of the estate, may also have dictated the title which was assigned to the manager of an estate. However, due to the fact that the land agency was not deemed an exclusive or full-time calling, agents revelled in the fact that they were free to explore their own pursuits and most happily did so.[21]

Regardless of the duties, for many eighteenth-century agents the position brought the opportunity for their accession to the highest social echelons. The remarkable rise of Henry Hatch (1680–1762) was a case in point. A grazier from county Meath, his qualifications for the position of Lord Blundell's agent in King's County were merely that he was 'a man of fortune and character'. However, for the Blundells the fact that Hatch was regarded as 'one who would not allow sympathy to delay ejectment of a tenant who was in arrears' was the characteristic

[18] E. Laurence, *The Duty of a Steward to his Lord* (London, 1727), preface.

[19] See, for example, PRONI, Blundell papers, MIC/317, Francis Blundell to Nathaniel Taylor, 11 May 1705.

[20] G. E. Mingay, 'The management of landed estates', in *English Landed Society in the Eighteenth Century* (London, 1963), p. 157. Others have argued that the term or definition of 'agent' was not stable and was often substituted by 'steward' depending on the estate; see S. Webster, 'Estate management and the professionalization of land agents on the Egremont estates in Sussex and Yorkshire 1770–1835', *Rural History*, 18:1 (2007), pp. 47–69.

[21] Barnard, *New Anatomy of Ireland*, p. 209. For example, Andrew Armstrong was left in charge of the family estates at Clara and Ballycumber, King's County, only receiving advice intermittently from his father, Warneford, in England on how best to proceed with the estate management; see Cornwall Record Office, Armstrong papers, X/819/1, Warneford Armstrong to Andrew Armstrong, 22 August 1752.

which was most needed in mid-eighteenth-century Edenderry.[22] Agent from 1746 to 1762, Hatch was described as 'tough' and competent in his duties. He needed to be for on commencing the agency he found things in a confused manner owing to Joseph Misset's mismanagement and fraudulence, and immediately set about putting things right. Although he was faced with threats to his life, the collection of rents soon regularised.[23]

Like most Irish land agents Hatch had no formal training for the position. However, what he lacked in formal training he made up for in social intercourse. A churchwarden in the parish of Saint Brides, Dublin, Hatch was also a subscriber to the Incorporated Society for Promoting English Protestant Schools in Ireland. In Dublin he was a man of high social standing, and according to William McCormack, Hatch was frequently mentioned in the letters of Jonathan Swift.[24] From the 1740s onwards this social mobility allowed for the creation of his land agency business. In turn, his son John Hatch (1733–99) was both politically and socially astute. A solicitor by trade, John Hatch was elected a Member of Parliament in the House of Commons, serving two terms for Swords in 1769–76 and 1783–90.[25] Like his father, his estate management had its shortcomings, but between them they served in the agency of the Blundell property (and later Downshire) estate for over fifty years, from 1746 to 1797.

Henry Hatch took over the Blundell agency in 1746 following the dismissal of Joseph Misset. Angered by the move, Misset subsequently made the role difficult for the incoming agent by taking with him the administrative papers of the estate. This was a frequent occurrence in eighteenth-century Ireland (and indeed later), and a landlord had to be careful when removing an agent deemed to be dishonest or incompetent. The situation created considerable problems for Hatch as it prevented him from putting new tenants in place that would readily pay rent.[26] The

---

[22] Barnard, *New Anatomy of Ireland*, p. 235; see also W. J. McCormack, *The Silence of Barbara Synge* (Manchester, 2003), p. 32.

[23] Barnard, *New Anatomy of Ireland*, p. 229.

[24] McCormack, *Silence of Barbara Synge*, p. 32.

[25] John Hatch entered Trinity College in May 1736, from where he graduated with a BA in 1739, and later was admitted to London's Lincoln's Inn. In 1749 he was called to the Irish Bar. Hatch was a significant landholder in his own right. His holdings included land in Swords (Dublin); Roundwood (Wicklow); York Street, Cuffe Street and French Street (Dublin city); and Edenderry; see NLI, 'Reports on Private Collections, 18, 494–506'.

[26] PRONI, Blundell papers, MIC/17, Henry Hatch to Lord Blundell, 21 February

confusion caused by Misset's departure meant that Hatch was forced to visit every tenant personally and examine the counterparts of their leases. This was a task that would have been particularly non-desirable to an eighteenth-century agent.[27] As late as 1760 the Misset issue was still unresolved when the Blundell sisters (co-heiresses) complained of 'this most tedious and vexatious law suit between us and Mr Misset'.[28] It had been hoped that Misset would be forced to pay what he owed to the estate, but he was never 'in the circumstances to discharge the debt'.[29] Misset, however, had undertaken to 'never cause disquiet' to Hatch 'either by word or otherwise'.[30]

Misset's departure also created the opportunity for agitating tenants to withhold their rents, and although Hatch would claim that he had suppressed a 'new rebellion', his tenure was largely one of conflict. Although, in 1749 he proudly reported that the tenants were 'now a quiet and industrious set of people', harmony soon dissipated.[31] In 1755, for example, the agent claimed that some of the tenants had refused to pay the rent and had 'spirited up the other tenants to follow their own example'. In order to contain dissension, Hatch was reluctant to allow 'new comers' to take a lease.[32] It was probably for this reason he found it necessary to 'keep in' with a Catholic, who had been appointed to collect the tithes. This was a calculated appointment as he was used to keeping other Catholic tenants in line.

1746.

[27] PRONI, Blundell papers, MIC/17/1, A. M. Blundell to Henry Hatch, 11 March 1758.

[28] PRONI, Blundell papers, MIC/17/1, William Trumbull to Henry Hatch, 8 March 1760.

[29] PRONI, Blundell papers, MIC/17/1, Miss Blundell to Henry Hatch, 2 August 1759.

[30] See PRONI, Downshire papers, D671/D/6/1/25, 'Deed of mutual release. Irish Estates. Hon. Anna Maria Blundell, Administratrix for Father to Joseph Misset'.

[31] Quoted in Barnard, 'World of goods and county Offaly', p. 374.

[32] Other examples of Hatch's tenure as agent can be seen in a letter of December 1759 when the issue of a lease at Edenderry was discussed. Hatch noted how two applicants were wishing to be instated as the tenant, namely Thomas Baily, 'an old tenant who has laid out a good deal of money in the town', and John Sharkey, 'a new comer'. A rental of the estate for 1797 shows that Thomas Baily was a resident of the town, but makes no mention of Sharkey; see PRONI, Blundell papers, MIC/17/1, Henry Hatch to Miss A. M. Blundell, 16 December 1759.

NEW EMPLOYERS

With the death of Lord and Lady Blundell in 1756 (in August and December respectively) the estate passed to their three daughters. For the most part, William Trumbull, married to Mary Blundell, conducted the transitional estate business with Henry Hatch. In effect, they asked him to 'act for us in the same manner as you did for my Lord Blundell'.[33] In December of that year Hatch was instructed to draw up a full account of 'the money you have now in your hands', an indication that it was unknown what rents had been collected up to that point.[34] The new owners were determined to bring their affairs to order and receive sufficient profit from the estate. However, they did not understand the intricate details of estate management in Ireland, a fact which in turn hindered the agent in his duties. For example, there was widespread disappointment when it was learned that all three had to sign the leases before they could be registered in Ireland. On each occasion a lease had to be sent to London, which meant that several weeks (in some cases months) elapsed before the new agreements were finalised. Nor did the sisters understand the fact that Catholic tenants and labourers were necessary for the estate to function. Their religious bias was evident in correspondence with Hatch, outlining that 'it would be always more agreeable to us to have if we could Protestant tenants, and we would be glad if you note in your next rent roll which of our tenants are Papists'. It was particularly vexing when they learned that Hatch had given consent to two new Catholic tenants to reside at Edenderry.[35]

The Irish custom of the 'hanging gale', where tenants paid their rent six months in arrears, was also something which hindered effective estate management and was said to have greatly perplexed the co-heirs.[36] In effect it meant that the agent was always collecting arrears. To overcome this shortfall in the rental, agents were required to have 'ready money', which would be made available to their employer whenever it was

---

[33] PRONI, Blundell papers, MIC/17, William Trumbull to Henry Hatch, 21 September 1756.

[34] PRONI, Blundell papers, MIC/17/1, Henry Hatch, Dublin to William Trumbull, 24 December 1756.

[35] PRONI, Blundell papers, MIC/17, A. M. Blundell, M. Raymond, W. Trumbull to Henry Hatch, 1 March 1758; see also Henry Hatch to Miss Blundell, 24 November 1759.

[36] PRONI, Blundell papers, MIC/17, Henry Hatch to Lord Blundell, 26 August 1755.

needed.[37] It was this ability to advance money which meant that agents were handsomely remunerated. By the 1780s, for example, John Hatch was amongst the best-paid land agents in Ireland, his salary amounting to over £500, although it should be remembered that this probably had much to do with the fact that he was then a sitting Member of Parliament and that the Blundells were determined to retain him as agent.[38]

The revival of interest in the late 1750s by the Blundell family made Henry Hatch somewhat uncomfortable in pressing tenants in arrears. If to this point he had been conciliatory towards tenants, William Trumbull pressed Hatch to make a proper return of the rental, the dates of respective leases and an account of tenants holding at will. The co-heirs also pressed to know the exact terms of the 'agreement concerning the mines', a reference to a number of mining ventures at Blundell Hill, which overlooked the town of Edenderry. Just how successful this silver- and lead-mining venture was is uncertain, but the fact that it was revived several times in the nineteenth century would indicate that it had been somewhat successful.[39]

Like his employers, Henry Hatch was an absentee, which of course brought its own problems. At Edenderry many of the day-to-day affairs were overseen by Adam Williams, an attorney, who resided at nearby Williamstown House in Carbury, County Kildare. Williams was married to a daughter of Shawe Cartland, a substantial middleman who held several hundred acres from the Blundell estate. It appears that Hatch and Williams were incapable of collecting rent from Cartland and by the 1790s he owed more than £4,000 in arrears. This awkward arrangement, whereby middlemen and strong farmers dictated the agenda, was something which hindered the management of the estate. The rise of Cartland in the latter half of the eighteenth century epitomised this, and his authority was bolstered by the fact that he was elected as a magistrate for King's County in 1774.[40] The treatment of middlemen such as Cartland was in stark contrast to Hatch's approach to the management of the Blundell estate at Dundrum, County Down. Here he pressed tenants for rent, perhaps safe in the knowledge that he would not have to face down riot or run the risk of assassination. Such bravado

[37] In 1756, for example, Hatch sent £900 to the co-heirs of the estate.

[38] PRONI, Downshire papers, D607/A/294, Miss Blundell, Lord Robert Bertie and Lord Sandys to John Hatch, 6 August 1785.

[39] PRONI, Blundell papers, MIC/17, Co-heirs to Henry Hatch, 9 September 1756.

[40] C. Reilly, 'The Cartlands of Ballykillen and Lumville: landowners, middlemen, yeoman and magistrate', *Offaly Heritage*, 5 (2007–8), pp. 45–51, especially p. 47.

was underlined in the comments of the under-agent, Robert Isaac, who informed the Blundell tenants in Dundrum that:

> if you or any of you misbehave in anything before-mentioned, I advise all of you to think with yourselves and consider that, if you fly in my face, the consequence will be that you also fly in the face of my Lord Blundell, your landlord, by whose authority I act. What I have premised, I hope will rectify all your mistakes that has [sic] happened hitherto, and if no more such happen for the future, then all of you may depend on my friendship as far as with justice I can extend it.[41]

A DIFFICULT TASK

Essentially, effective estate management at Edenderry hinged on the leasing arrangements which were put in place, and Hatch was frequently admonished for taking bribes and payment for granting the renewal of leases. However, leases were problematic and to a large extent beyond the control of the individual agent. The expiration of a lease, or indeed the death of a named lessee, was something which greatly troubled agent–tenant relations. Further complicating matters was the fact that many named on leases emigrated from the estate during these years. In 1757, for example, the settlement of a lease depended on two men who had since died in the East Indies and America.[42] In a number of instances Hatch's refusal to facilitate individual tenants meant that they brought their case directly before the co-heirs. In 1758 the Church of Ireland minster and churchwardens of the parish petitioned the co-heirs with regard to the plight of Elizabeth Murray, the schoolmistress whose lease expired with the death of Nathaniel Taylor. Arguing that Murray had provided greatly for the poor children of the parish and that money had been left in a will to pay annually 'a person capable of instructing the poor children of the parish together with a cabin for a school house', they believed that a lease should be granted to her. As this case indicated, both Hatch and his sub-agent, Williams, favoured family and friends in the granting of leases.[43]

---

[41] PRONI, Downshire papers, D607/A/52, Robert Isaac, Clough, to Henry Hatch, Dublin, 21 November 1747.

[42] See, for example, PRONI, Blundell papers, MIC/17, Miss Blundell to Henry Hatch, 18 June 1857.

[43] Taylor claimed that his information was trustworthy as his great-grandfather and grandfather had acted as agents of the Blundell estate at Edenderry 'for more than four score years', having come 'from their native place with Sir George Blundell'; PRONI, Blundell papers, MIC/17/1, Thomas Taylor to Miss Blundell, 16 June 1758.

Nepotism aside, it was sometimes difficult to encourage new tenants; in 1759 Hatch noted that 'the cottages are in such bad repair that if they cannot get tenants they will fall into decay'.[44] He did have some success attracting entrepreneurs to Edenderry including gunsmiths, brewers and chandlers. This of course complemented the fact that in the early years of the eighteenth century Blundell's leasing arrangements had allowed for the emergence of a merchant class in Edenderry, spearheaded in the main by the Quaker community. For example, in May 1755 a delighted Hatch informed Lord Blundell that two Quakers, Bewley and Wilson, were excellent proponents of industry in the area. In particular, Wilson was described as a 'man of fortune' who intended to establish a woollen manufacture in the town. Hatch advised that no new leases should be granted as they would be worth far more when Bewley and Wilson were 'up and running'.[45] In September some of the products of the woollen manufacture at Edenderry were sent to the Blundells, which it was hoped would 'answer in colour and goodness'.[46] Maintaining the estate as a centre of industry and commerce was central to Hatch's management. For example, he was opposed to the making of a new road connecting the villages of Clonbullogue and Portarlington, as this would have a detrimental effect on the Edenderry market. He was backed in his objections by the merchants of the town, who were willing to repair the roads leading to Edenderry at their own expense which were said to be in 'extreme bad order'.[47]

Although his visits to Edenderry were infrequent, Hatch was very much the landlords' 'man of business' and where possible undertook to represent them at official functions. Of upmost importance was his presence 'on the spot' at election time, something Henry Hatch took quite seriously, to ensure tenants voted in line with the landlords' wishes.[48] In 1757, for example, Hatch spent fourteen days at Philipstown (now

---

[44] PRONI, Blundell papers, MIC/17, John Hatch to William Trumbull, 15 March 1759.

[45] PRONI, Blundell papers, MIC/17/1, Henry Hatch to Lord Blundell, 5 May 1755.

[46] PRONI, Blundell papers, MIC/17/1, Henry Hatch to Lord Blundell, 25 September 1755.

[47] PRONI, Blundell papers, MIC/17/1, Henry Hatch to A. M. Blundell, 12 April 1757.

[48] In 1757 the Blundells lent their support to Richard Malone of Pallas, near Tullamore, for his election to the House of Commons, if he would oppose the building of new road from Edenderry to Portarlington in Queen's County; see PRONI, Blundell papers, MIC/17/1, William Trumbull to Henry Hatch, 14 May 1757.

Daingean) representing the Blundells at the election and was sorry to inform William Trumbull that 'their candidate was unsuccessful' owing to the fact that 'some of your tenants voted against us and others of them stayed at home'.[49] This must have been a disappointment to landlords and agent alike as prior to this Hatch had declared that although 'some of your tenants are wavering in their determination how they shall vote . . . I hope my being present will keep them steady'.[50]

While Hatch, and later his son, were praised for their efforts on official business, their continued absence during the eighteenth century negated against maintaining social order, and Edenderry was frequently troubled by crime and the presence of secret societies.[51] In 1781, for example, John Hatch's efforts to prevent several hundred trees from being cut on the estate were futile.[52] On most occasions Hatch avoided confrontation with the 'mob', which in the eyes of the tenantry weakened his authority.[53] When he did target the 'mob' Hatch regularly met with success. In 1784 he wrote that he 'got a most vile villain out of three parcels of land he held under you and out of a house which I had fitted up for myself and only put him into it to keep it for me'.[54] But for the most part it appears that it was not in their nature to be confrontational. In 1757 Henry Hatch advised William Trumbull that the tenants had not paid their rents owing to the 'calamitous season' but that he was 'convinced they are doing all in their power, do not choose to press them least it should disable them from tilling their grounds and consequently from providing the payment of their future rents'.[55]

Of course, there were also a number of factors outside of their control which often mitigated against effective estate management. A bad harvest and prolonged wet weather, for example, had the potential to generate unrest amongst the tenantry. This was particularly problematic when

[49] PRONI, Blundell papers, MIC/17/1, Henry Hatch to William Trumbull, 15 November 1757.

[50] PRONI, Blundell papers, MIC/17, Henry Hatch to William Trumbull, 9 October 1757.

[51] PRONI, Blundell papers, MIC/17, John Hatch to Miss Blundell, 17 February 1781.

[52] PRONI, Blundell papers, MIC/17, John Hatch to Miss Blundell, 17 February 1781.

[53] See, for example, PRONI, Blundell papers, MIC/17/1, John Hatch to Miss Blundell, 20 June 1783.

[54] PRONI, Blundell papers, MIC/17/1, John Hatch to Miss Blundell, 10 May 1784.

[55] PRONI, Blundell papers, MIC/17/1, Henry Hatch to William Trumbull, 9 October 1757.

turf ('the peculiar fuel of the people of those parts'[56]) was unavailable
for cutting. A far greater problem was the fact that neither Henry nor
John Hatch had recourse to the law or constabulary force. Without
recourse to the law, the agent was often prevented from carrying out
his duties. The Hatches were often prevented from ejecting tenants or
seizing farms as tenants came together to oppose them. In these difficult
times the agent was required to keep a watchful eye on all proceedings
on the estate. In this vacuum agrarian agitators regularly tormented
improvement at Edenderry, ranging from the building of churches to the
arrival of the Grand Canal. Towards the end of 1777, for example, John
Hatch was happy to report that the building of the Protestant church
progressed rapidly, despite the fact that it was frequently the target of
secret societies who stole building materials and disrupted work.[57] There
was widespread optimism in the mid-1780s with the news that the canal
would proceed towards the estate, which Hatch reckoned 'will be the
making of Edenderry'.[58] And there were further grounds for optimism
with the visit of the new owner of the estate, Lord Kilwarlin (and future
second Marquess of Downshire) in April 1789 when he was warmly
greeted by the tenantry.

However, the renewed interest did little to alter John Hatch's percep-
tion of the land agency business and, as already alluded to, by the early
1780s he had grown tired of his role and wished to be relieved of his
duties. In 1780 he wrote somewhat despondently to Lord Robert Bertie:

> I shall be ready to hand over the care of your affairs together with everything
> belonging to them to anyone your Lordship shall think more fit for that trust
> than me; it is a matter I have long wish'd to be discharged from, as I have
> been a slave the best part of my life to it.[59]

Five years later Hatch was once again anxious to resign his agency, citing
health reasons as his main concern.[60] Infirmity, old age and despondency
all contributed to an apparent lack of interest in the position of agent. In
addition, he conceded that Edenderry was merely a 'drooping town' and

[56] *Finns Leinster Journal*, 14 August 1790.
[57] PRONI, Downshire papers, D607/A/281, John Hatch to Miss Blundell, 7 January 1778.
[58] PRONI, Downshire papers, D607/A/316, John Hatch to Miss Blundell, 27 November 1786.
[59] PRONI, Blundell papers, MIC/17/1, John Hatch to Lord Robert Bertie, 28 November 1780.
[60] PRONI, Downshire papers, D607/A/297B, Miss Blundell, London, to John Hatch, Dublin, 8 September 1785.

that he could do little to revive it.[61] On another occasion he described the estate as 'in a very poor state and provisions of all kinds monstrously dear'.[62] So anxious was Hatch to be removed from the position that he was willing to settle the arrears on the estate himself in order to relinquish the agency, admitting that it could be attributed to negligence on his part.[63] The suggestion apparently appalled the Blundells who believed that their affairs were in the hands 'of a gentleman of so much integrity, truth and honour'.[64] It was enough to persuade Hatch on this occasion that he should not retire.[65]

The marriage of Mary Sandys, granddaughter of Lord Blundell to Arthur Hill in 1786 brought the estate under the control of the Hill family. By 1791 Hill, Lord Kilwarlin (and later Viscount Hillsborough) demanded support from Hatch on political matters, something which the agent greatly resented. Once more Hatch indicated his desire to resign, but Kilwarlin would not entertain the idea, arguing that he had 'successfully managed the estate for so long' that 'we all think that you are incapable of any misconduct towards us'.[66] The matter was obviously resolved and Hatch remained in the agency until his death in September 1797.

CONCLUSION

The evolution of the Irish land agency business was a long and arduous process, fraught with numerous difficulties. The case of the Hatches, father and son, highlights that their duties were numerous and sometimes confused, thereby hindering the effective management of the Blundell estate. While the renewed interest of the Blundell co-heirs from the 1750s meant that the agents were required to be more thorough in their dealings, these certainly were not professional in nature. However, the

---

[61] PRONI, Downshire papers, D607/A/302, John Hatch to Lord Sandys, 25 February 1786.

[62] PRONI, Blundell papers, MIC/17/1, John Hatch to Miss Blundell, 10 May 1784.

[63] PRONI, Downshire papers, D607/A/338, John Hatch to Miss Blundell, 24 August 1787.

[64] PRONI, Downshire papers, D607/A/340A, Miss Blundell to John Hatch, 1 September 1787.

[65] PRONI, Downshire papers, D607/A/356, John Hatch to Miss Blundell, 18 February 1788.

[66] NLI, Hatch papers, MS 10,212, Lord Hillsborough to John Hatch [n.d. but 1791].

Hatches can be said to have been clever in their approach to estate management, cultivating the local community to their own advantage and
avoiding confrontation where possible. For the Hatches it was deemed
more advantageous to ride out dissent, offering relief to tenants during
times of acute distress. These varied from periods of inclement weather
when the harvest (and more importantly the turf) was affected, to times
of economic depression. For example, in November 1759 a compassion-
ate Henry Hatch told the sisters that he would give 'indulgence' to the
tenants on account of the 'bad times experienced at present, owing to
two of the principal banks in Dublin stopping payment'.[67] Reciprocating
such an approach, the new co-heirs were careful to develop their reputation or at least to show that they had the interests of their tenantry
at heart. In March 1757 Anna Blundell gave £20 to help the poor of
Edenderry, a gesture praised by Hatch as it 'was never more wanted'.[68]
Moreover, through careful alliances, marriages and the use of Catholic
tenants (although frowned upon by their employers), the agents were
able to control an entire community. The examination of their land
agency business also reveals much about the enforcement of the Penal
Laws and in general the treatment of Catholic tenants throughout the
eighteenth century. As early as 1703, for example, Blundell allowed
tenants to 'keep papist cottiers or labourers, each to have one acre and
one cabin'.[69] Although by the 1750s the trustees of the estate insisted
that it would be 'more agreeable' to have Protestant tenants, in reality it
was impossible to implement such measures, particularly where labour
was concerned.[70] While Catholic tenants were an inevitable presence at
Edenderry, part of the problem with effective estate management lay
in attempts by agents to use middlemen to help in the management of
the estate vis-à-vis the collection of rent. Where middlemen defaulted,
as was often the case, the system crumbled as Henry and John Hatch
found to their detriment when dealing with Shawe Cartland.[71] The situation arose because eighteenth-century land agents were largely left to

[67] PRONI, Blundell papers, MIC/17/1, Henry Hatch to Miss Blundell, 24
November 1759.
[68] PRONI, Blundell papers, MIC/17/1, Henry Hatch to A. M. Blundell, 7 April
1757.
[69] See, for example, Fingal County Library, Hely Hutchinson papers, Box 59/14,
Francis Blundell to John Lawrence, 3 August 1703.
[70] PRONI, Blundell papers, MIC/17, A. M. Blundell, M. Raymond, W. Trumbull
to Henry Hatch, 1 March 1758.
[71] PRONI, Blundell papers, MIC/17/1, Lord Robert Bertie to John Hatch, 18
December 1781.

their own devices. Where they lacked the necessary skills and business acumen, it was hardly surprising that many foundered, or like John Hatch, wished to resign. It was only in the nineteenth century that landlords began to scrutinise the management of their estates, by then too late for some.

10

'Between two interests':
Pennant A. Lloyd's Agency of the Penrhyn Estate, 1860–77

Shaun Evans

INTRODUCTION

'I CAN TRULY SAY that I have served both landlord and tenant faithfully and honestly.'[1] So asserted Pennant A. Lloyd (1821–1909) at the ceremonial banquet held in December 1877 to bring a close to his eighteen-year stint as chief agent on the Penrhyn estate in north-west Wales (see Figure 7). Earlier in his career he stated his belief that 'the duties of men in his position [i.e. a land agent] were more difficult to perform than those persons in either higher or lower positions, [because] they stood between two interests'.[2] He concluded his retirement speech hoping that he would be remembered as someone 'who endeavoured conscientiously to do his duty by all – high and low, rich or poor'.[3] This sense of dualism and impartiality, of having responsibility for representing and intermediating between two factions, forms the primary focus of this chapter, and in this respect, reinforces one of the central themes highlighted across the case studies featured within this collection; that of the challenges land agents had to face. Though landlords and tenants usually had a strong mutual interest in sustaining good relations, maintaining a balance between their priorities could be fraught with difficulties. In his assessment of the land agent in nineteenth-century Wales, Richard J. Colyer noted the 'virtual impossibility of attaining universal popularity by steering the middle course', whereas G. E. Mingay concluded that the 'complexities and uncertainties of the work made estate management a thankless career'.[4]

---

[1] *The North Wales Chronicle* [hereafter *NWC*], 8 December 1877.
[2] *Caernarvon & Denbigh Herald* [hereafter *CDH*], 11 August 1866.
[3] *NWC*, 8 December 1877.
[4] R. J. Colyer, 'The land agent in nineteenth-century Wales', *Welsh History Review*, 8:4 (1977), pp. 401–25 (quote at p. 401); G. E. Mingay, 'The eighteenth-

Figure 7 Pennant A. Lloyd (1821–1909), by James
Sant (1820–1916), presented to Lloyd on his retirement
from the Penrhyn agency in 1877.

On his retirement, Lloyd concluded that his role at Penrhyn had been
'no ordinary agency'.[5] The specification and extent of the estate alone
presented a daunting challenge to the person charged with overseeing
its management. On his appointment in 1860, he took responsibility for
overseeing the third-largest estate in Wales, estimated at 43,974 acres in
1873 and continuing to expand across the period of his custodianship.[6]
The Penrhyn estate occupied a prominent feature in the life of the region,
and the role of chief agent was vested with considerable status, authority
and responsibilities. This was reflected in the size and appearance of

century land steward', in E. L. Jones and G. E. Mingay (eds), *Land, Labour and
Population in the Industrial Revolution: Essays Presented to J. D. Chambers*
(London, 1967), pp. 3–27 (quote at p. 7).

  [5] *NWC*, 8 December 1877.

  [6] B. Ll. Jones, 'The "great landowners" of Wales in 1873', *National Library of
Wales Journal*, 14:3 (1966), pp. 301–20. By 1893 it was claimed that the estate had
grown to 72,000 acres; *NWC*, 23 September 1893.

the agent's house at Lime Grove, Llandygái, which during the 1860s
was transformed into a three-storey Tudor-Gothic mansion.[7] In the
months prior to Lloyd's appointment, Penrhyn Castle hosted a visit by
Queen Victoria.[8] His new employer, Colonel Edward Douglas-Pennant
(1800–86), was in the highest rank of British landowners: the custodian
of an immense political, social and economic influence which radiated
throughout much of Caernarfonshire and surrounding areas.[9] A younger
brother to the 17th Earl of Morton, Douglas-Pennant had inherited
the Penrhyn estate in 1842 through his marriage to Juliana Isabella
Mary Douglas (1808–42), the heiress of George Hay Dawkins-Pennant
(1764–1840) of Penrhyn. Member of Parliament for Caernarfonshire
from 1841, Douglas-Pennant was appointed Lord Lieutenant of the
county in 1866, the same year in which he was elevated to the peerage
as Baron Penrhyn of Llandygái. R. Merfyn Jones has called him 'the
crucial element in Gwynedd society in the nineteenth century'.[10] On
top of his landed influence, Lord Penrhyn owned one of the largest and
most prosperous slate quarries in the world, which dominated local
industry.[11] In 1859 he employed 2,500 men at his quarries in Bethesda,
which generated an output of 120,000 tons and £100,000 annual net
profit.[12]

Partly driven by the income from their sugar plantations in Jamaica,
from the late eighteenth century Douglas-Pennant's predecessors at
Penrhyn had invested in an immense scheme of estate improvement and
diversification, overseen by the multitalented Benjamin Wyatt (1745–
1818) and his son James (1795–1882), who served as chief agents on
the estate successively between 1786 and 1859.[13] Benjamin was brother

---

[7] Lime Grove was originally built in the 1780s by Samuel Wyatt for his brother
Benjamin (see below); J. Davidson, *Plas y Coed: Bangor – Archaeological Mitigation:
Building Record*, Gwynedd Archaeological Trust Report No. 1254 (Bangor, 2015).

[8] Lloyd played a part in orchestrating the celebrations; *NWC*, 22 October 1859.

[9] For basic biographical details, see E. H. Douglas-Pennant, 'The Penrhyn estate
1760–1997: the Pennants and the Douglas-Pennants', *Caernarvonshire Historical
Society Transactions* [hereafter *CHST*], 59 (1998), pp. 35–54.

[10] R. M. Jones, *The North Wales Quarrymen, 1874–1922* (Cardiff, 1981),
p. 9.

[11] J. Lindsay, *A History of the North Wales Slate Industry* (London, 1974);
D. Gwyn, *Welsh Slate: Archaeology and History of an Industry* (Aberystwyth,
2015).

[12] *Mining Journal*, 10 September 1859, p. 639. In August 1866 it was reported
that Lord Penrhyn employed 2,700 men at the quarry; *NWC*, 11 August 1866.

[13] P. E. Jones, 'The Wyatts of Lime Grove, Llandygai', *CHST*, 42 (1981),
pp. 81–117; J. M. Robinson, *The Wyatts: An Architectural Dynasty* (Oxford,

to the celebrated architects Samuel (1737–1807) and James Wyatt (1746–1813). In addition to the development of the slate industry, the long-term vision of estate improvement, inherited and augmented by Douglas-Pennant, extended to increased agricultural productivity, major afforestation, significant building works (including the construction of a model village at Llandygái), enhanced transport infrastructure (including the narrow gauge Penrhyn Quarry Tramway) and the construction of Porth Penrhyn to facilitate the export of slate on a global scale.[14] On his retirement in 1859, James Wyatt was presented with a silver candelabrum by Douglas-Pennant 'in grateful remembrance of the zeal, talent and probity with which he conducted for forty-five years the agency of the Penrhyn properties'.[15] The task faced by Lloyd in stepping into the shoes vacated by the Wyatts was an intimidating one.

On top of this complex role specification, during Lloyd's time as agent, Penrhyn and its environs was emerging as a primary theatre for the playing out of a fierce confrontation about the nature and future of Welsh society. As David W. Howell has stated, 'during the 1860s and 1870s longstanding criticism of the gentry as political leaders ripened into a total attack on their very existence as a class'.[16] This attack was spearheaded by a radical Nonconformist movement, positioning as the true representatives of Welsh national consciousness and demanding emancipation from the traditional structure of society embodied by the power and privilege of landlordism in general, and Penrhyn in particular.[17] Land reform, disestablishment of the Anglican Church and the overthrow of Tory hegemony formed key planks in the campaign, all of which impinged upon the credentials of Douglas-Pennant. The highly effective narrative constructed in pursuit of this agenda often centred on drawing fundamental divisions in society, between the caricature of a Tory, Anglican and English-speaking landholding elite on the one hand, and the Liberal, Nonconformist and Welsh-speaking characteristics of a mythicised Welsh populace or *gwerin* on the other.[18] In the words of

1979), pp. 136–41. For the family's sugar plantations, see M. Gwyn, 'The heritage industry and the slave trade' (unpublished PhD thesis, Bangor University, 2014).

[14] Jones, 'Wyatts of Lime Grove', pp. 86–93.

[15] *NWC*, 21 January 1860.

[16] D. W. Howell, *Land and People in Nineteenth Century Wales* (London, 1978), p. 152.

[17] K. O. Morgan, *Wales in British Politics, 1868–1922* (Cardiff, 1991), pp. 1–27; Jones, *North Wales Quarrymen*, pp. 49–71.

[18] P. Morgan, 'The *gwerin* of Wales – myth and reality', in I. Hume and W. T. R. Pryce (eds), *The Welsh and their Country* (Llandysul, 1986), pp. 134–52.

K. O. Morgan, 'from this clash of two societies, modern Wales was to be forged'.[19] This all-pervading political context directly impacted on the relationship between landlord and tenant, and the traditional hierarchal way of life which Lloyd had responsibilities for upholding in his position as chief agent. A vibrant radical Nonconformist press – fronted by *Baner ac Amserau Cymru*, established in the year prior to Lloyd's appointment – used every opportunity to 'depict landlords as totally out of sympathy with their tenants', creating a 'myth of oppression' which only occasionally had a basis in fact.[20] 'There is a terrible diversity and antagonism between the proprietors of the soil and their tenants in Wales', claimed Rev. Henry Richard (1812–88), the prominent Nonconformist Member of Parliament for Merthyr Tydfil.[21] This climate provided a constant challenge to Lloyd as every action and decision made and implemented by the estate risked being commandeered as political capital. Preventing the polarisation of rural society became a crucial part of his role.

THE AGENT IN THE MAKING

Lloyd was born in 1821 as Pennant Athelwold Iremonger, the fourth son of William Iremonger (1776–1852) of Wherwell Priory in Hampshire.[22] Following the example of his father, he initially pursued a career in the army, progressing from the rank of ensign in 1838 to captain in 1845, with a considerable part of his service spent in India.[23] These military credentials echoed those of Colonel Douglas-Pennant (who served for thirty-two years in the Grenadier Guards until 1847) and provided Lloyd with the credentials of 'respectability' deemed necessary for the role: on his appointment, his new employer introduced him as a 'thorough gentleman and a man of honour'.[24] However, his background as a former army officer and the younger son of a relatively modest English

[19] Morgan, *Wales in British Politics*, pp. 9–10.

[20] Howell, *Land and People*, pp. 149, 151; see also p. 42; M. Cragoe, *Culture, Politics and National Identity in Wales 1832–1886* (Oxford, 2004), pp. 208–12.

[21] *The Llangollen Advertiser*, 9 July 1869. In response to this narrative, see M. Cragoe, *An Anglican Aristocracy: The Moral Economy of the Landed Estate in Carmarthenshire, 1832–1895* (Oxford, 1996), p. 26.

[22] For biographical details, see S. Evans, *The Lloyd Family of Pentrehobyn, Flintshire* (Mold, 2017), pp. 65–78.

[23] Ensign in the 8th Foot (King's) Regiment in April 1838; Lieutenant in the 84th (York and Lancaster) Regiment in April 1842; Captain in the 3rd West India Regiment in October 1845; and Captain in the 56th Regiment.

[24] *NWC*, 21 January 1860.

landowner also followed a pattern of appointment which was subject to criticism and grievance across the period.[25] He formed part of the large body of so-called 'untrained interlopers', including retired army officers, bank clerks, auctioneers and solicitors, who were regularly appointed to manage the landed estates of England and Wales during the nineteenth century.[26] These 'outsiders' usually had insufficient experience of agricultural practice, and in the case of Wales were recurrently brought in from England or Scotland without any understanding of the Welsh language, which formed a mainstay in rural life. In the prevailing political climate, land agents in Wales were 'frequently the recipients of abuse and vilification from the chapel pulpit and the radical press' – tarnished as incompetent, linguistically ignorant and, at worst, rapacious enforcers of their masters' schemes of tyranny.[27]

Iremonger did have existing links to Wales, through his mother, Pennant Thomas (1781–1872) of Coed Helen – a relatively small yet long-established Caernarfonshire estate – which allowed him to connect into the landholding network of north Wales.[28] His mother's Welsh lineage also featured at least two prominent land agents, which may have provided him with a familial grounding in the profession: Thomas Trevor Mather (d. 1846) of Pentrehobyn was resident agent on the Chirk Castle estate in Denbighshire during the early nineteenth century; and Peter Lloyd of Llanfyllin (d. 1775) served as Montgomeryshire steward and rent-collector on the sprawling landholdings of Sir Watkin Williams-Wynns.[29] On his mother's death in 1872, Iremonger inherited the Pentrehobyn estate in Flintshire, adopting the 'Lloyd' name and coat of arms under the instructions laid out in his grandmother's will.[30] Thus, Captain Iremonger became Pennant A. Lloyd.[31] In April 1850 he married Mary Elizabeth (c. 1823–1908), daughter of Pryce Jones of Cyfronydd, Montgomeryshire, a match which further bolstered his Welsh connections. After marrying, the couple settled in Caernarfon, living at Bryn Helen for much of the

---

[25] Howell, *Land and People*, pp. 44–5; E. Richards, 'The land agent', in G. E. Mingay (ed.), *The Victorian Countryside* (London, 1981), vol. 2, pp. 439–56, especially pp. 443–4, 450–1.

[26] Richards, 'Land agent', pp. 443–4, 450–1.

[27] Colyer, 'Land agent', p. 403; see also Morgan, *Wales in British Politics*, p. 5.

[28] Evans, *Pentrehobyn*, pp. 54–9.

[29] Evans, *Pentrehobyn*, pp. 44, 52.

[30] Evans, *Pentrehobyn*, pp. 54–9, 66; see also The National Archives, PROB 11/1713/391–3; Flintshire Record Office, D/KK/1121.

[31] *The Times*, 13 July 1872; NWC, 20 July 1872.

1850s with Lloyd serving as Adjutant and Captain of the Royal Caernarfon Regiment of Militia.[32]

Though he did not assume the agency of Penrhyn as a complete outsider, the enormity of the task faced by Lloyd only became clear during the course of his first couple of years in the role; a period which was hampered by injury, caused by a nasty fall from his horse in November 1860.[33] By September 1861 he had been forced to resign the captaincy of the 6th (Bangor) Corps of the Caernarfonshire Rifle Volunteers (which he had helped establish with Douglas-Pennant in c. 1860) on account of his growing workload on the estate.[34] At the end of his agency, Lloyd reflected with pleasure on the fact that 'for eighteen years, except on two occasions, I have never had an uncivil or disrespectful word from anyone'.[35] One of these occasions took place early on in his agency, when he was targeted by a local contingent wanting to vent publicly their condemnation of Douglas-Pennant. As part of the miscellaneous public responsibilities accompanying Lloyd's role, he served as chair at the meetings of the Llanllechid Vestry; Llanllechid being a large parish at the heart of the estate, forming part of Dyffryn Ogwen and including the Glynderau and Carneddau mountains. At one such meeting held on 21 February 1861 discussions veered towards the status and condition of 'the mountain', with Richard Hughes of Bethesda proposing that the land be free to all ratepayers, further claiming that 'since the poor had been excluded from the mountain, it was said to be under a curse'.[36] In 1858 Douglas-Pennant had purchased Llanllechid waste lands from the Crown and had quickly taken steps to enclose the area, employing a 'watcher' to protect his rights.[37] The conversations quickly morphed into a fiery debate on the general poverty and injustices of the neighbourhood, with the brunt of the blame placed squarely on the

[32] Gwynedd Archives (Caernarfon Record Office), XL1 14/6–7.

[33] NWC, 17 November 1860.

[34] B. Owen, Welsh Militia and Volunteer Corps, 1757–1908: 1 – Anglesey & Caernarfonshire (Caernarfon, 1989), pp. 152–5; NWC, 11 February 1860, 9 March 1861, 31 August 1861.

[35] NWC, 8 December 1877.

[36] NWC, 23 February 1861.

[37] Bangor University Archives and Special Collections [hereafter BUASC] Penrhyn PFA/3/116, PFA/15/30. Douglas-Pennant's predecessors had previously leased the lands; BUASC Penrhyn PFA/1/310. For estate plans of the lands in question, see BUASC Penrhyn Add. 1797, 2210. For the general context of enclosure in nineteenth-century Wales, see Howell, Land and People, pp. 38–41; and for Caernarfonshire in particular, see A. H. Dodd, A History of Caernarvonshire, 1284–1900 (Denbigh, 1968), pp. 235–40.

shoulders of Douglas-Pennant. In a violent verbal attack, Robert Jones (one of the overseers of the poor of the parish) claimed that the sheep were dying on the mountain and that the poor – who previously had the right to 'cut turf for firing' – were being prevented from cutting peat 'and even a few rushes to put under their pigs'.[38] Jones further alleged that the level of wages issued for work at the Penrhyn Quarry was deplorable.[39] Unprepared for the onslaught and unable to follow the flow of the Welsh-language attack, Lloyd insisted that the Vestry meeting was not the appropriate place to discuss estate matters, yet found himself singlehandedly having to defend his employer's character and rights and values as a landlord.[40]

The outpouring of public criticism caused ripples in local society. At the next meeting of the Bethesda Local Board of Health, Lloyd, who served as one of the commissioners and chaired meetings in the absence of his employer, opened proceedings with a lengthy speech on the 'uncalled-for attack made upon Col. Pennant' at the recent Vestry meeting, criticising its 'general tone' and resenting the fact that nobody had supported him in contradicting the claims.[41] Providing a full refutation of the allegations, he narrated the rights and conditions of tenure on the wastes and praised his employer's efforts to protect against the destruction of the pasture. He insisted that Douglas-Pennant was fully committed to 'improving' the agricultural potential of the mountain, outlining the proceedings of a meeting he had recently held in his estate office, where it had been agreed not to over-stock the sheep-walks.[42] Painting a picture of local prosperity, he argued that 'there was scarcely a cottage or a family in the neighbourhood which did not disprove' the allegations of poverty, and issued a staunch defence of the levels of wages issued to quarrymen.[43] Lloyd announced that in response to the attack, Douglas-Pennant was resigning from the Board of Health with

[38] NWC, 23 February 1861, 2 March 1861. Lloyd later confirmed that though the poor were not allowed to 'pare the grass sods generally', six places were set aside for people to cut peat; NWC, 9 March 1861.

[39] NWC, 23 February 1861.

[40] NWC, 23 February 1861. Lloyd claimed that 'his ignorance of the language and [the] novelty of his position' had been seized upon by the complainants; NWC, 9 March 1861.

[41] NWC, 9 March 1861. For Lloyd's and Douglas-Pennant's involvement in the local boards of health, see P. E. Jones, 'The Bangor Local Board of Health, 1850–83', CHST, 37 (1976), pp. 87–132.

[42] NWC, 9 March 1861; BUASC Penrhyn 1802, fos. 220–4.

[43] NWC, 9 March 1861.

immediate effect, a move which was replicated by Lloyd himself and other members of Board closely associated with the Penrhyn interest, all using the occasion to defend the position of Douglas-Pennant – 'our kind benefactor' – and to criticise the 'ungratefulness' shown towards him.[44]

Over the next few days a series of public meetings was arranged in the vicinity to reaffirm the community's outward projection of loyalty and attachment to Douglas-Pennant and 'to contradict the personal attack made upon him'.[45] The assembled crowds were eager to ensure 'that a whole neighbourhood should [not] suffer' as a consequence of Douglas-Pennant's withdrawal from the Board of Health, and the proceedings were packed with praise for his benevolence and liberality. Mr Roberts of Brynmeurig affirmed that 'Col. Pennant has given at least £1,700 to Bethesda during the past 2–3 years'; with Mr J. Hughes of the Douglas Arms listing his expenditure on bringing water through the town, contributing towards the work of the Improvement Board and Gas Company, supporting the erection of new National and British schools and paying £12,000 for the building of a new church.[46] At a special meeting of tenant farmers, Elias Williams of Bronydd heaped praise on his landlord's support of new agricultural methods, commenting on the rewards he made available for good farming practice; his introduction of bulls to improve breeding; and for materially improving the land through drainage. At this meeting William Parry of Corbri's motion 'that it is not oppression on the part of the Hon. Col. Pennant, *nor his agents*, which is the cause of the poverty in the parish', was unanimously accepted.[47] However, the underlying sense of grievance and resentment articulated at the Llanllechid Vestry meeting did not disappear. Douglas-Pennant's drive to transform the productivity of his landholdings often cut across local customary practice and communal rights, exacerbating feelings of social and cultural injustice.[48] When in 1867 the newly ennobled 1st Baron Penrhyn intervened in his capacity as Lord Lieutenant to quell the 'disorder' and 'lawlessness' emanating from the 1858 enclosure of Caerhun and Llanbedr-y-Cennin mountain commons, his actions were

[44] *NWC*, 9 March 1861.
[45] *NWC*, 9 March 1861.; see also *NWC*, 23 March 1861.
[46] *NWC*, 9 March 1861.
[47] *NWC*, 9 March 1861 (emphasis added).
[48] This theme is discussed in R. W. Hoyle, 'Introduction: custom, improvement and anti-improvement', in R. W. Hoyle (ed.), *Custom, Improvement and the Landscape in Early Modern Britain* (Farnham, 2010), pp. 1–38.

encapsulated in a couplet which persisted in local consciousness for the next half-century:[49]

Mi gewch chi'ch crogi am ddwyn dafad oddi ar y mynydd;
Ond am ddwyn y mynydd mi gewch chi'ch gwned yn Arglwydd

(You will be hung for stealing a sheep from the mountain; / but for stealing the mountain you will be made a Lord)

The Llanllechid episode shone a spotlight on a number of issues which contextualised the entirety of Lloyd's agency. The Penrhyn estate had a reach and relevance in local society well beyond the sphere of landlord–tenant relations; its management, actions and standing were the subject of intense and often highly polarised public discourse. Much of this discourse took place through the medium of Welsh, a language which Lloyd did not speak nor fully understand. For example, at a meeting arranged by Lloyd with tenant farmers in February 1866, Rev. John Evans, Rector of Llanllechid, was called upon to translate his proposals for the benefit of monoglot Welsh tenants.[50] For a role so dependent on the formation and maintenance of good relations, the inability to communicate in the primary language of the community formed a significant barrier.[51] Throughout his agency, language remained a divide between landlord and the vast majority of tenants, which Lloyd was unable to bridge.

The reaction to the Llanllechid attack also emphasised that Lloyd had responsibility for representing the interests of a landowner who was deeply concerned with his own public image and the preservation of his position of pre-eminence. The management of the estate – the appearance and condition of its landscapes and built environments, the quality of agricultural practice, the state of relationships with tenants, the economic output of its quarries and its wider contribution towards the welfare and well-being of the community – formed an essential part of Douglas-Pennant's self-image. He remained continuously, extensively

---

[49] NWC, 17 August 1867, 26 October 1867; see also BUASC Penrhyn PFA 8/10, PFA 8/22; J. Chapman, *A Guide to Parliamentary Enclosures in Wales* (Cardiff, 1992), pp. 42, 45. For Lloyd's evidence to the Welsh Land Commission on this subject, see NWC, 8 September 1894. For context, see C. W. J. Withers, 'Conceptions of cultural landscape change in upland North Wales: a case study of Llanbedr-y-Cennin and Caerhun parishes, c. 1560–c. 1891', *Landscape History*, 17 (1995), pp. 35–47.

[50] NWC, 10 February 1866.

[51] For the status of Welsh language on the Penrhyn estate, see Jones, *North Wales Quarrymen*, pp. 56–7.

194   SHAUN EVANS

and actively engaged in the management of his estate and local affairs,
even during the periods he spent away from his landholdings, particularly
at his Mortimer House residence in London.[52] The landscape and the
built environment of the estate were socially appropriated as a discourse
through which Lord Penrhyn sought to frame his identity and his hierarchal relations with his tenants and other individuals residing within his
geographical sphere of interest and influence.[53] The interlinked tools of
paternalism and philanthropy were employed to their full capacity, as
primary antidotes to the criticisms levelled at him. Lloyd had an essential
role to play in promoting and delivering his employer's desired image.
During Lord Penrhyn's absences and with routine matters, Lloyd was
permitted to 'take a certain amount of responsibility upon myself' and
'acted on behalf of and personally represented' his employer in a range
of local contexts.[54] As with every good land agent, all public credit for
his successes was channelled to Lord Penrhyn. In his retirement speech
he referred to the 'purchases, improvements, church building, parson-
age house and shop building, re-erecting farm houses and buildings
continuously added by purchase to the estate [and] plantation making',
concluding that 'I can safely say that all this work was as much looked
after as one man could look after it.'[55]

Good landlord–tenant relations formed an essential part of the rhetoric of proprietorship, paternalism and philanthropy espoused by the
Penrhyn estate. Reflecting on this agenda, Lloyd stated:

I have never spared myself in going away among them [the tenants] and
learning their wants in ascertaining the condition of every farmhouse, farm
building and cottage to know where the money allowed me should be spent;
and of Lord Penrhyn's 800 cottages, there is not one that I do not know the
condition of.[56]

In 1868 it was asserted that 'the comfortable and beautiful farmhouses
and outbuildings erected upon [Lord Penrhyn's] estate here are substantial monuments of his generosity and of his care for the health

[52] For further arguments against the established narrative of absenteeism, see
Howell, *Land and People*, pp. 42–3; Cragoe, *Anglican Aristocracy*, p. 16, n. 10.
[53] Based on the approach outlined in D. E. Cosgrove, *Social Formation and
Symbolic Landscape* (London, 1998).
[54] See, for example, NWC, 15 April 1865.
[55] NWC, 8 December 1877. The letter books kept by Lloyd during his time as
agent detail all aspects of his role and activities; BUASC Penrhyn 1801–7; see also
BUASC Penrhyn PFA 8/5, PFA 14/401.
[56] NWC, 8 December 1877.

and happiness of his tenants'.[57] Towards the end of the nineteenth century about a third of gross rental income was being reinvested in improvement works.[58] Amidst a political narrative centred on insecurity of tenure, rent increases and eviction, in 1869 Lord Penrhyn issued a rigorous defence of his tenancy agreements at a meeting of the Anglesey and Caernarfonshire Agricultural Society.[59] He claimed that:

> for the past 20 years on his estates, every tenant had had guaranteed security, viz. a term of 30 years for improvements such as the erection of buildings, 20 years for drainage and levelling and for 2 or 3 years for lime, guano or bone manure.[60]

He kept a team of men at his own expense to destroy rabbits on his tenants' farms, and received praise for bringing in West Highland, Angus and Galloway bulls to improve the quality of his tenants' cattle stock.[61] In February 1866 he reacted quickly, in tandem with Lloyd, to meet with tenants to discuss precautions for a potential cattle plague, supporting a scheme of vaccination and the creation of a joint fund to buy infected livestock.[62] The illustrated address presented to him on elevation to peerage praised him as:

> the first to adopt the most approved methods of modern agriculture, thereby converting fields, which a few years ago were barren and unproductive, into lands teeming with produce and in a stage of cultivation unsurpassed by any other lands in the kingdom.[63]

Messages of gratification, flattery and appreciation formed key parts of the ceremonies and celebrations accompanying events such as the visit of Queen Victoria (1859) and Lord Penrhyn's elevation to the peerage (1866), with the *North Wales Chronicle* content to act as a regular mouthpiece for Penrhyn's agenda. Beyond the realms of agriculture, he supported and funded the erection and rebuilding of schools, churches, chapels, hospitals and infirmaries, model cottages and other public buildings on an epic scale, right across his dominions, 'bringing all the appliances of great wealth to foster and promote every good work'.[64]

[57] *NWC*, 14 November 1868.
[58] Howell, *Land and People*, p. 51.
[59] *NWC*, 25 September 1869, 2 October 1869, 16 October 1869.
[60] *NWC*, 25 September 1869; see also 2 October 1869, 16 October 1869.
[61] *NWC*, 20 April 1867, 6 October 1860.
[62] *NWC*, 10 February 1866.
[63] *NWC*, 11 August 1866.
[64] Lord Penrhyn's obituary, printed in *NWC*, 3 April 1886, which lists many of his building works and charitable contributions; see also M. L. Clarke, 'Church

Lloyd played an important role in facilitating the development and
delivery of these investments, which sought to link the promotion of
well-being and welfare in the region to the material prosperity of the
estate and its owner. In 1871, for example, Lloyd arranged for a lease
of land to accommodate the building of an entrance for the new Treflys
Independent Chapel in Bethesda. In response to Lord Penrhyn's generosity, the prominent Independent Minister William Nicholson (1844–85)
issued a public statement which declared that 'in spite of false reports
that were circulated about his lordship in recent years, they [the parish-
ioners] cherish the profoundest feeling of respect towards him'.[65]

THE AGENT UNDER PRESSURE

Despite the depiction of harmony, munificence, welfare and improvement promoted through the work of the estate, an equally assertive
counternarrative centred on themes of privilege, subjugation, ignorance
and neglect gathered considerable traction over the course of the late
nineteenth century. This impinged upon the operation of Lloyd's agency
in a variety of ways. Throughout 1867, for example, he faced a series of
terse interviews at the Bethesda Local Board of Health (chaired by Lord
Penrhyn) on drainage provisions for ten new leasehold cottages in the
Henbarc/Coetmor part of the district, the suggestion being that Lloyd
had reneged on a promise to drain the land to the rear of the properties.[66] Lord Penrhyn and Lloyd both felt that their fellow commissioners
were continuously resurrecting the case in an effort to undermine and
discredit the estate's image of liberality, with Lloyd further complaining
that the allegations were 'calculated to seminate among the tenants an
idea that the manager had broken faith with them'.[67] In the same year
Lloyd was also reprimanded by the Bangor and Beaumaris Board of
Guardians for the poor standard of repairs made to cottages in Aber,
recently purchased by the estate and designated as 'not fit for human
habitation' by the inspector.[68] Lloyd's response was to point out that
'during the last five years his lordship has expended no less than £10,000
in cottage improvements alone'.[69]

building and church restoration in Caernarvonshire during the nineteenth century',
CHST, 22 (1961), pp. 20–31.
  [65] *NWC*, 2 December 1871.
  [66] *NWC*, 20 April 1867, 12 October 1867.
  [67] *NWC*, 31 August 1867.
  [68] *NWC*, 16 February 1867.
  [69] *NWC*, 16 February 1867.

The following year witnessed the biggest affront to the political power of Penrhyn since Douglas-Pennant's assumption of the patriarchy. The election of 1868, held with a widened electorate, is viewed in Liberal tradition as a 'national awakening' which fundamentally altered the balance of power in Wales; in the words of David Lloyd George (1863–1945), 'the political power of landlordism in Wales was shattered'.[70] George Sholto Douglas-Pennant (1836–1907), Lord Penrhyn's son and heir, lost the county seat to the Liberal candidate Sir Love Jones Parry (1832–91) of Madryn, who fought the campaign on the anti-Penrhyn slogan of 'trech gwlad nag arglwydd' ('a land is stronger than its lord').[71] At the Great Welsh Reform Meeting held in Liverpool in 1868, Rev. Dr William Rees ('Gwilym Hiraethog', 1802–83) declared to the assembled audience that in Caernarfonshire 'you will find a lord alien in blood and language, exercising supreme control over the minds and consciousness of the whole population'.[72] During the campaign, Lord Penrhyn was allegedly attacked by some 1,500 quarrymen when out canvassing on behalf of the Tory cause.[73] It is unknown what role Lloyd played, if any, in canvassing for the Penrhyn interest amongst the tenantry, though in general the land agent was recognised as forming part of the established wielders of power capable of applying electoral pressure through what was colloquially known as *y scriw*.[74] In return, the Tories complained of an equally potent chapel *scriw*. From February 1868 Lloyd had been corresponding with Richard Parry ('Gwalchmai', 1803–97) about a request for the Penrhyn estate to make land available for the building of a new Congregational Chapel at Chwarel Goch, Tregarth.[75] Lord Penrhyn refused to cede to the request, arguing that he had already supported the erection of chapels at Nant y Benglog and Tyn y Maes. Parry, however, was persistent in his agitation and succeeded in politicising Penrhyn's refusal. The long sequence of letters between Parry and Lloyd on the subject was published in the local press, including lines

[70] Morgan, *Wales in British Politics*, pp. 22–5; see also P. Jenkins, *A History of Modern Wales, 1536–1990* (London, 1992), pp. 321–4.

[71] *CDH*, 28 October 1868; E. Douglas-Pennant, 'The second Lord Penrhyn (1836–1907)' (unpublished MPhil thesis, Bangor University, 1994).

[72] *NWC*, 20 June 1868, 11 July 1868.

[73] Cragoe, *Culture, Politics and National Identity*, p. 233, referencing *CDH*, 7 November 1868, 14 November 1868.

[74] Dodd, *History of Caernarvonshire*, p. 360. Despite backing the Penrhyn interest throughout his agency, on retirement Lloyd became a vocal proponent of Gladstone's reform agenda; Evans, *Pentrehobyn*, pp. 76–7.

[75] *NWC*, 7 November 1868, 14 November 1868.

from Parry aimed at galvanising support for the Liberal candidature: 'His lordship ought to be informed that the Welsh, being a nation of Nonconformists can never be satisfied by the multiplication of State Church buildings'; 'there are duties as well as privileges in connection with property'.[76] *Baner ac Amserau Cymru* accused Lord Penrhyn of religious intolerance, promoting a line that he and his agent had refused permission for a new chapel because of their opposition to the Liberal politics of its chief proponents.[77]

Although much of the electorate inhabiting the sphere of the estate remained loyal in their deference to the Penrhyn interest – out of 'a mixture of habit, ignorance, fear and genuine loyalty' – the loss of the seat represented a major blow to Penrhyn's standing.[78] On the day of the poll, two of Penrhyn's gamekeepers – George Hunter and William Thomas – became embroiled in a confrontation at the Horseshoe Inn at Penmachno, which led to accusations that Hunter had attempted to shoot two quarrymen who were celebrating the Liberal victory, and in turn faced accusations of battering the keeper.[79] In his position as chief agent, Lloyd had to deal with the repercussions, with the resulting court case perpetuating political divisions on the estate over several months. Similarly, Penrhyn did not escape the Wales-wide pattern and narrative of eviction which accompanied the aftermath of the election.[80] It was alleged that eighty quarrymen were dismissed from the Penrhyn Quarry on account of their political leanings, a claim which was strenuously denied by Lord Penrhyn.[81] Similar allegations were repeated in 1870 after between eighty-five and a hundred men were laid off from the Cae-Braich-y-Cafn quarry on account of the depressed state of the market.[82] The quarry was increasingly emerging as the primary focus for discord on the estate.

If 1868 was the year that broke Lord Penrhyn's political hold over

[76] *NWC*, 14 November 1868.

[77] *Baner ac Amserau Cymru*, 24 October 1868; *NWC*, 17 October 1868.

[78] Howell, *Land and People*, p. 151; see also Jones, *North Wales Quarrymen*, pp. 51–2.

[79] *Baner ac Amserau Cymru*, 23 December 1868, 6 January 1869, 7 April 1869; *CDH*, 2 January 1869; *NWC*, 19 December 1868, 9 January 1869, 3 April 1869.

[80] M. Cragoe, 'The anatomy of an eviction campaign: the General Election of 1868 in Wales and its aftermath', *Rural History*, 9:2 (1998), pp. 177–93; Jenkins, *History of Modern Wales*, p. 324; Morgan, *Wales in British Politics*, pp. 25–6.

[81] *Yr Herald Cymreig*, 24 October 1868, referenced in Morgan, *Wales in British Politics*, p. 26; see also Gwynedd Archives (Caernarfon Record Office), XPQ/1175.

[82] *Baner ac Amserau Cymru*, 6 July 1870, 13 July 1870, 30 July 1870, 3 August 1870; W. J. Parry, *The Penrhyn Lock-Out* (London, 1901), p. 7.

the region, it was 1874 that signalled a loosening of his capitalist control over his extensive quarry workforce. As evidenced by the Llanllechid Vestry controversy, tensions had been simmering for some time about the management of the Penrhyn Quarry and the working and living conditions of its quarrymen.[83] Lord Penrhyn's insistence on managing the quarry as he saw fit was increasingly at odds with significant parts of his workforce who were pressing on the right to form a union to canvass on conditions, wages and management.[84] In April 1874 a North Wales Quarrymen's Union was established, instigating strikes throughout Caernarfonshire, including at Lord Penrhyn's works in Bethesda from 31 July.[85] Both sides stuck stubbornly to their principles, embodied by Lord Penrhyn's assertion that 'I shall resist any such interference with the rights of proprietors of quarries and shall if such support [for the Union] be continued, immediately close the quarry.'[86] In return the quarrymen's representatives attacked at the heart of Penrhyn's strategy of philanthropic paternalism, declaring that 'we are perfectly willing that his lordship should keep his charities to himself – if those in any way interfere with him in his giving us proper wages'.[87] As chief agent, it was Lloyd who was called upon, on the recommendation of the workforce, to manufacture a compromise. This nomination recognised the fact that his role made him best placed to secure an agreement between capital and labour, landlord and tenant, which in this instance were largely synonymous – 1,600 of the men working in the Penrhyn Quarry also lived on the estate.[88]

With some reluctance, Lloyd agreed to negotiate with W. J. Parry (1842–1927) and the Quarrymen's Committee on behalf of Lord Penrhyn.[89] By 12 September he had managed to secure a deal on rates of pay, conditions of employment and changes in management which

[83] Parry, *Penrhyn Lock-Out*, p. 1. There were strikes at the Penrhyn Quarry in 1825, 1846, 1852 and 1865; Lindsay, *North Wales Slate Industry*, pp. 201–6.

[84] On 13 December 1873 the *CDH* published an editorial on the 'wretched' working conditions in the quarry.

[85] For the background to the formation of the North Wales Quarrymen's Union and chronology of the strike, see Jones, *North Wales Quarrymen*; Parry, *Penrhyn Lock-Out*, pp. 7–34; Lindsay, *North Wales Slate Industry*, pp. 213–18.

[86] Parry, *Penrhyn Lock-Out*, p. 8.

[87] Parry, *Penrhyn Lock-Out*, p. 13.

[88] Jones, *North Wales Quarrymen*, pp. 19–20, 25–6.

[89] For Lloyd's correspondence with Lord Penrhyn on the negotiation of the agreement, see BUASC PQS/324–405; see also Gwynedd Archives (Caernarfon Record Office), XPQ/1177–1202.

convinced the quarrymen to return to work after a seven-week strike.[90] This arrangement included Lloyd's appointment as Supreme Manager, to oversee the quarry managers, proposed by the Committee as 'an arrangement [which] would gain the confidence of the men'.[91] An employee-controlled Quarry Committee was to be formed to consider grievances and bring them to the attention of Lloyd who was to act as arbitrator.[92] The negotiations had been incredibly tense and closely followed by the local and national media. During this period Lloyd faced bouts of criticism from his employer and appears to have suffered a heart attack, which came close to taking his life, causing him to spend some time recuperating in France and Luxembourg soon after the finalisation of the accord. Lloyd later described the whole episode as intolerable.[93] Although not without controversy, the principals of what became known as the 'Pennant Lloyd Agreement' remained in force between 1874 and 1885. The agreement delivered profound change to the way the quarry was managed, giving a meaningful voice to the workforce. Many quarrymen looked upon it as their 'Great Charter', and the occasion was celebrated through the production of a souvenir print.[94] It earned Lloyd a reputation for bridging the gap between the quarry workforce and the industrial proprietorship of Lord Penrhyn, which was to endure for the rest of his life. The agreement evidenced the full potential of a land agent to mediate between landlord and tenant, identifying a solution which eased, at least temporarily, parts of a tension which threatened to tear apart local society and the integrity of the estate. In his retirement speech Lloyd commented that 'it was very satisfactory to me at the time of the quarry strike to find the confidence of the men placed in me, by which I was able to name a settlement to both sides'.[95]

---

[90] Parry, *Penrhyn Lock-Out*, pp. 28–9. The agreement is printed as appendix 2 in Jones, *North Wales Quarrymen*, p. 331. Further strike action followed during the autumn, which ensured that the agreement was implemented to the Union's satisfaction; *CDH*, 21 November 1874.

[91] Parry, *Penrhyn Lock-Out*, pp. 17–18; BUASC PQS/375; Gwynedd Archives (Caernarfon Record Office), XM/1647/4.

[92] He was later replaced in this role by Arthur Wyatt; Gwynedd Archives (Caernarfon Record Office), XPQ/1239.

[93] *North Wales Weekly News*, 29 January 1909.

[94] D. Gwyn, 'Vaunting and disrespectful notions: Charles Mercier's portrait of the Penrhyn Quarry Committee and Lord Penrhyn', *CHST*, 61 (2000), pp. 99–110.

[95] *NWC*, 8 December 1877.

CONCLUSION

Lloyd announced his intention to resign from the agency in March 1877, to take up his inheritance of the Pentrehobyn estate in Flintshire.[96] He was to be replaced by Colonel the Honourable W. E. Sackville West (1830–1905) who served in the post until 1898.[97] In December 1877 Lloyd was presented with an oil painting of himself by the artist James Sant (1820–1916) (see Figure 7) and an illustrated testimonial album bearing the signatures of the 562 tenants, neighbours and friends who had raised a total of 350 guineas for the artwork through subscription.[98] The address noted that 'for eighteen years you have held the management of the Penrhyn estates, a position charged with great responsibilities and duties of an important character':[99]

> The cheerful cooperation, active assistance and practical sympathy accorded to the testimonial committee by all classes of the tenantry – from the largest farmer down to the humblest cottager – afford the best proof of the ability, fidelity and impartiality [with] which those important duties have been fulfilled and how the interests both of landlord and tenant have been conscientiously and honourably regarded and maintained by one who, in his deeds, has shown himself:
>
> Of soul sincere
> In action faithful, and in honour clear,
> Who broke no promise; serv'd no private end;
> Who made no foe, and lost no friend.[100]

[96] *Wrexham Guardian*, 3 March 1877; Evans, *Pentrehobyn*, pp. 69–78.

[97] *Wrexham Guardian*, 24 November 1877; CDH, 27 May 1898, 24 June 1898.

[98] NWC, 8 December 1877. Lord Penrhyn though, was conspicuously absent from the ceremony.

[99] NWC, 8 December 1877.

[100] NWC, 8 December 1877.

PART IV

Social Memory and the Land Agent

11

John Campbell ('Am Baillidh Mor'), Chamberlain to the 7th and 8th Dukes of Argyll: Tradition and Social Memory

Robin K. Campbell

The Cottar Tribe, who are the Locusts of the Land ... they comprise the indolent, uncivilised and pauperism of the Estate ... His Grace of Argyll never speculated money to such advantage as to get rid of them by all possible speed.[1]

I would watch them and all those who are not industrious would most assuredly be deprived of their possessions. Nothing but harshness and dread I find will do, they are so naturally slothful and indolent.[2]

I have daily, numerous applications for food ... unless they work they must just starve.[3]

INTRODUCTION

AT 1 P.M. ON a Saturday afternoon at the end of August 1872, on the island of Mull within a small, felt-roofed blackhouse in the Ardfenaig steading, a very tall and heavily built man who had been feared the length and breadth of the islands of Mull, Iona and Tiree, and who had lain stretched out on a bed for the previous two weeks, gasped his last breath and died, having collapsed earlier at the steading. So began the myth of a man still passionately spoken about today, 145 years after his death. Vivid oral traditions have survived about his life on Mull during his twenty-six years there and his eighteen years on Tiree as Chamberlain for the Duke of Argyll. He is regarded in oral tradition as being one of the most notorious chamberlains in Argyllshire, if not Scotland, during the nineteenth century. His name was John Campbell, a Gaelic speaker from the island of Islay (see Figure 8). He became

---

[1] Inveraray Castle Papers [hereafter IC], National Register of Archives for Scotland [hereafter NRAS] 1209, bundle 1522, [n.d.] 1847.

[2] IC, NRAS1209, bundle 1522, 14 March 1847.

[3] IC, NRAS1209, bundle 1804, 19 December 1850.

Chamberlain of the Inner Hebridean islands of Mull, Iona and Tiree at the time the potato blight arrived in the 1840s, which had such devastating consequences for all who lived there.

Oral tradition relates that dogs howled all night the day before he died with a premonition of his imminent death and that maggots had infiltrated his body so that 'he became alive like a maggoty sheep'.[4] After he died, 'animals broke their ties and the barking of the Ardfenaig dogs were heard in Ardtun'.[5] A frequently told story on Islay relates to Campbell's old family home, where it was said that on the day he died every bell in Ardmore House rang.[6] Even after his death, stories still abounded. One oral tradition bearer, who had spent all his life in Bunessan in the Ross of Mull, remembered listening to old people recalling ghostly sightings of John Campbell walking across the Ardfenaig Marches to the Tiraghoil burn, dragging chains behind him.[7] He had spoken to many men who had witnessed this spectre. Another recalled her relation who worked for Campbell, referring to an uncomfortable and disturbing presence felt inside Ardfenaig House after his death and her reluctance to enter.[8]

During his life he had been known on Mull and Iona as *Am Factor Mor* ('the Big Factor') and on Tiree as *Am Baillidh Mor* ('the Big Baillie') and *Am Baillidh Dubh* ('the Black Baillie'), with two of the epithets emphasising the physical size and social authority of the man who had administered the islands on behalf of the duke until his death in 1872. The latter sobriquet, for some, referred to his dark hair but, for others, to his dark deeds during his time as chamberlain. Some described him as being completely devoid of pity and compassion and pointed to the evidence presented to the Napier Commission in 1883 as proof.[9]

This Royal Commission had been established in 1883 by the Home Secretary, Sir William Harcourt, on the orders of the Prime Minister, William Gladstone, to look into the 'condition of the crofters and cottars in the Highlands and Islands of Scotland, and all matters affect-

[4] E. M. MacArthur, *Iona: The Living Memory of Crofting Community* (Edinburgh, 1990), p. 138.
[5] Campbell of Ardmore Papers [hereafter CAP], J. Campbell, Bunessan, correspondence with the author, 5 July 1986.
[6] School of Scottish Studies, University of Edinburgh, SA 1969028.
[7] CAP, recording of oral tradition bearer, Ian MacFadyen, Mull, 4 June 1986.
[8] CAP, recording of oral tradition bearer, Mull, 8 October 2014.
[9] *Evidence Taken by Her Majesty's Commissioners of Inquiry into the Condition of the Crofters and Cottars in the Highlands and Islands of Scotland* [hereafter *Napier Commission Evidence*] (Edinburgh, 1884).

Figure 8 John Campbell (1801–72), the Duke of Argyll's chamberlain, and his wife Flora MacNeil. Image courtesy of Robin K. Campbell.

ing the same, or relating thereto'.[10] Six Commissioners (Lord Francis Napier, Sir Kenneth MacKenzie of Gairloch, Sir Donald Cameron of Lochiel, Charles Fraser-Mackintosh MP, Sheriff Alexander Nicolson of Kirkcudbright and Professor Donald MacKinnon of Edinburgh University) and a secretary (Malcom M'Neill) were appointed for the task under the chairmanship of Lord Napier, and their report was published in 1884. Within two years the Crofters Holdings (Scotland) Act was passed in 1886 providing security of tenure for crofters, compensation for improvements to the land and a review of rents through the Land Court. However, there appeared no solution for the landless cottars.[11] Mounting public and political pressure had been gathering pace in the years running up to the establishment of the Napier Commission as a result of increasing resistance by crofters and cottars to high rents and forced evictions. Rent strikes and seizures of land exacerbated an already tense situation in the Highlands. During the 1880s the deteriorating economic conditions and increased newspaper coverage helped to raise public concern and place further pressure on

[10] *Report of Her Majesty's Commissioners of Inquiry into the Condition of the Crofters and Cottars in the Highlands and Islands of Scotland* (Edinburgh, 1884), p. 1.

[11] E. A. Cameron, *Land for the People?: The British Government and the Scottish Highlands, c. 1880–1925* (East Linton, 1996), pp. 16–39.

the government to take action over the plight of the crofters and cottars in the Highlands.

The complaints and grievances produced to the Napier Commission in 1883 against Campbell and many other estate officials, both past and present, in many respects followed a familiar pattern. There were charges of oppression, misrule and harsh treatment against the crofters and cottars, unreasonable increases in rent, the removal of common pasture, insecurity of tenure and no compensation for improvements in cases of removal. The common view of the factor was summed up by one Sutherland crofter, Donald Macdonald:

> the then factor stood in our way like a flaming sword, so that until this year, we have not ventured to give public expression to our grievances. So long, then, we have crouched under the iron heel of the oppressor without a groan.[12]

The grievances presented against Campbell and others were not made under oath, in common with other statements made by the delegates to the Commission, and therefore could not be corroborated. This was acknowledged by the Commissioners in their report:

> In judging of the validity of much of this evidence, we shall do well to remember that these depositions, regarding acts and incidents often obscure and remote, are in many cases delivered by illiterate persons speaking from early memory, or from hearsay or from popular tradition ... Many of the allegations of oppression and suffering with which these pages are painfully loaded would not bear a searching analysis.[13]

Nevertheless, the grievances against Campbell, who had died eleven years previously, were numerous and consistent and fed social memory and tradition. They also touched upon areas which were not as common in other complaints made against estate officials elsewhere. Nepotism was one particular criticism levelled against Campbell due to the favouritism he showed to Islay incomers, friends and family as well as the coterie of estate officials working directly for him. *Morlanachd* – the provision of forced free labour from the cottars and crofters, for so many days of the year, for himself and the duke – was another injustice bitterly remembered. One crofter from Iona stated that 'we were forced to work for him with our horses and carts, without food or wages, any time he thought proper to ask us'.[14] The descriptions of the forced evic-

---

[12] *Napier Commission Evidence*, p. 2621.
[13] *Napier Commission Evidence*, p. 2.
[14] *Napier Commission Evidence*, Q. 44074.

tions by Campbell of the elderly, the blind, the mentally and physically disabled, pregnant women and children within the evidence presented to the Commission were particularly disturbing and portrayed him as a heartless and cruel man, unwilling to show any mercy or compassion.[15] Anyone found providing shelter to those evicted were told that they and their families would be instantly removed.

It was also significant that in the evidence produced when the Commission sat in Argyll, Campbell was repeatedly named as one of the main causes of grievance and hardly any other estate official was remembered with such resentment and bitterness by the delegates. One crofter stated that 'I never heard a complaint scarcely against the Duke or Factor until the end of 1846 or 1847. I was acquainted with three factors.'[16] One writer mentioned that Campbell was still being referred to in 'hushed tones' on Mull in the 1950s; even in the 1970s children were still being ushered to bed with the threat of the *Factor Mor* coming for them.[17] As recently as 2010, a play was performed in Oban, set in the now-deserted township of Shiaba on the Ross of Mull, where Campbell was portrayed as the arch-villain masterminding and coldly executing the clearance of the local community.[18]

By all accounts Campbell was a large and very tall man, noted especially for his exceedingly long legs. One Tiree bard referred to his legs like 'candlesticks with treachery at the back of his throat'.[19] His old Islay friend, the noted Gaelic folklorist John Francis Campbell (Iain Og Ile), remarked in one letter to him: 'I have a vision of your long shanks by the fire at the cottage looming though a baccy reek . . . I may be mistaken as to the tales, the legs I cannot forget.'[20] His brother Dr Archibald Campbell, at the time of Campbell's funeral, referred to the 'longest coffin I ever saw being carried shoulder high by twelve of the tenants who were relieved by others at short intervals'.[21] He also

---

[15] *Napier Commission Evidence*, Q. 33607.

[16] *Napier Commission Evidence*, Q. 35378.

[17] F. Carothers, *A Grass Bank Beyond: Memories of Mull* (Edinburgh, 2014), p. 146; W. Orr, *Discovering Argyll, Mull & Iona* (Edinburgh, 1990), p. 115.

[18] 'History of Mull comes alive at Corran Hall', *Oban Times*, 14 January 2010.

[19] E. Cregeen and D. W. Mackenzie, *Tiree Bards and their Bardach* (Isle of Coll, 1978), p. 18.

[20] F. Thompson and D. A. MacDonald, *Lamplighter and Story Teller: John Francis Campbell of Islay 1821–1885* (Edinburgh, 1985), p. 26; National Library of Scotland [hereafter NLS], Adv. MS 50.1.14, fo. 45, 17 February 1859.

[21] CAP, Dr A. Campbell to Josephine Campbell, 13 September 1872.

referred to 'his giant frame reclining on the dining room couch'.[22] He must have struck a threatening, imposing, formidable and unforgettable figure. His striking physical appearance may have contributed to his enduring memory to this day.

The obituary refers to Campbell's 'tall and commanding presence, possessed of great discrimination, of equable temper which nothing could ruffle or disturb'.[23] He was a man of few words. His brother mentions that he had 'a large and kind heart altho [sic] he said but little'.[24] The obituary continues that he was 'genial and kind', 'his hospitality was quiet and unassuming' and that

> no one who had access to Ardfenaig will ever forget the regularity and order of the household, the hearty shake of the hand, and smile more expressive than words, with which they were welcomed nor the warm and kindly invitation at leaving, to return.[25]

These descriptions are in stark contrast to the grim evidence placed before the Napier Commission in 1883 and the surviving oral traditions. There is a remarkable and curiously disconcerting pencil portrait of Campbell in the journals of John Francis Campbell, drawn in September 1870. He was staying at Campbell's family home at Ardfenaig House in the Ross of Mull whilst collecting material for his book *Leabhar na Feinne*, published in 1872.[26] It could be mistaken for a deathbed scene as the sitter is drawn whilst asleep.

It is interesting that Campbell himself was seen as a valuable source for the tales that John Francis Campbell was collecting. He asked his son Donald, an oil merchant working in London, to forward material on to Campbell.[27] John Francis Campbell wrote in 1871 to the minister in Tiree, the Rev. John Gregorson Campbell:

> The stories to which I referred were told me by John Ardfenaig [the Duke of Argyll's factor in the Ross of Mull] as facts . . . If you know these you have got far, but if not you have a good deal to learn in Tiree.[28]

---

[22] CAP, Dr A. Campbell to Josephine Campbell, 13 September 1872.
[23] *Oban Times*, 'The late Mr Campbell of Ardfenaig', 7 September 1872.
[24] CAP, Dr Archibald Campbell to Josephine Campbell, 13 September 1872.
[25] CAP, Dr Archibald Campbell to Josephine Campbell, 13 September 1872.
[26] NLS, Adv. MS 50.2.2, fo. 158v.
[27] CAP, Flora Campbell to Donald Campbell, 6 December 1860.
[28] J. G. Campbell, *Waifs and Strays of Celtic Tradition, Argyllshire Series: No. V. Clan Traditions and Popular Tales of the Western Highlands and Islands* (London, 1895), p. 139.

EARLY LIFE

John Murdoch, the radical Highland and Irish land reformer and journalist, referenced in his autobiography the families living on Islay at that time: 'there was a stock of gentry there of which any chief might have been proud'. Amongst them he includes 'John Campbell, Ardmore'.[29] Campbell was the son of Archibald and Helen Campbell of Ardmore in Islay and descended from several generations of tacksmen, known for their agricultural improvements on Islay.[30] His mother was a Campbell of Ormsary from the Mull of Kintyre. There are fine portraits by Henry Raeburn of Helen's brother, James Campbell of Dunmore, and his wife Eliza Hope Baillie, daughter of Lord Polkemmet. Campbell's father Archibald was descended from the Cawdor branch of the Campbells and a half-brother of The Campbell of Glendaruel.[31]

Campbell's younger brother Archibald dedicated his medical thesis at Edinburgh University to his uncle, Prince Jules de Polignac, who became Prime Minister of France in 1829. The prince was married to Barbara Campbell, his mother's stepsister. Archibald became a senior diplomat in India and became a close friend of Sir Joseph Hooker, plant collector and Director of Kew Gardens. *Magnolia campbellii* was named in his honour, and *Rhododendron campbelliae* after his wife Emily. He was one of Darjeeling's founding fathers and is chiefly remembered today for being the first to have successfully introduced the tea plant there. A sister, Mary, married John Lorn Stewart of Glenbuckie and later of Coll, Chamberlain to the Duke of Argyll, on his estates in the Mull of Kintyre. Another sister, Margaret, married a son of the Gaelic scholar the Rev. Donald Macnicol, well known for his lambast in 1781 against Dr Johnson.[32]

LAND AGENTS AND OFFICIALS OF THE ARGYLL ESTATE

By the time of John Campbell's death, the 8th Duke of Argyll, one of Scotland's largest landowners, had an estate comprising some 168,315

---

[29] J. Hunter, *For the People's Cause: From the Writings of John Murdoch* (Edinburgh, 1986), p. 47.

[30] J. Macdonald, *General View of the Agriculture of the Hebrides, or Western Isles of Scotland* (London, 1811).

[31] CAP, *Family Tree of the Campbells of Ormsary.*

[32] Rev. D. Macnicol, *Song of Alarm to Scotland against the English Doctor* (Glasgow, 1781).

acres.[33] This figure had been even higher until the disposal of the Morvern estate by the 6th duke between 1819 and 1825.[34] The duke's lands were divided up into distinct areas and administered by four chamberlains. On the eve of Campbell's appointment in 1846 they comprised James Robertson, Chamberlain in Inveraray until his resignation due to ill health in 1869; John Lorn Stewart of Glenbuckie and later of Coll, Chamberlain in the Mull of Kintyre until his death in 1878; John Stewart of Achashenaig, Chamberlain in Mull and Tiree until he was replaced by John Campbell of Ardmore; and finally Lorne Campbell, Chamberlain in Rosneath in Dumbarton until his death in 1859 after being 'seized with a paralytic stroke'.[35] These key officials reported directly to the duke.

The term 'chamberlain' was not peculiar to Argyllshire and was commonly used across a number of landed estates in Scotland including Skye, South Uist and Lewis during the nineteenth century. Sir James Matheson used the term for the unpopular Donald Munro, Chamberlain of the Lews; and the Dukes of Hamilton and Atholl amongst others also used the same designation for their factors.[36] Alternative synonymous terms include 'baillie' and 'factor', which did not indicate another level of land agent. For example, John Campbell was known as *Am Baillidh Mor* ('the Big Baillie') in Tiree, *Am Factor Mor* ('the Big Factor') in Mull and Iona and was also formally and officially addressed as 'Chamberlain'. The word 'chamberlain' had been regularly used during the eighteenth century on the Argyll estates.

The 7th duke, whose health had been poor, died in April 1847, not long after Campbell's appointment. John Stewart of Achadashenaig had been 'deprived of his Factory' in December 1845 but continued until Campbell was able to take up the position during 1846.[37] He set up home at Ardfenaig House with his wife, Flora Macneill of Ardnacross. It contained both his family quarters as well as the Argyll estate office from where meal was distributed during the famine years from a stone bench still standing outside the house. A family of Maclean tenants had

---

[33] A. Campbell of Airds, *A History of Clan Campbell, Volume 3: From the Restoration to the Present Day* (Edinburgh, 2004), p. 171.

[34] P. Gaskell, *Morvern Transformed: A Highland Parish in the Nineteenth Century* (Cambridge, 1968), p. 25.

[35] *Greenock Telegraph & Clyde Shipping Gazette*, 15 February 1859.

[36] J. MacLeod, *None Dare Oppose: The Laird, the Beast and the People of Lewis* (Edinburgh, 2010).

[37] J. B. Loudon, *The Mull Diaries: The Diary of James Robertson, Sheriff Substitute of Tobermory (1842–1846)* (Dunoon, 2001), p. 171.

to make way for Campbell and this resentment was expressed by a niece. Upon hearing that her uncle, the Rev. Donald Macvean, minister of the Free Church, had taken lunch with Campbell, she cried, 'How could you do such a thing! I wonder the first mouthful did not choke you!'[38] One of Campbell's duties as chamberlain was to represent the duke on official occasions. In 1847, not long after his appointment, Queen Victoria and Prince Albert toured the west coast of Scotland in the royal yacht. The Queen did not come ashore but Prince Albert landed on Iona, and Campbell personally guided the Prince Consort around the abbey ruins.[39]

ESTATE POLICY

The 8th duke had a strict and uncompromising view on how his island estates should be managed. His desire to create an economically viable estate involved dramatically reducing the populations of Tiree, Iona and Mull. The duke, when marquess, felt that the

> laziness, ignorance and intractability induced by an over population subsisting on potatoes and having small possessions of land is such as to increase one's dread of the system and one's anxiety to put an end to it, the more one sees of its effects. Out of a population of 7000, at least half ought to be sent to Canada.[40]

The duke complained of 'the many young men on those islands on whom the wretched potato system has produced the same listless idleness which exists in Ireland, and who would rather starve on their family's croft than leave it in search of active work'.[41] He felt that the responsibility for the consequences of the potato famine lay plainly with the people: 'When the potato famine came and the people seemed likely to starve ... no prudence had withheld them from multiplying on a wretched soil.'[42] He wished to create more productive and economically viable farms by the consolidation of land holdings, ending the generational

---

[38] MacArthur, *Iona*, p. 130.

[39] *London Daily News*, 23 August 1847.

[40] *Correspondence from July 1846 to February 1847 Relating to the Measures Adopted for the Relief of the Distress in Scotland, Presented to both Houses of Parliament by Command of Her Majesty* (London, 1847), Marquis of Lorne to Sir G. Grey, 19 November 1846, p. 160.

[41] *Correspondence from July 1846 to February 1847*, Marquis of Lorne to Mr Trevelyan, 6 January 1847, p. 241.

[42] Duke of Argyll, *Passages from the Past*, Volume 2 (London, 1907), p. 528.

subdivision of land and thereby increasing his rental income. Above all he was determined to see the voluntary or forceful removal of the landless cottar class from the islands, those sons and daughters of the crofting tenants who squatted on crofts or common grazings illegally and who provided no financial benefit to his coffers at Inveraray.

Campbell's views on the laziness of the crofters and cottars and on the relief for destitution fully and personally reflected the views of his master the duke and the prejudices of the day. The depiction of Highlanders as lazy and indolent was not an isolated view, as the 1846–7 correspondence relating to the measures adopted for 'the relief of the distress in Scotland' presented to both Houses of Parliament shows.[43] The index to the Command White Paper even contained an entry for 'Highlanders – Their characteristic indolence etc.' As reported at the highest levels of government, 'they are *lazy*, however, and sadly want the persevering energy of the Anglo-Saxon race'.[44] 'I described the people of these isles as presenting the wretched remains of a selfish feudal system, divested of all its chivalry', admitted one observer to the senior officials in charge of relief.[45]

Campbell was cross-examined by the Board of Supervision in 1851 and claimed that the relief from the Destitution Committee 'has deteriorated the character of the people. It has made them seek to subsist by charity rather than by industry.'[46] He blamed the relief for persuading people to stay rather than emigrate. He stated that the population could not be made self-sustaining unless it was reduced by at least one half. Again this fully reflected the views of the duke. Campbell's argument was that for any man to pay his rent and bring up his family in tolerable comfort, he needed to pay a rent of not less than £20 per annum. Crofters paying rent between £12 and £15 per year were getting poorer every day. 'The classes amongst whom destitution exists … are the cottars and the small crofters.'[47] Campbell's systematic reasoning simply echoed the establishment line expressed by the duke, the Church and the secular authorities.

Campbell's strict moral stance on issues was always foremost in his

---

[43] *Correspondence from July 1846 to February 1847*, pp. 160–3.

[44] *Correspondence from July 1846 to February 1847*, Captain Rose to Mr Trevelyan, 7 February 1847, p. 334 (emphasis in original).

[45] *Correspondence from July 1846 to February 1847*, Captain Pole to Sir E. Coffin, 14 October 1846, p. 66.

[46] *Report of the Board of Supervision by Sir John M'Neill on the Western Highlands and Islands* (Edinburgh, 1851), p. 5.

[47] *Report of the Board of Supervision*, p. 4.

business and family correspondence and aligned neatly with his particularly close relationship with the Free Church and his strong religious principles. These strict ethical standards played a major part in Campbell's far-reaching decisions on individual cottar and crofter families on both islands and whether they remained or left on the emigrant ships to America, Canada and Australia. Campbell appeared to take a very strict and narrow approach to life, and those who breached his moral code could expect no compassion. His 'Special Rules and Regulations as to the Removing of Crofters' drawn up in the 1860s provides a fascinating insight into who he regarded as deserving of removal:

1. Indolent crofters who cultivate their land in a careless, slovenly manner and do not adhere to the given rules as to cultivation.
2. Widows and families of deceased crofters with a few exceptions when there is a young family with grown up sons of industrious habit.
3. Crofters who are quarrelsome and troublesome to their neighbours and of reputed bad character.
4. Crofters taking married sons and daughters into possession when the rent is under 20 pounds.
5. Crofters who keep idle grown up families about them and of no benefit to the property.
6. Crofters keeping dogs or infringing any of the regulations laid down for the management of the estates.
7. All crofters who do not pay up their rents at the stated periods of collection and not having sufficient stock on their land.[48]

However, it should not be overlooked that Campbell proposed important measures to alleviate the general distress on both island estates during his time as chamberlain including the setting up of a soup kitchen, the distribution of clothing, proposing the introduction of oyster farming, flax-growing and establishing a tile kiln, providing a newly built vessel for the crofters on Tiree to encourage fishing and the provision of employment on public works in return for meal.[49] The latter included the construction of the 'Indian Meal' pier at Bunessan in Mull in 1871, employment on draining land, and the construction and repair of roads and dykes.[50] He even wrote to the duke to persuade him to pay a higher

[48] C. Riddell, *Tireragan – A Township on the Ross of Mull: A Study in Local History on the Island of Mull* (n.p., 1995).

[49] IC, NRAS1209, bundle 1804, 19 December 1850.

[50] IC, NRAS1209, bundle 1523, 12 February 1852; bundle 916, January 1847; bundle 1763, 14 January 1864; bundle 1523, 12 February 1852; bundle 1533, 5 November 1847; bundle 1537, [n.d.] 1861; bundle 1804, 19 December 1850; bundle 1763, 1 November 1871.

price for knitting by the cottars and crofters to help their impoverished state.[51]

As we have seen already, there was mounting resentment towards Campbell amongst the cottar and crofter classes in the critical evidence placed before the Napier Commission and this has been reflected in the oral traditions of Tiree and Mull. Some have argued that this anger helped to lay the foundations for the land agitation in Tiree in 1886, which was challenging enough for a Royal Navy gunboat to be dispatched. The duke strongly defended Campbell's memory and his reputation by repudiating the charges of embezzlement implied by the radical member of the Napier Commission, Charles Fraser-Mackintosh MP.[52]

Campbell undoubtedly had inherent natural abilities as an administrator, accountant and skilful breeder of horses (Clydesdales) and cattle, including his outstanding herds of West Highlanders. In addition, he had skills as an agricultural improver and ensured that Ardfenaig would become a model farm for the area. This would bring credit not only to himself (and act as an example for others to follow) but also to the duke in illustrating how forward-thinking his chamberlains had become at a time when agricultural improvement was being actively encouraged. The duke was impressed with the improvements that Campbell had undertaken and this was reflected in family correspondence: 'we have had a visit from the duke about 10 days ago, he is so much pleased with the improvements going on here'.[53] Contemporary commentators added their glowing observations.[54]

ADMINISTRATIVE HIERARCHY ON THE ARGYLL ESTATES

Campbell had a clerk resident on both islands. One local oral tradition related that the clerk who lived in a house along Loch Caol would sail or row up the loch to the jetty at Ardfenaig House before noon each day and receive his daily instructions.[55] In Tiree, Campbell's clerk was Lachlan Macquarie, a Gaelic speaker from Mull, who combined

[51] IC, NRAS1209, bundle 1804, 19 December 1850.

[52] Duke of Argyll, *Crofts and Farms in the Hebrides, Being an Account of the Management of an Island Estate for 130 Years* (Edinburgh, 1883), pp. 67–8.

[53] CAP, Flora Campbell to Donald Campbell, 11 September 1861.

[54] W. Maxwell, *Iona and the Ionians* (Glasgow, 1857), p. 42; *Journal of Agriculture*, January 1868.

[55] CAP, I. Bowles, conversation with the author at Ardfenaig House, August 1972.

Figure 9 Lachlan Macquarie (1818–93), ground officer
in Tiree, his wife Marion MacIntyre and son Duncan,
15 September 1864. This is a rare photograph of a
ground officer. Image courtesy of Robin K. Campbell.

the post with that of ground officer (see Figure 9). He became a loyal
and trusted lieutenant of Campbell along with Angus Macniven, his
farm manager at Ardmore in Islay who moved to Mull to serve him.
Additionally, on each island there was to be a ground officer, otherwise
known as a sub-factor. They would normally be drawn from the crofting class, though not in the case of Macquarie, who was a farmer,
merchant and tacksman. He was the mouthpiece of the chamberlain
and the duke, as well as their eyes and ears. On Tiree and Mull, where
Gaelic was the predominant language, the ground officer would usually
be a Gaelic speaker. He would be actively involved in serving notice on
the tenants to quit as well as superintending their eviction. This must
have been an unenviable position, especially for a local man, and he and
his family faced the prospect of isolation and animosity from the rest of
the community. The ground officers and clerks were vital components
of Campbell's efforts to implement the duke's policies in his administration of the islands. These roles were supported directly and indirectly
by a coterie of local officials including solicitors (Sproat & Cameron,
in Tobermory), sheriff officers and police constables. Both islands had
their own sheriff officers responsible for serving documents and enforcing court orders as well as supporting police constables. They would be
present when families, having been served with summons of removal,
were evicted from their houses along with their personal possessions.

Macquarie's unpopularity is highlighted in a remarkable oral tradition regarding the last clay image made in Tiree: 'the greatest evil that witches can do is to make, for a person whose death they desire, a clay body or image (corp creadha)'.[56] It was made of Macquarie by women at Balephetrish with the aim of physically injuring him. They were challenged by a man, who seized the clay body and smashed it and warned the women that they would be burnt at the stake as witches if any harm should come to Macquarie.[57] If true, the fact that clay bodies were still being made on the island in the mid-nineteenth century is noteworthy. This is the only known surviving oral tradition in Tiree relating to clay images during the nineteenth century and none is known for Mull.

The role of factor or chamberlain could be a difficult path to tread. As one historian has noted, 'breakdowns in discipline, health (mental and physical), occasional criminality and lastly, mismanagement and incompetence dogged estate management'.[58] Campbell also had to endure the constant stress of living daily with a population on the edge of starvation and the very real feeling of helplessness in being unable to provide an instant solution. He must have felt very isolated at times. Throughout the period Campbell was chamberlain, there are regular comments in his letters to the duke on the acute conditions facing the local populations of Mull and Tiree. In 1848 he writes: 'yesterday they were at me in numbers begging for food, some of them actually in tears'.[59] And again in 1851:

> the people in a worse state for want of food than I ever anticipated . . . Some of whom were actually starving. I think the people are more destitute this year than in 1846 . . . impossible to describe the state of destitution.[60]

In 1863 he writes regarding Tiree:

> the destitution is very considerable indeed, there has been nothing like it since 1847 . . . I did not anticipate there could have been so much real want among them. The weather was very bad while I was there and the poor

---

[56] J. G. Campbell, *Witchcraft & Second Sight in the Highlands & Islands of Scotland* (Glasgow, 1902), p. 46.

[57] *Tocher: Tales, Songs, Tradition*, 18 (1975), p. 57.

[58] A. Tindley, '"They sow the wind, they reap the whirlwind": estate management in the post-clearance Highlands, c. 1815–c. 1900', *Northern Scotland*, 3 (2010), pp. 66–83.

[59] IC, NRAS1209, bundle 1522, John Campbell to Duke of Argyll, 3 September 1848.

[60] IC, NRAS1209, bundle 1805, John Campbell to Duke, 18 March 1851.

people suffered much from wet and cold in their anxiety to earn a subsistence for themselves and families, coming out in the morning with the wet clothes they put off the night before for want of fuel to dry them.[61]

And in 1868: 'Many of them are actually starving having little else than shellfish to live upon.'[62] Finally in 1872, the year of his death, he writes that those on the Ross of Mull are 'on the very next step to starvation'.[63] Being constantly surrounded by these appalling conditions over such a long period of time must have had a profoundly deleterious effect upon Campbell.

To administer and look after two disparate and extensive estates for the duke must have been exhausting and logistically very difficult given the poor roads, difficult terrain and inhospitable nature of some of the land, isolated communities on the southern coast of Mull and inclement weather. Campbell may have used his four-wheeled carriage on occasions, but probably his horse for the majority of the time he spent travelling around the islands. The fact that Campbell was able to carry out these duties successfully over so long a period across three islands into his seventies testifies to his physical stamina and mental strength, undoubted ability and dogged determination to carry out the tasks with which he had been entrusted. Annie Tindley's work on the role of factors and the fact that many of them failed to last the course due to alcoholism, mental illness or fatigue underlines his achievement.[64]

The island estates were separated by the Atlantic Ocean. Lieutenant Buchan of HMS *Firefly* wrote to the Secretary of the Admiralty that the island of Tiree, 'during the winter months ... is often impossible to communicate with by boat'.[65] And even if you survived the rough passage across from Mull, there was no pier, so 'the landing there is at all times difficult, and the anchorage not safe'.[66] Edward Stanford, who set up a kelp factory in Tiree, said in his evidence to the Napier Commission in 1883 that

---

[61] IC, Argyll Papers Letter Book, John Campbell to Duke, 8 January 1863.

[62] IC, NRAS1209, bundle 1763, John Campbell to Duke, 25 February 1868. For a discussion of the handling of the same crisis in Sutherland, northern Scotland, see A. Tindley, '"Actual pinching and suffering": estate responses to poverty in Sutherland, 1845–1886', *Scottish Historical Review*, 90:2 (2011), pp. 236–56.

[63] IC, NRAS1209, bundle 891, John Campbell to Duke, 29 March 1872.

[64] Tindley, '"They sow the wind"'.

[65] *Correspondence from July 1846 to February 1847*, p. 136.

[66] *Correspondence from July 1846 to February 1847*, Sir E. Coffin to Mr Trevelyan, 5 October 1846, p. 69.

boating to Tiree ... is one of extreme danger and has caused the loss of several lives, the boats having to encounter one of the wildest seas on the west coast. There is no heavier sea on the west coast than that between Tiree and the mainland, where the Atlantic comes in ... and anyone who has crossed that sea in a smack on a stormy day in the winter, is not likely to forget it.[67]

In January 1847 Campbell was detained in Tiree for over three weeks due to heavy seas, and it was felt that he would be further delayed 'until a change of wind and weather takes place'.[68] Shortly after Campbell's appointment, his friend Captain Donald Campbell of Quinish, factor to Maclean of Coll, wrote that the 'report of your being drowned on your passage to Tyree reached me here ... until I traced it to be without foundation and that you were still in the land of the living in which may you long continue'.[69] Campbell's wife Flora constantly worried about her husband's regular sea journeys to Tiree and was relieved when in 1864 he relinquished the post of Chamberlain of Tiree and a non-Gaelic speaker from Perthshire, John M. M. Geekie, replaced him as chamberlain. 'I am very glad of it, the constant boating was so dangerous it kept my mind in constant anxiety.'[70] She was only too aware of the dangers of the sea having lost one brother, Neil, by drowning. Flora even referred to these concerns in a warm and tender Gaelic love song, *Oran do Bhaillidh Iain Caimbeul*, that she composed in Campbell's memory and published in 1879:

Yester night I was dejected ... by my weeping, speech had left me, since your vessel sailed not ... Now that you are with us safely, let us, as we ought live happily. May you long in life be spared us and we in gratitude remain.[71]

Campbell personally possessed two smacks, the *Flora* and the *Jane*, which he kept moored at his jetty at Ardfenaig, overlooking Loch Caol. They are described as 'two decked smacks, each 40 tons, with float, boats, furniture and apparelling and ready for sea'.[72] They were used for his regular trips to Tiree and for miscellaneous duties including transporting cattle, horses and sheep and for carrying oatmeal, Indian meal and corn, and potatoes from Ireland during the destitution crisis. His

[67] *Napier Commission Evidence*, p. 3061.
[68] *Correspondence from July 1846 to February 1847*, p. 312.
[69] Mull Museum, Tobermory, Donald Campbell to John Campbell, 21 January 1848.
[70] CAP, Flora Campbell to Donald Campbell, 17 March 1864.
[71] A. Sinclair, *The Gaelic Songster: An T – Oranaiche* (Glasgow, 1879), p. 9.
[72] CAP, Displenishing Sale Poster for Ardfenaig, 21 March 1873.

letter book refers to the use of his smack *Jane* in importing these goods from Londonderry.[73] In an eight-page Gaelic praise poem published in 1868, *Moladh Do Mhaighstir Iain Caimbeul*, especially dedicated to Campbell by the Morvern bard John MacDougall (*Am Bard Ruadh*) of Ardgour, who was both a panegyrist and a satirist, specific reference was made in the second verse to the importation of meal from Ireland: 'you were bringing meal from Ireland with your valiant, expert crew and your rare lucky boat and giving it out on credit'.[74] MacDougall's eleven verses praised Campbell, his wife, his shooting and dancing ability, his talent for playing the fiddle, his skill as a steersman, his wise judgments as magistrate and his military prowess as commander of the Volunteers. Campbell was one of the nine members of the Special Committee for the Mull Volunteers in 1860, representing the Duke of Argyll, with the task of forming and organising a force of voluntary soldiers. A Tiree bard from Balephuil may well be referring to Campbell's Volunteer uniform when he sneeringly said, 'Since you got the suit of pilot cloth, you bear a faint resemblance to a soldier.'[75]

MacDougall's Gaelic praise poem for Campbell was originally composed, published and circulated as a pamphlet in 1868 and in 1870 it was included with other compositions in his book *Gaisge nan Gaidheal: Orain agus Dain*. The poem also referred to Campbell's generosity in providing the bard with meal which his clerk had denied him. It is remarkable and indeed extremely rare to find a printed Gaelic praise poem in honour of a duke's chamberlain or, for that matter, any estate official in Scotland.

To supplement Campbell's income of £200 per year as chamberlain, he operated a fishing concern, as evident from the auction at Ardfenaig in May 1873 which included: 'three fishing boats, 12 barrels of herring nets, 1 trawl net'.[76] Sales of wool from his flocks of sheep also provided extra income as well as breeding from his renowned stock of Ayrshire and pure West Highland cattle. He also bred from his American trotting horse 'Yankee', which went on tour to mainland Argyll including Oban, Kilmartin and Inveraray.[77] In addition, further valuable revenue

[73] IC, Argyll Papers Letter Book, John Campbell to Messrs J. & R. Wilson, Londonderry, 5 June 1866.

[74] J. MacDougall, 'Moladh Do Mhaighstir Iain Caimbeul', in *Gaisge nan Gaidheal: Orain agus Dain* (Sandbank, 1870), pp. 65–71 (quote at p. 65).

[75] Edinburgh, School of Scottish Studies, SA 1968143, *An Seiclear*.

[76] CAP, John Campbell to Donald Campbell, May 1864; CAP, Displenishing Sale Poster for Ardfenaig, 21 March 1873.

[77] 'Wool sales, Ardfinaig', *Edinburgh Evening Courant*, 20 September 1862;

was received from Campbell's numerous farms in Mull: Ardfenaig, Tiroghoyle, Knockafenaig and part of Creich. Two hundred acres were arable and capable of keeping about 2,500 blackfaced sheep and about 35 cows with their followers, beside a number of young horses. He also had farms at Fidden, Pottie, Salchur and the island of Erraid numbering 1,950 acres, 125 acres of which were arable and capable of keeping about 300 blackfaced sheep and about 50 cows with their followers. The total acreage came to 5,500 acres.[78] In addition, in Tiree he had the farm of Heylipoll which was able to graze around 900 sheep and over 70 black cattle. He died a wealthy man in 1872, leaving over £24,000 in his estate.[79]

CONCLUSION

In August 1872 John Campbell lay dying in a small blackhouse on his steading at Ardfenaig, considered too ill to be moved to the family house. The duke wrote to John Francis Campbell, 'My poor John Ardmore was lying at death's door when we were in Loch Laigh.'[80] Oral traditions related that Campbell was eaten alive by maggots. It was said that 'he came alive like a maggoty sheep . . . a curse came upon him . . . hens were put under his arms to see if it would draw out the maggots . . . coming out of his ears and mouth'.[81] Another recounted that hens every three days were cut in half and placed under his armpits to draw out the pus from his body.[82] Vivid and disquieting stories recounted the way he died with the presence of lice, maggots and even fleas on his body while lying on his death bed.[83] A disease transmitted by lice could result in a maggoty infestation. His clothes could have provided a suitable home for the insects, neither too hot nor too cold. The sudden loss of body heat on death would account for the disturbing and dramatic sight of heavy infestations of lice rapidly leaving the dead body by the ears, nose and mouth. Oral tradition referred to Angus Macniven, his right-hand man, and Lachlan Macquarie, the former

'The celebrated trotting horse "Yankee"', *Oban Times & Argyllshire Advertiser*, 4 May 1872.

[78] *Glasgow Herald*, 25 December 1872.

[79] This translates into approximately £1,096,800 in today's values.

[80] NLS, Adv. MS 50.2.17, 8th duke to John Francis Campbell, 16 September 1872.

[81] MacArthur, *Iona*, p. 138.

[82] CAP, recording of informant, Argyll, 8 October 2014.

[83] CAP, recording of oral tradition bearer, Ian MacFadyen, Mull, 4 June 1986.

ground officer, hurriedly sweeping the lice off the body by means of a brush and a shovel into the fire.[84] The presence of body lice may well have led to epidemic typhus and hence the 'disease of the heart' shown on his death certificate.

An eyewitness account of the funeral described the body being taken by the ship *Dunvegan Castle*, along with ninety grieving tenants and family members, to Islay and buried at Kildalton in the family tomb.[85] Over a month after his death, Campbell's wife Flora still remained in her bedroom at Ardfenaig House unable to come to terms with her sudden loss.[86] Only a few miles away, in Ardtun, Eugene Rose, an elderly boat carpenter, was busily composing and celebrating the death of the 'beast' in his bitter and gloating satirical mock lament 'Cumha a'Bhaillidh Mhoir' ('Lament for the Great Factor'), 'laughing', 'toasting' and 'praising God that you had died'.[87]

What of Campbell's legacy? The organisational restructuring of the management of the Argyll estates was effected immediately after his death in 1872 and again upon the departure of John Geekie as Chamberlain of Tiree in 1877 to become a farmer in Canada. The death of Campbell saw the end of Gaelic-speaking resident chamberlains on the island estates and placed increased reliance on the resident ground officers. The departure of Geekie finally saw the disappearance of resident island chamberlains on the Argyll estates. Power henceforth was centralised in Inveraray with the chamberlain James Wyllie, who had formerly been factor on Lord Breadalbane's Perthshire estates until his appointment by the duke in 1869. He took over the administration of both Mull and Tiree and continued as chamberlain until his retirement in 1900, some thirty-one years later.[88]

Campbell's reputational legacy amongst the crofters and cottars lives on to this day, through many unfavourable traditions recalling his time as chamberlain on both island estates. His blemished reputation may not have been helped by his appointment as chamberlain in 1846, at precisely the same time that the potato blight affected both Mull and Tiree, at a time of acute economic hardship. The large body of surviving oral traditions for Campbell held by the School of Scottish Studies at Edinburgh

[84] *Tocher: Tales, Songs, Tradition*, 17 (1975), p. 27.

[85] CAP, Dr Archibald Campbell to Josephine Campbell, 13 September 1872.

[86] Argyll and Bute Council Archive, Lochgilphead, Sproat and Cameron Papers, Lachlan Macquarie to William Sproat, 4 October 1872.

[87] D. E. Meek (ed.), *The Wiles of the World, Caran an T-Saoghail: Anthology of 19th Century Gaelic Verse* (Edinburgh, 2003), pp. 170–1.

[88] *Scotsman*, 27 September 1872.

University far outweighs surviving material for any other chamberlain in Argyllshire during the eighteenth and nineteenth centuries. This fact alone bears witness to the deep impression Campbell's reign as chamberlain had made upon the inhabitants of Tiree and Mull. He was a feared man, no doubt enhanced by his imposing physical appearance.

However, this menacing and villainous reputation was not reflected in his personal life and relationships within his own social class or amongst the many grieving tenants who attended his funeral:

> These rough looking men on shouldering the Bier sobbed and cried like children and all who understood Gaelic – which embraced all present could hear them muttering regrets for the loss of their best friend; and all agreeing that they should never see his like again.[89]

He was highly regarded within his own social group, amongst his peers and family, a view which was dramatically at odds with the traditional view of Campbell. His wife's love song bears testament to the deep affection she bore for her husband. He was held in deep regard by the duke, impressed no doubt by his sharp financial acumen in bringing in revenue to the Argyll estate during a very difficult period for the property and the western Highlands and Islands more broadly. The agricultural improvements he undertook on both islands no doubt enhanced his reputation. The respect and affection which the 8th duke expressed for Campbell and his wife is reflected in his book *Crofts and Farms in the Hebrides, Being an Account of the Management of an Island Estate for 130 Years*, published in 1883.

Finally, Campbell's visual legacy of the years he was chamberlain can still be seen in the crumbling ruins of the former townships at Shiaba and Tireragan in Mull, which he cleared. But on a more positive note, the granite-built school at Bunessan in Mull along with a pier, both of which he officially 'opened', are still in use today. During his lifetime Campbell had been a hugely controversial figure, and his memory lives on, some 145 years after his death. There had not been a more infamous or enigmatic chamberlain in Argyllshire either before his appointment in 1846 or after his death in 1872.

---

[89] CAP, Dr Archibald Campbell to Josephine Campbell, 13 September 1872.

12

'Castle government':
The Psychologies of Land Management in Northern Scotland, c. 1830–90

Annie Tindley

INTRODUCTION

> Factors [land agents] find themselves placed in remote districts with enormous and almost absolute power over nearly every person there, and the more they exercise this power, the more the love of power increases, and impatience of all opposition increases; these men in these circumstances would be more than human if they did not sometimes commit excesses in the exercise of this power, and do things which it would be painful to bring to light, and which they can hardly see in their true colour unless set before the eyes of the public.[1]

THIS DIAGNOSIS OF THE neuroses and monomania generated by nineteenth-century estate management was given to a Royal Commission, appointed to inquire into the conditions of the small tenants in the Highlands and Islands of Scotland, when it heard evidence in the remote crofting township of Bettyhill, Sutherland in late 1883. It was given by a local Free Church minister, and represents a strikingly moral and yet empathetic description of the profession.[2] We might note that the minister does not target any individual factor, but instead outlines the fundamental fractures and tensions in the nature of the profession; although, given the personality of the long-standing factor for the Sutherland estates in the north of the county, John Crawford, the minister could perhaps not be blamed for including some personal criticism as well.[3]

---

[1] In Scotland, land agents are commonly termed 'factors'; *Evidence taken by Her Majesty's Commissioners of Inquiry into the Condition of the Crofters and Cottars in the Highlands and Islands of Scotland* [hereafter *Napier Commission Evidence*] (Edinburgh, 1884), evidence of Rev. Mr James Cumming, p. 1633.

[2] For a fuller elucidation of Cumming's views on the land question, see National Library of Scotland [hereafter NLS], Acc. 5931, papers of Rev. James Cumming, 'Observations on our Land Laws', March 1883.

[3] For further background on the career and personality of John Crawford,

The management of landed estates in an era of high paternalism, the professionalisation of land management and – in direct tension with these broad factors – sustained attack on landed privilege represented far more than any simple economic or asset management. It was a cultural and moral exercise and as such often generated more heat than light; it was a contentious, tangled operation with a significant attrition rate.[4] This is perhaps unsurprising when we consider the scale of the power held by later nineteenth-century estate managers. The focus of this chapter is the Sutherland estates, the largest landed estate in western Europe in this period. The factors employed by the ducal family were in charge of territories as large as many counties – even countries or colonies – and as such, an examination of their methods, strengths, weaknesses and responses in a period of enormous change and challenge is instructive.[5]

By the early 1830s the Sutherland estates covered over one million acres of land in the county of Sutherland, in northern Scotland. In addition, the family owned small but valuable English estates at Trentham, Staffordshire and Lilleshall, Shropshire as well as a London palace, Stafford House, on the Mall. As such, they were by far the largest landowners in Britain (and most of Europe) at that time, with agricultural as well as industrial and imperial concerns and investments making up their portfolio.[6] Unsurprisingly, the management of such large, varied and far-flung assets was complex. This complexity was deepened with the problematic public reputation of the ducal family, stemming from the first two decades of the nineteenth century and the notorious events of the Sutherland clearances. These clearances were a huge, nearly twenty-year project, during which the estate restructured its tenancies to accommodate commercial sheep farming. As part of this, nearly 25,000 people were relocated from the interior glens of the estate to the coastal areas, with great insensitivity and occasional violence.[7] This process was overseen by the estate management, and the

---

see A. Tindley, *The Sutherland Estate 1850–1920: Aristocratic Decline, Estate Management and Land Reform* (Edinburgh, 2010), pp. 15–18, 74–5.

[4] A. Tindley, '"They sow the wind, they reap the whirlwind": estate management in the post-clearance Highlands, c. 1815–c. 1900', *Northern Scotland*, 3 (2012), pp. 66–85; E. Richards, *The Highland Estate Factor in the Age of the Clearances* (Laxay, 2016).

[5] Tindley, *Sutherland Estate*, pp. 1–14, 174; E. Richards, *The Leviathan of Wealth: The Sutherland Fortune in the Industrial Revolution* (London, 1973).

[6] Tindley, *Sutherland Estate*, pp. 3–7.

[7] See E. Richards, *Debating the Highland Clearances* (Edinburgh, 2007), pp. 55–6, 63–5, 73–6.

population of Sutherland never forgot nor forgave their role in the hated policy, generating a legacy of bitterness and sullen challenge towards later generations of factors.[8]

This chapter will explore a number of key themes in relation to the drivers and philosophies of estate management in post-clearance Sutherland. As the chapter focuses on estate management, the ducal family will play almost no role in this analysis. The ducal family, the Leveson-Gowers, essentially left all management in the hands of the three resident factors and the commissioner, the chief overseer and man of business for all the Sutherland operations.[9] The management structure was somewhat elaborate: at the pinnacle was the commissioner, who oversaw all landed, industrial, financial and political matters for the family, and who also managed the staff below him. These constituted, first, the factors, substantial men in their own right, each overseeing roughly a third (approximately 300,000 acres each) of the land area of the northern estates, known as managements. In their turn, they appointed and managed local ground officers, usually one per parish. Each factor kept detailed letter books, logged monthly reports under fixed subject headings and curated the financial records of their managements.[10]

Highland factors – like those across Scotland, Britain and Ireland – were men of immense social, political and economic influence over often extensive territories and populations. The factor was the symbolic figure of estate authority, in place of often absentee or disinterested owners.[11] The concentration of land ownership into a small number of hands in Scotland generally and (famously) Sutherland in particular, led to a similar concentration of the management of those estates within a limited circle of administrators.[12] This put a burden of immense responsibility and pressure on factors, with often negative results. This

[8] See the classic apologia, J. Loch, *An Account of the Improvements on the Estates of the Marquis of Stafford* (London, 1820); see also F. McKichan, 'Lord Seaforth and Highland estate management in the first phase of clearance (1783–1815)', *Scottish Historical Review*, 86 (2007), p. 53 for a discussion on a proximal estate.

[9] For a full description of James Loch, see Richards, *Leviathan of Wealth*, pp. 3–19, 23, 25–6, 32.

[10] Tindley, *Sutherland Estate*, pp. 2, 6, 174.

[11] See, for example, Alexander Macdonald, factor for multiple estates on Skye, *Napier Commission Evidence*, pp. 480, 498, 523.

[12] Figures detailing the concentration of landholdings in the hands of a few can be found in D. Cannadine, *The Decline and Fall of the British Aristocracy* (London, 1990), pp. 8–11. In c. 1880 in Scotland, 92.8 per cent of the land was held by 1,758 owners; Cannadine, *Decline and Fall*, p. 8.

remained the case until well into the twentieth century, when factoring agencies began to become the established norm in estate management.[13]

The challenges of the post-clearance period were largely faced by the estate factors who developed and executed estate policy and managed the land and its people on a day-to-day basis. This chapter will examine the Highland factor, through the prism of the Sutherland estates – his reputation, training, education, duties and social and political roles – in the post-clearance environment. What did the system consist of and how successful was it in managing the interests of the estate owners? The almost universal unpopularity of Highland factors is well documented, and this was heightened in Sutherland because of their role in organising and executing the hated clearance policies.[14] Decades after the clearances, however, the factors were habitually despised in their own communities, accused of tyranny and seen as the oppressive instruments of unpopular estate polices – increasing rents, small-scale evictions and removals.[15] Was the factorial system successful enough to justify this unpopularity and if not, why was it left unreformed?

One possible reason may be posited: the continuing, even accelerating, pace of change in the region in the nineteenth century, and the impact this had on the factor's role. Factors managed a population that lived in poverty-stricken conditions with periods of acute destitution (as in 1836–7, 1846–9, 1861–5 and 1868–9); after 1886 they had to deal with direct government intervention in the administration of estates and the surge of crofter agitation – sometimes violent – against their rule.[16] In this they stood aligned with their Irish and Welsh brethren, as other chapters in this collection discuss. How they responded, and how successfully, to these challenges will be discussed here. Arguably, there was

[13] Tindley, '"They sow the wind"', pp. 82–3.

[14] See similar examples on the Isle of Lewis: J. S. Grant, *A Shilling for your Scowl: The History of a Scottish Legal Mafia* (Stornoway, 1992), pp. 137–41; J. Macleod, *None Dare Oppose: The Laird, the Beast and the People of Lewis* (Edinburgh, 2010), p. 256.

[15] See accusations made directly to the estate management: Staffordshire County Record Office [hereafter SCRO], Sutherland estates papers, D593, K/1/3/70/a, John MacKay of Hereford to Sir Arnold Kemball, 24 June 1882; and extensively in the *Napier Commission Evidence*, pp. 167, 1645, 1738.

[16] T. M. Devine, *The Great Highland Famine: Hunger, Emigration and the Scottish Highlands in the Nineteenth Century* (Edinburgh, 1988), pp. 83–94; J. MacAskill, '"It is truly, in the expressive language of Burke, a nation crying for bread": the public response to the Highland famine of 1836–1837', *Innes Review*, 61 (2010), pp. 169–206; E. Richards, 'Highland emigration in the age of Malthus: Scourie, 1841–55', *Northern Scotland*, 2 (2011), p. 65.

nothing particularly special in the land agent experience in Sutherland, but the size and wealth of the estate, combined with the practical and reputational legacies of its clearance policy, serves to focus and heighten the emotive and cultural tension and conflict inherent in the factorial condition over many contentious decades.

THE LIFE AND TIMES OF A SUTHERLAND FACTOR

Highland estate management as a profession developed significantly as the age of improvement dawned, and men with new and specialised skills were required.[17] These included detailed bookkeeping and financial acumen, scientific agriculture and land surveying. As Highland landowners, seeking to stay abreast of activities in the Lowlands and England, developed their estates along commercial lines, a more painstaking approach towards estate management was required. Landowners had to buy in the specialist skills of a new class of men: those who had a detailed legal knowledge, a head for finances and a solid, practical grounding in agriculture. They also had to be respectable and well educated enough to take up a prominent position in local society; indeed, as the personal representative of the landlord, who might often be absentee for at least part of the year, this was arguably one of the most important aspects of their role.[18]

With a move towards commercial agriculture and the reorganisation of population and tenancy structures on estates, landowners looked to consolidate expertise into a single individual, a trend led by the Sutherland estates in the appointment of James Loch as commissioner in 1812, succeeded on his death by his son George in 1855.[19] James Loch was appointed to the premier position in the Sutherland estates – and indeed in British and Irish estate management – and his role was far

[17] For a general discussion of the Scottish development of the profession, see I. H. Adams, 'Economic process and the Scottish land surveyor', *Imago Mundi*, 27 (1975), pp. 13–18; I. H. Adams, 'The agents of agricultural change', in M. L. Parry and T. R. Slater (eds), *The Making of the Scottish Countryside* (London, 1980), pp. 155–76, especially pp. 159–60, 167–9; T. M. Devine, 'The transformation of agriculture: cultivation and clearance', in T. M. Devine, C. H. Lee and G. C. Peden (eds), *The Transformation of Scotland: The Economy since 1700* (Edinburgh, 2005), pp. 71–99, especially pp. 79, 87.

[18] J. Hunter, *The Making of the Crofting Community* (Edinburgh, 1976), pp. 121–2.

[19] See Chapter 1 in this volume by David Gent for more on Loch's English appointments and activities; Tindley, *Sutherland Estate*, p. 174. James Loch was commissioner from 1812 to 1855, and his son George from 1855 to 1879.

above that of even influential local factors. He was equivalent to a chief operating executive in the early Victorian period, with oversight and management of all the Sutherland estates, in England and Scotland, as well as their industrialising activities in the Staffordshire potteries and extensive investment portfolio. He managed all of the estate employees on behalf of the family, and all this while a long-standing Member of Parliament.[20] His employer, the 1st duke, may have been the 'leviathan of wealth', but Loch was the 'Sutherland Metternich', governing extensive and remote territories with his pen from the principal family seats in London or Trentham, Staffordshire.[21]

Loch had been selected and employed by the Sutherlands in the hope that he might be able to work some financial and social magic in Sutherland, undertaking a transformation of their estates in northern Scotland, which were limping – economically and in every other sense, as it seemed to the owners – behind their English holdings.[22] As such, he picked up and pushed through the most extensive clearance project undertaken in Scotland.[23] Men of Loch's position were rare, in part because operations the size of the Sutherland estates were unusual, but his example serves to emphasise the great variation in scope and responsibility within the estate management profession, even in one estate.

Much more common were the resident factors (of whom Loch managed three for the northern territories); even so, they still represented a small coterie of men numerically, but their influence far outstripped their numbers. They were generally well paid, but the post was challenging; the responsibilities were heavy and the expectations of their employers high.[24] They were required to collect rents (and later, rates) from their tenants, twice a year, sometimes across huge swathes of remote and inaccessible territory. They had to manage the bookkeeping for the estates, monitor existing properties and organise new building; they were also often required to plan and execute major improvements to the estates – either in mapping and surveying, agricultural changes or via the enforcement of 'improving' leases granted to the bigger tenants. They had to be educated to a relatively high level and it was generally preferred by estate owners that their staff were not native to the areas

---

[20] Richards, *Leviathan of Wealth*, pp. 3–19.

[21] Richards, *Leviathan of Wealth*, pp. 23, 25–6.

[22] Richards, *Leviathan of Wealth*, pp. 155–6.

[23] Richards, *Debating the Highland Clearances*, pp. 55–6.

[24] By the mid-1820s factorial salaries on the Sutherland estate were £200 per annum, with the use of a house and a home farm; by c. 1900 this had increased to £600–£1,000.

they managed as it was felt that they would be less subject to the petty feuds and disagreements that flared up from time to time among the tenantry and have some degree of impartial authority over them.[25]

The combination of all of these requirements meant that a factor's life was one of hard work in challenging conditions, peppered with conflict and loneliness, especially for those without wives or families. It was also immensely physically demanding, and this remained the case until well into the twentieth century, particularly in the more remote areas of the Highlands such as Sutherland. Many factors worked in far-flung and inaccessible places where transport links were rudimentary at best; roads were infrequent in many areas, and factors had to rely on ponies, small boats and their own physical stamina to carry out their duties.[26] They were required to maintain this level of fitness in all weathers and over many years; they could only work as long as they were physically able to do their job. Evander McIver, factor for the Sutherland estates in the Scourie management in the remote north-west of the country (see Figure 10), was faced with the stark realities of this as regards a land surveyor he had employed at Clashmore in Assynt. When they had walked back to Lochinver one evening (a round journey of some twenty miles), McIver wrote that he had 'walked the legs off him!' and that he would necessarily have to be retired soon, leaving a significant skills gap in the estate management.[27]

But most challenging of all was the socio-economic inheritance of post-clearance Sutherland; a poverty-stricken, dense and sullen crofting community on one side, and a commercially driven sheep-farming and sporting tenantry on the other. Factors had to maintain good relations and high rents with the latter, and were expected to address the 'problem' of the former by their employers and latterly, the government. This was not a social and economic structure unique to Sutherland; it could be found in numerous variations across the Scottish Highlands

[25] For example, Evander McIver, factor of the Scourie district of the Sutherland estate, attended Edinburgh University in the 1820s before taking up his first post; E. McIver, *Memoirs of a Highland Gentleman: Being the Reminiscences of Evander McIver of Scourie*, ed. Rev. G. Henderson (Edinburgh, 1905), pp. 20–4.

[26] This may explain why they were to a man supporters of schemes for new or improved roads and railways, as discussed by John McGregor in Chapter 3 of this volume.

[27] SCRO, Sutherland estates papers, D593, K/1/3/62, Evander McIver to George Loch, 14 May 1873; see also Highland Council Archives, Cameron of Lochiel papers, CL/A/3/1/2/6, Mackenzie to Lochiel, 31 December 1892 for a similar example on a West Highland estate.

Figure 10 Evander McIver, factor for Sutherland
Estates from his book, *Memoirs of a Highland
Gentleman* (1902), showing him aged eighty-one.

and Islands, western Ireland and parts of Wales. Factorial responses differed according to context, naturally, but patterns emerge, as discussed in the next section.

CHANGE IN THE POST-CLEARANCE HIGHLANDS AND THE FACTORIAL RESPONSE IN SUTHERLAND

After the upheaval and turmoil of the decades of clearance, the 1850s and 1860s in Sutherland were a period of consolidation within the estate management.[28] Large-scale removals ended, although smaller-scale reorganisations, generally to enhance the grazings of sheep farms or to extend the boundaries of the newer deer forests, were constantly rumbling on.[29] Meanwhile, the vast majority of the population – the crofters and cottars – struggled to reclaim and make productive their new plots of poor land. Many fell onto the poor rolls and a significant majority were in arrears of rent by the early 1860s, and for the estate managers, they were the most troublesome – economically and morally

[28] Hunter, *Making of the Crofting Community*, pp. 119–20; A. Tindley, '"Actual pinching and suffering": estate responses to poverty in Sutherland, 1845–1886', *Scottish Historical Review*, 90:2 (2011), pp. 236–56.

[29] See, for example, SCRO, Sutherland estates papers, D593, K/1/3/70, McIver to Kemball, 2 May 1884.

– aspect of their difficult jobs.[30] For the Sutherland factors, on their salaries of £600 per annum, house and sheep farm attached, dealing with the grinding, degrading poverty of the dense populations around them generated anger, frustration, disdain and despair.[31]

There was worse to come, however; from the 1870s, a new challenge appeared: the growing expression and organisation of crofter and landless cottar disaffection. By the early 1880s this had blossomed into outright agitation in parts of the Highlands, particularly in Skye and Lewis, and Sutherland would not escape.[32] The Crofters War, as it was known, represented a nightmare for all Highland factors, including those in Sutherland; crofting communities across the region agitated for reform of land tenure and for more land, and it was factors who were on the front line of this protest. Tactics used by crofting and cottar communities ranged from rent strikes to intimidation; enough for most factors to think carefully about enforcing estate policy in the face of angry and mobilised crofting communities.[33] The landlords' right to evict small tenants at forty days' notice or to raise rents as they pleased could no longer be utilised with impunity. Crofter protest and critical coverage in the local and national press were now the almost inevitable consequences, and even if the factor was still willing to run this gauntlet, many found that their employers did not have the stomach for it.[34] In addition, agitation in the region attracted the attention of the government, concerned as it was with similar rural breakdowns in Ireland and Wales. In 1883 William Gladstone's Liberal government appointed a Royal Commission to inquire into conditions for the crofters and cottars in the Highlands and Islands – the Napier Commission – which travelled

[30] Tindley, '"Actual pinching and suffering"'; see Evander McIver's evidence on this to the Napier Commission, *Napier Commission Evidence*, p. 1709.

[31] See E. Richards and A. Tindley, 'Turmoil among the crofters: Evander McIver and the "Highland Question", 1873–1903', *Agricultural History Review*, 60:2 (2012), pp. 191–213.

[32] Hunter, *Making of the Crofting Community*, pp. 128–30, 132–3; E. A. Cameron, *Land for the People?: The British Government and the Scottish Highlands, c. 1880–1925* (East Linton, 1996), pp. 16–18.

[33] On the genesis of protest and the politicisation of the crofters and the land question in the Highlands in the 1880s, see E. A. Cameron, 'Poverty, protest and politics: perceptions of the Scottish Highlands in the 1880s', in D. Broun and M. Macgregor (eds), *Miorun Mor nan Gall, The Great Ill-Will of the Lowlander: Lowland Perceptions of the Scottish Highlands* (Glasgow, 2009), pp. 218–31.

[34] See the instructions issued to all Sutherland factors by head office in 1881, limiting their powers and imposing a moratorium on evictions, SCRO, Sutherland estates papers, D593, K/1/3/66, Kemball to all factors, 9 March 1881.

to all corners of the region to interview and record the views of the small tenants and the history of their treatment. This exposed factors to the full force of appalled public opinion for the first time.[35] The spotlight of hostile and detailed investigation told heavily on them, most of whom did not recognise the picture painted of themselves by their communities as tyrannous oppressors. The emotional turmoil generated from this, as well as that within politics and land management, was significant.

This was very pronounced on the Sutherland estates. The 3rd Duke of Sutherland and his son, Lord Stafford (later the 4th duke), were both highly sensitive to any degree of public criticism of their estate policy, both past and present, an attitude embedded within the family since the great clearances of the early nineteenth century and the waves of criticism and controversy that followed.[36] This aversion to public condemnation was filtered down to the factors, who once the Crofters War started, were forbidden to raise crofters' rents, evict any crofter or issue summons of removal – essentially removing all weapons in the factors' armoury to impose financial and social discipline on their mass of crofting and cottar tenants.[37] It was intended to be a more sensitive approach to management, but for the factors themselves, it was an unworkable plan; how could rent payment, one of the central planks of estate (and factorial) discipline, be enforced? As well as the practical and financial implications for day-to-day management, the factors felt that their personal authority – the fundamental basis of their powers of control – had been damaged by the removal of their powers. Evander McIver wrote to his colleague John Crawford at Tongue in the far north, giving him his impressions of the new social order in the Highlands:

> I have only just come back from Assynt where the rents have not been well paid. I found that the [Napier] Commission has left its mark decidedly on the minds and manners of the people and that they look upon Factors with jaundiced eyes and smirks, it is the teaching the people have received from their masters![38]

The undercurrents of deference, opposition and control had been fundamentally disrupted by the agitation and government investigation into it.

[35] The Napier Commission was chaired by Lord Napier; see Chapter 11 in this volume by Robin K. Campbell for a different regional perspective on its work.

[36] Tindley, *Sutherland Estate*, pp. 76–80, 170.

[37] SCRO, Sutherland estates papers, D593, K/1/3/66, Kemball to all factors, 9 March 1881.

[38] NLS, Sutherland estates papers, Acc. 10225, Policy Papers, 214, McIver to Kemball, 14 December 1882.

A new era was dawning in Sutherland and the long-standing, autocratic factors were utterly ill-equipped to adjust to the new reality.

Part of the nightmare that was estate management in Sutherland and the wider Highlands from the early 1880s was the requirement that factors contribute to the great public inquiries set up in response to the continuing agitation and poverty of the region. In effect, the factors were being held to public account for their past and present administration, as well as offering their diagnosis of and solutions to the wider 'Highland problem'. Evidence for both the 1883 Napier Commission and the later Highlands and Islands Commission, 1892–5, was taken in public and often highly charged settings, a context many factors were not familiar or happy with. The arrival of these commissions also meant a significant increase in factorial workloads; the collection of detailed statistical evidence for the commissioners as to tenancies and rentals, as well as preparation of statements and for questioning, added to the already heavy burdens of the factors.[39]

The work of these commissions was watched with trepidation; most factors (and their employers) regarded them as fundamentally biased towards the crofters, and the arrival of the Napier Commission in particular, with its focus on the crofting and cottar population, led to many estate factors auditing their crofting rents in advance, making repairs to crofting housing and fencing stocks and otherwise trying to add as much polish as possible.[40]

Some factors rejected the very notion that they had to defend themselves against public attacks, highlighting again the fundamental disjoint between their self-perception and changing political and public opinion on their work and methods. Evander McIver, by 1883 factor for forty years, had certainly long felt that estate management should not be subject to the whims of public opinion. McIver instead pointed to the 'peculiar and opposite ideas' held by the public and asked, 'are we on that account [to] cast our convictions to the winds and be guided wholly

---

[39] Principally the inquiries surrounding the Highland famine of the 1840s and in the later nineteenth century, the Napier Commission (1883) and the Deer Forest Commission (1892–5): *First Report from the Committee on Emigration, Scotland* (1841); *Evidence and Report of the Commissioners of Inquiry into the Condition of the Crofters and Cottars in the Highlands and Island of Scotland* (1884); *Royal Commission (Highlands and Islands, 1892), Report of Evidence, 1895* [hereafter *Deer Forest Commission Evidence*].

[40] See, for example, NLS, Sutherland estates papers, Acc. 10225, Factor's Correspondence, 357, Peacock to Kemball, 10 November 1884.

by what the public think and say? Surely not.'[41] Regardless of their
personal views on the question of public accountability, factors had
to face the new reality. In this, many landowners were ahead of them,
sensitive about their reputations particularly when seeking election or
political office, and put pressure on their factors to meet, rather than
dismiss, the challenge of hostile public opinion.[42]

Taken as a whole, factorial evidence to the Napier Commission in
Sutherland confined itself to discussion (sometimes very detailed) of
past management decisions, generally consisting of changing economic
contexts and managerial responses, much of it stretching back seventy
or eighty years.[43] They had to work through the archives of their managements, unpicking the history of the decision-making and activities
of decades ago. Perhaps surprisingly, they were remarkably consensual
in the pictures they painted of the estate management. Fundamentally
coloured by the drivers of economic change, industrialisation and com-
mercialisation, their history of estate management was one of attempted
– often aborted – progress and improvement in the face of an inert,
primitive and sullen population.[44] In an attempt to avoid the emotive
histories of clearance, their evidence was resolutely quantitative, with
detailed tables outlining estate expenditure on improvements, marshalled
to paint a picture of selfless expenditure and financial loss on the part
of the estate and family, sacrificed for the ungrateful tenantry.[45] They
were also well aware that the crofters and cottars would not be able to
access or present the same kind of evidence when making their case.
When asked by the commissioners what measures they thought would
improve conditions in the Highlands, the factors to a man – in tune with
their employers – suggested large-scale emigration and a crackdown on
subdivision of crofts.[46] For the factors, the 'Highland problem' equated

[41] NLS, Sutherland estates papers, Dep. 313, 1542, McIver to George Loch, 22
March 1858.
[42] Tindley, *Sutherland Estate*, pp. 167–8. Similar tensions were evident on the
estate of Cameron of Lochiel a little later; see Highland Council Archives, Cameron
of Lochiel, CL/A/3/1/2/6, Mackenzie to Lochiel, 3 September 1894.
[43] For a discussion of the evidence overall, see I. M. M. MacPhail, 'The Napier
Commission', *Transactions of the Gaelic Society of Inverness*, 48 (1972–4), pp.
446, 458–9, 462; for a discussion of the Sutherland estate evidence, see Tindley,
Sutherland Estate, pp. 168, 171.
[44] For example, *Napier Commission Evidence*, pp. 1709–11.
[45] Evander McIver, Scourie factor, summed up this feeling when he said, 'I don't
think that any land is profitably occupied by crofters'; *Deer Forest Commission
Evidence*, pp. 718–19.
[46] Richards, 'Highland emigration in the age of Malthus', p. 65.

to over-population on difficult and uneconomic ground. They resolutely defended landowning policies of creation of large sheep farms, and later commercial sporting tenancies, as the only possible economic direction for estates to take.[47]

Sutherland factors had to work within a rapidly changing and challenging context across the nineteenth century. The background to their work was the post-clearance inheritance of an elite and demanding caste of wealthy sheep-farming and sporting tenants on one side, and a dense mass of poverty-stricken crofters and cottars on the other. The factors had to guide this divided community through economic crisis and changing expectations as to the duties of landlordism. Economically, things began to improve from the mid-1860s, but politically, Highland landownership and its management through factors was increasingly challenged, until in the 1880s all-out war erupted over reform of land tenure.[48] Factors were on the front line of both crofter agitation and government inquiry into their management both past and present. After decades of immense influence over remote communities, the hostile light of public and government interest began to shine on their management, and many reacted negatively. Stress and anger at this turn of events led to a rash of resignations: no fewer than five in the Sutherland management in the mid-1880s.[49] This period was a watershed in estate management, as a new, moderate style of factor was introduced as a response to the heavily critical assessment of traditional estate management generated at this time.

CONCLUSION

One of the striking aspects of factorial work in the nineteenth century was the level of consensus among factors as to first, what the economic interests of Highland estates were, and second, how these interests could best be catered for. It was almost universally accepted among the managers by 1815 that clearance and the introduction of large-scale commercial sheep farming was the only way to make the Sutherland estates

---

[47] See NLS, Sutherland estates papers, Dep. 313, Policy Papers, 1228, George Loch to Joseph Peacock, Dunrobin factor, 26 July 1859. McIver had argued this point for decades; see NLS, Sutherland estates papers, Dep. 313, 1520, McIver to Loch, 26 August 1856; Richards, 'Highland emigration in the age of Malthus', p. 65.

[48] W. Orr, *Deer Forests, Landlords and Crofters: The Western Highlands in Victorian and Edwardian Times* (Edinburgh, 1982), pp. 3–5.

[49] See Tindley, *Sutherland Estate*, pp. 74–5, 86, 155.

economically viable; by the early 1860s a similar level of agreement was reached over the conversion of sheep walks to commercial sporting lets.[50] The other key area of consensus was over the small tenant population; the great reorganisations of the early nineteenth century had been designed in part to funnel this community to the coasts, where in theory they would find ample employment opportunities and lift the financial burden they represented from the shoulders of landowners, however broad they might be in the Sutherland case. In fact, the new system failed, the people became dependent on their small patches of land, and congestion, poverty and chronic land hunger followed: this was the post-clearance inheritance that estate managers had to face. Acting in the interests of their employers, the Sutherland factors were condemned to carry out what were effectively damage-limitation exercises; nearly all estate factors regarded crofting as a failed system, as fundamentally uneconomic and detrimental to the interests of the landowners they served.[51] Whether it was beneficial for Sutherland society to be managed by men who rejected the economic and social system they had inherited, or even played a part in imposing, is questionable.

How successful were the Sutherland factors in managing the reputation of their estate? For the 'old guard', it was the financial health and social discipline of the estate they administered which dominated their day-to-day management; the often conflicting requirement of a sympathetic public image was less important to them, and it took many factors a long time to come to terms with these changed priorities. The ducal family, deeply embedded in British and imperial political and public life, recognised the power of a good reputation, and was prepared to offer concessions to the crofters' lobby to enhance theirs. Their factors took much longer to make the same adjustment, unsurprising given their local dominance and unchallenged superiority over so many decades.[52] The evidence given to the great government inquiries of the 1880s and 1890s exposed this tension both internally and to external observers, and combined with factorial unhappiness about the new social order, leading to a wave of retirements and the appointment of a new generation of politically moderate managers in these decades.

[50] Cameron, *Land for the People?*, pp. 192, 202; Hunter, *Making of the Crofting Community*, pp. 185, 197, 205–6.

[51] Tindley, *Sutherland Estate*, p. 32.

[52] NLS, Sutherland estates papers, Acc. 10225, Policy Papers, 217, McIver to Wright, 21 June 1890; *Napier Commission Evidence*, p. 1707; McIver, *Memoirs of a Highland Gentleman*, p. 213.

Lastly, how effective were the Sutherland factors in their dealings with the tenantry they managed? That they were generally troubled in this respect can be seen by the degree of their unpopularity in the crofting community, which occasionally reached infamous levels.[53] It must also be asked whether this unpopularity constituted a handicap on their effectiveness as managers of large populations facing serious problems, as well as their own will to rule. Added to this was the almost universal unpopularity of factors, and the high rate of professional collapse through illness and misconduct. Although not all Sutherland factors deserved the level of contempt and resentment heaped upon them, as a model of estate management, the system was flawed. Perhaps too much depended on isolated individuals overburdened with numerous and at times conflicting roles; these were men who believed in the march of rational progress in the Highlands, but whose working lives were dominated by the maintenance of what they perceived to be an uneconomic and backward-looking crofting system. As the Rev. James Cumming noted in 1883, however, estate management was about far more than economic development; it was both a driver and a victim of wider social and cultural realities – hence the turmoil and conflict at its heart.

[53] Such as with McIver: McIver, *Memoirs of a Highland Gentleman*, p. 310.

Postscript

13

The Land Agent in Fiction

Lowri Ann Rees, Ciarán Reilly and Annie Tindley

She didn't know much about horses and she didn't know anything about Patrick Sellar [land agent for the Sutherland estates]. Nor, for that matter, did he know much about her. As far as he was concerned, she was a disposable object . . . She didn't particularly like the look of him. His head wasn't Highland. It was too heavy and the face was too fat and red, and the eyes in the head were small and burning.[1]

A S MANY OF THE chapters have touched upon individually, the legacy and memory of the land agent in Britain and Ireland made a strong impression on both contemporary and subsequent poetry, fiction, drama and folklore. This is unsurprising, given the wide range of powers, personalities and activities of land agents in all corners of the British and Irish isles, as well as the sheer scale of their dominion. Despite the urbanisation and industrialisation overtaking much of society in this period, large sections of it remained rural and agricultural, and the power of the landed and aristocratic classes, though subject to challenge, remained strong.[2] Ireland – Belfast, Dublin and Cork aside – remained a fundamentally rural society and agricultural economy well into the twentieth century.[3] As such, the requirements for, and scope of activities of, land agents remained significant and the raw materials for fictional presentations of such powerful figures prevalent.

---

[1] I. Crichton Smith, *Consider the Lilies* (London [1968] 1998), pp. 1, 3.

[2] S. W. Martins, *Farmers, Landlords and Landscapes: Rural Britain, 1720–1870* (Macclesfield, 2004); T. Williamson, *The Transformation of Rural England: Farming and the Landscape, 1700–1870* (Exeter, 2002); J. Finch and K. Giles (eds), *Estate Landscapes: Design, Improvement and Power in the Post-Medieval Landscape* (Woodbridge, 2007).

[3] D. Dickson, *Old World Colony: Cork and South Munster, 1630–1830* (Cork, 2006); T. Barnard, *A New Anatomy of Ireland: The Irish Protestants 1649–1770* (London, 2004); M. Dowling, *Tenant Right and Agrarian Society in Ulster 1600–1870* (Dublin, 1999).

A number of common stereotypes of the land agent can be traced in fiction and poetry from the eighteenth to the twentieth centuries, which had a powerful impact on their image in social, communal and popular memory. These shared stereotypes act as linking membrane between the four nations of the British and Irish isles, right into the present day, differences in traditions, languages and religion notwithstanding. The first of these was a will to rule, an overweening desire for the exercise of power, not simply on behalf of their employers, but for its own sake. This mania was used by authors to illustrate the untrammelled and corrupt power of an old, hereditary aristocratic class over a struggling tenantry, and both fed into, and fed off, contemporary land and political reform debates. Land agents were used by writers as the symbolic conduits of this power, to demonstrate its emotional, communal and social destructiveness. A further aspect of this stereotype was the way in which the land agent was used to symbolise the unbridgeable gap between the landed and powerful, and the landless and powerless. Whether by class, culture, gender or – very commonly – language, the factor is written as a figure apart, both unable and unwilling to integrate into the communities over which they wielded so much power. Various conclusions are drawn from this division, from state-of-the-nation condemnations on the decline of traditional cultures to micro-historical analyses of fracturing communities. Either way, the land agent, as both instrument and symbol of power and its negative consequences, rarely receives a good press in fiction or poetry.

A final aspect to comment on generally relates to gender. Reflecting the prevailing characteristics and history of the profession, fictional land agents are all male; as, with a few exceptions, are the authors who write about them.[4] As such, they provide a rich seam for presentations of masculinities in the modern period, particularly within small, tightly knit and hierarchical rural communities. Fictional land agents are rarely supplied with a hinterland of wives, mistresses, children or other family members, never mind friends or colleagues. They are most often presented as intensely isolated figures – both professionally and personally – and therefore display certain forms of masculinity; domineering, emotionally repressed and repressing, and obsessed by the exercise of power.

These power relations on Scottish – especially Highland – estates have been a rich vein of material for creative writers. The land agent's ultimately destructive power over the crofters dominates both Neil Gunn's classic *Butcher's Broom* (1934) as well as the recent novel *His Bloody*

---

[4] Maria Edgeworth being a notable exception.

Project by Graeme Macrae Burnet (2016).[5] This book turns on the capriciousness of the township constable, a lowlier but intimately more powerful local figure than the factor, although the latter also figures in the plot. Taken together they uphold and represent a system so malign that it leads to an extreme outburst of violence. The fictional Scottish land agent is drawn principally from the popular memory and poetry of the clearances and figure prominently in Fionn MacColla's, *And the Cock Crew* (1945) and Iain Crichton Smith's, *Consider the Lilies* (1968). They are used as symbols of the oppressive and unequal tyranny of the landed over the landless in rural Scotland, and are often put in opposition to female characters, perhaps to enhance the drama of binary opposition and moral corruption being portrayed.

These binaries were also commonly played out through linguistic divisions and misunderstandings, especially in the Welsh case. The linguistic barrier between English-speaking land agents and monoglot Welsh tenants is strongly portrayed in the novel *Elisa Powell, or Trials of Sensibility* (1795), by Edward Davies, which presents several parallels of concern regarding language. The works of the Nonconformist minister Samuel Roberts, in particular *Farmer Careful of Cilhaul Uchaf* (1850) and *Diosg Farm: A Sketch of its History* (1854), also drew attention to the uneasy relationship between landlord and tenants in nineteenth-century Wales. Such works helped cultivate the popular image of the Welsh land agent as a tyrannical force oppressing the Welsh tenantry, something that land reformers were able to incorporate into their cause to build support for it.

Claire Connolly has noted that in Irish fiction and drama one of the most popular stereotypes has been that of the villainous land agent.[6] This negative depiction of land agents in works of fiction had begun even before the Great Famine, with Maria Edgeworth's novels highlighting the perils of oppressive agents, as shown in *Castle Rackrent* (1800) and *The Absentee* (1812). Interestingly, these portrayed the agent as an enemy of the landed elite 'who slowly and inexorably displaces the hereditary proprietor'.[7] Pre-Famine novels such as Charles Lever's *Jack*

---

[5] N. Gunn, *Butcher's Broom* (Edinburgh, 1934); G. Macrae Burnet, *His Bloody Project* (Glasgow, 2016); see also E. A. Cameron, 'Growing up with Gunn', in A. McCleery (ed.), *Neil Gunn Circle: Nation and Nationalism* (Dunbeath, 2013), pp. 25–31.

[6] Quoted in J. Cleary and C. Connolly (eds), *The Cambridge Companion to Modern Irish Culture* (Cambridge, 2005), p. 323.

[7] V. Kreilkamp, *The Anglo-Irish Novel and the Big House* (Syracuse, NY, 1998), pp. 50–1.

Hinton, the Guardsman (1843) and *Tom Burke of Ours* (1844) depict the eviction of impoverished tenants and the distraining of crops and animals for rent.[8] As a result, attacks perpetrated on land agents are features of the novels of William Hamilton Maxwell including *The Fortunes of Hector O'Halloran* (1843) and the earlier *The Wild Sports of the West, with Legendary Tales and Local Sketches* (1838).[9] Likewise, in H. G. Curran's novel *Confessions of a Whitefoot* (1844), Hynes, the leader of the peasantry, believed that the agents' use of the hanging gale was a means to keep the tenants in continued subjection.[10]

The immoral actions of the land are also depicted in Lever's *St Patrick's Eve* (1845), where the agent is portrayed as ruthless and impersonal. According to Lever, 'the agents get a guinea for every man, woman and child they turn out of a houldin [sic]'.[11] Similarly, the novelist Anthony Trollope, who spent much of the 1840s in the Irish midlands at Banagher, King's County, used real-life agents as the basis for his fictional characters. In his novel *The Kellys and the O'Kellys* (1848), Trollope claimed that an agent managed property 'in that manner most conducive to the prosperity of the person he loved best in the world and that was himself'.[12] It is likely that Trollope's agent was based on the real-life Arthur Baker who managed the nearby Armstrong estate. Canon John Guinan also included real-life agents in his early-twentieth-century works of fiction. In Guinan's novels agents were generally depicted as cruel and oppressive or weak and inferior characters. Overtly pro-Catholic in tone, Guinan's novels depict Protestant agents as being the root cause of the people's woes. Indeed, in the novel *Priest and People in Doon* (1907), Guinan writes of Mooney, a Catholic agent, who after thirty years' service was considered 'a true friend to the tenantry, beloved by all and universally respected'.[13] By contrast when a new Protestant agent, Toler Garvey, was put in place, 'his will was law and his power despotic'.[14]

---

[8] Quoted in P. G. Lane, '"The boys was up": Connacht agrarian unrest in fiction, c. 1800–1850', *Journal of the Galway Archaeological and Historical Society*, 58 (2006), pp. 42–52, especially p. 43.

[9] Lane, '"The boys was up"', pp. 44–5.

[10] Lane, '"The boys was up"', p. 47. In some cases the hanging gale suited tenants, especially where the agent was lax in collecting the rent.

[11] Lane, '"The boys was up"', pp. 48–9.

[12] A. Trollope, *The Kellys and the O'Kellys: A Tale of Irish Life* (London, 1848), p. 20.

[13] Rev. Canon J. Guinan, *Priest and People in Doon* (6th edn, Dublin, 1925), p. 95.

Perhaps most influential with regard to the memory and representation of agents in Ireland was the work of William Carleton who created a number of memorable characters such as 'Greasy Pockets' and 'Yellow Sam', both of whom personified the stereotypical representation of agents. In Carleton's novels these agents were seen as being a source of ridicule, greed and tyranny, highlighting the many wrongdoings which were perpetrated against the Irish peasantry. 'Yellow Sam', who appears in the novel *The Poor Scholar* (1833), was metaphorically born without a heart and carries 'black wool' in his ears to keep out the cries of widows and orphans 'who are now long rotten in their graves through his dark villainy'.[15] He takes advantage not only of the tenants but also his employer, the absentee Colonel B, a 'good hearted and principled man' whom he has been cheating for many years. Carleton believed that 'needy men' made for bad agents. While agreeing that they were necessary in the day-to-day management of an estate, Carleton urged that agents should be respectable men and never left in complete control.[16]

All of the fictional work discussed here had an agenda, of course; some contemporary, others retrospective. They are all to some degree critiques of social, communal and gender structures and expectations that were fundamentally unequal. These impersonal historical structures and forces are dramatised through the character of the land agent – oppressive, impersonal, heartless; the instrument of the application of power. This volume ends, fittingly, with a new short story by Kirsty Gunn, 'Poor Beasts', which considers the contemporary understanding of the land agent, and the land question more broadly, in an age of democracy. Her story demonstrates that the land agent as a symbol still carries great weight in contemporary rural cultures in Britain and Ireland, and the various reasons why this has been the case have been considered in this volume. The continuing influence of land agents in

---

[14] Guinan, *Priest and People*, p. 100. Toler Garvey was the son of George Garvey. The Garveys remained as agents of the Rosse estate until the 1940s; see also P. Maume, 'A pastoral vision: the novels of Canon Joseph Guinan', *New Hibernia Review/Iris Eireannach Nua*, 9:4 (2005), pp. 79–98, especially pp. 83, 89. See Guinan's other novels, *The Moores of Glynn* (1907), *The Island Parish* (1908), *The Famine Years* (1908) and *Annamore* (1928).

[15] M. Chesnutt, *Studies in the Short Stories of William Carleton* (Gothenburg, 1976), p. 112.

[16] Chesnutt, *William Carleton*, p. 111; W. Carleton, *Valentine McClutchey: The Irish Agent or Chronicles of the Castle Cumber Property* (3 vols, London 1845), vol. 1, preface.

contemporary British and Irish society, as well as their particularly powerful influence on rural memory and culture, makes them rich subjects
for the historian and the writer alike.

14

Poor Beasts

Kirsty Gunn

'Y OU COULDN'T MAKE IT up,' says Aly.
He's sitting at the table in our kitchen, looking out over the hills.

'It's like a short story,' I reply. 'Only if I write it as one, I'll have to change the names of the estate, the people. You, even. We couldn't, you know, let it get around. How you feel about the changes they are making. You'd be out of a job.'

'I'm out of a job anyway,' says Aly. 'I reckon. But, yeah. I see what you mean.'

He takes a sip of his coffee. Spends a long time settling the mug back down on his plate, just so, beside the scone sitting there he's barely touched. I've known him and his wife for thirty years. More than thirty. They've looked after the Ben Mhorlaich estate for most of that time. His wife, Margaret, is one of the most practical and far-sighted people I know. If there's something I want to find out about – from pruning an apple tree to making a time-and-place line of all the characters in *War and Peace* – Margaret is the one who can tell me.

Right now, I wish she was here to comfort me about this news Aly's just served. While I was getting the scones out of the oven – a particular sort of scone I make – he told me then, while my back was to him and I couldn't react straight away with holding the hot tray, and then dealing with them, taking them off and getting them onto a cooling rack.

Only to say, 'What?' and, 'I don't believe it,' while I was putting them onto a plate and getting out the butter and cheese. Normally Aly loves these scones. I put herbs and olives in them. Today it was one bite, and that was it. I didn't feel like eating either.

'It is like a short story,' I say again, and break off a lump of olive and fiddle with the crumbs around it on the plate. 'It has all the elements. A lovely place, a way of living that seems unchanging, and then in one summer . . .'

'Margaret says it's the end of the Lodge,' says Aly quietly, as though to himself. 'She says they'll sell all the shooting to the Chinese or the Russians, whoever pays the most, and they'll just bring in their own parties from one of the fancy hotels – that one near Rosehall, say – for the day.'

'But –'

'And the helicopters,' Aly finishes. 'As I say, that's what these big outfits use in the Highlands now. So they can come in, get out . . .'

'Like a war,' I say.

'Some kind of awful thing, for sure,' Aly says. He goes to pick up his mug again, but then doesn't. 'I don't know what to think about it . . .' His voice trails off.

I can't bear it. I stand and go over to the window. It's early spring and the hills are greening. Under all the brown and grey and stone, it's there, the beginnings of the summer ahead and all the light. This morning, very early, before the rest of them were up, I was awake. I stood at the kitchen window then and watched the sun rise from behind the hills, everything brightening, second by second, a kind of photo coming into print, bleaching out all of the dark and gradually showing outlines, shapes. As I stood and watched, a herd of deer came running like water down off the side of the furthest hill, like a run of water, yes, then taking form as individual animals as they got closer. Closer they came, and closer, the entire herd on the move as though something were after them, driving them onwards. Down they came, making for the far field that used to be for the MacKays' sheep and is now all empty pasture, coming through that and across the river, over the high water like it was nothing, and then straight up towards the house, towards our house – me . . . Where I was standing as though waiting for them. For a second it really did seem like that. As though the deer were going to run straight through the walls of the house and into the kitchen and all around me in one great rush of movement, onwards, forwards, the house as invisible to them as the river had been, coming right up to just before the fenceline at the bottom of the garden before they veered off to the left, into the little wood that runs up by the farm road, disappeared into it and were gone.

The rest of them were still in their beds, my daughters, home from university with friends, and my husband, and my two cousins who were staying with us from Canada, a houseful of us – and all of them asleep – yet I'd seen this thing. I'd had this moment in my life when I'd thought, been overwhelmed by the feeling, that we could have all been surrounded by the deer that had been rushing across the land, that they might have run right through the house and out again. In the few seconds of my watching there had been no break in their stride.

'It doesn't bear thinking about,' says Aly now. 'I'll take some more of that coffee, Beth, since you've made it.'

I turn, reach for the pot on the bench beside me, and in that second of turning feel how old I am, how old we both are, Aly and I, two old friends sitting here. Though we may be going about the place as always, and I am riding as well as I ever have, and doing everything as fast, and still up and down to Edinburgh and London every few weeks or so with Robbie to see the girls and not even noticing it . . . Still. In that little old lady gesture of my turning I feel every one of my years built up within me, thirty years in this dear, dear place.

I fill Aly's cup, top up my own.

'They can't afford the taxes now,' he says, 'is just about the sum of it. Margaret and I have seen this coming. And now this guy, Povlsen. Buying up every estate in Sutherland and Caithness he can get his hands on, one by one like he's playing Monopoly and the Scottish Government are helping him. Nothing good can come from that either.' He takes up a scone, puts it down. 'We've been out of a job for a while, you could say, Margaret and I. And all of us. There'll be no more gamekeepers anywhere in Sutherland with the way things are going. But, after that meeting yesterday, the way it is there, in the Estate Office . . . Well . . .'

'It doesn't bear thinking about,' I repeat after him, using his own sentence, filling up his coffee again like someone with no mind or heart or will. Because how can I have will or mind or heart to hear what I am hearing though it's not for the first time. Margaret and Aly, Robbie and I . . . We've talked about these things before, seen all the changes that are afoot, the legislation that's going on with everything being put in place and none of us even aware of it most of the time, but still a deep feeling, gone deep in, that the land is gathering a different meaning to itself . . . Especially here, where we are, though there's no one much who'll talk about it, how the big estates are selling off one by one and not as going concerns, as it would have been in the old days, but for different reasons – wind turbines, fish farms, whatever will pay. That meeting Aly had yesterday . . . That says a lot. That there are these meetings and involving lawyers now, not anyone he knows, and with the old factor long gone. It was some guy from one of the government departments doing all the talking this time, Aly said. 'Centralised initiatives' – that was how he put it, and lodges closed up the length of Sutherland and even the shooting, the bit of fishing, not like it was once, but all day trippers coming up from London and going back the same night, bringing their own guns with them and god knows how they behave, out on the hill, these people who've bought up vast acreages in a place they know nothing about, and don't care to know except that it is there on their lists of assets.

'It's not the first time, though,' I say to Aly out loud, thinking about all of this. Three years ago he was in my kitchen telling me about a new manager brought in from Edinburgh who had been up seeing all the gamekeepers in the region, telling them their time was marked. It would be Knight Frank and Bell Ingram doing all the estate managing from now on, he said, no need to keep couples on in full-time work in these remote places. Things seemed to go quiet then, after that visit. But things never go completely quiet. Once change comes, change moves things on, and in the parts where it goes quiet it's just us, the people who live here, getting used to change, is all, that's it there in the back of our minds and so we come to expect it. Still, 'We have heard all this before,' I say, to comfort Aly, to comfort myself. 'We have seen all this coming.'

For months, yes. Longer. Aly and Margaret have known their time at Ben Mhorlaich was numbered to months, there were no longer years in it. The factor who was no longer the factor, a Bell Ingram agent, called a meeting with them, not long after the September Referendum. The estates all over Scotland were bringing in lawyers by then, 'to assess the situation' was the phrase Aly told me the Ben Mhorlaich people had used. Not all of them would be affected, of course, but with forthcoming changes due to new land legislation, and with – as Aly had looked into all this – 'the behind the scenes dismantling of powers', as it was described, in their bureaucratic jargon, of 'certain landholdings, contexts, situations', some of the larger estates were going to have to divest themselves of properties 'damn smartly', he had told him, this guy, Aly said, as though it was a fun thing, a wanted thing.

But it was only now, I am thinking, at this meeting yesterday . . . It was only yesterday that the estate actually informed their employees, only then that they told them, formally, told Aly and Margaret Sutherland, told them outright that they'd need to start looking for accommodation and alternative employment for the 'forthcoming period' – another phrase taken out of the paperwork, Aly said.

'They tell me they can find something for me to do over this winter,' he says now, draining his coffee. 'But I've had enough.' He lets out a short, bitter laugh. 'We're going back to Perthshire. An old friend has some fencing work he can give me, and some other bits and pieces. Margaret's sister is in Loch Tummell. We'll manage.'

All the time, during this grim talk, I am there doing nothing, saying nothing – just hearing his words and saying them back to myself, in my mind, arranging the things on the table, moving them from here back to there, like pieces on a chessboard: sugar, mugs. My dumb scones. Everything silent, actually. No life in anything at all. Despite Aly talking, the things he says, there are no words, really, for any of this. No expression for the weight of it, feeling the awful knowledge of time and what is ahead. Then, in the midst of that, the hopelessness of it, there in my mind appear the deer again, running down off the hills as they had been early in the morning, streaming down towards me in the kitchen as though I wasn't even there.

'But I can't think of this part of the world without you two in it,' I say then.

With the deer running, I can see them coursing down the hill.

'Margaret and I . . .,' I say. 'We've been talking about the situation for some time . . . But even so –'

The deer running still, streaming down the hill like water.

'Is there nothing we can do?'

The whole thing, the sight of them, had been over in seconds.

'Seems, Beth, nothing,' says Aly, standing up now to go. 'You'll see Margaret later,' he adds, leaning down to give me a hug goodbye. 'Say good morning to that lazy family of yours,' he says. 'Where are they anyhow?'

'Robbie's taken them to Dornoch,' I say. 'My sister wanted a run with him to see that new shop with all the tweed and the pottery, and my cousins have gone with them for the ride. The kids are around somewhere, though they may have gone too, a couple of them . . .'

'And I thought they were all sleeping,' Aly says. 'Well there you go.'

He's on his way to the door and I'm behind him. He ducks as he always has to, at the entrance to the porch. 'Margaret will call in around five, she said. She's got some cuttings for you. They might see her – your lot – in Dornoch.'

'Might,' I say. 'No, they weren't sleeping.' No, none of us were. Yet look at us all, it occurs to me, we may as well be. Sleeping and sleep-walking through all of this change as it collects around us, inevitable as the kind of weed you see in the loch up behind the hills now, bright green and strong, changing the colour of the water as you look at it, bright and strange and artificial, and killing the fish, killing everything as it grows.

'We may as well all be asleep . . .,' I say then. But Aly doesn't hear me. He is walking down the garden towards his truck parked out on the road. I feel like I am in the midst of a dream . . . A dream, only I am asleep in it. Asleep while the deer come down. Asleep while the land they come through is sold off, piece by piece – to Russia, China, this man Povlsen . . . Whoever pays most, fastest. I walk with Aly to the gate, unspeaking. Dumb and meek, with nothing to say, like one of his dogs who I guess soon he'll have to shoot or rehome because sure enough he can't take a kennel full of gun dogs and hounds to Margaret's sister's in Tummell. And over everything a feeling of heaviness, impending change and endings that have their beginnings in things that have been going on for a while now, I can see it, like a dreamer. First with the turbines and you couldn't go anywhere in Sutherland or Caithness without seeing them – what was it Robbie and I found out – that Sutherland had been designated a 'red zone' for windpower development? So-called 'renewables' as though the people who live here might get renewed energy, cheap and free as the wind when all we get are the monstrous white machines everywhere you look and the same high energy bills and the massive lorries carving up roads all over the places where we live and sinking aggregate into the peat in order that those huge towers have somewhere to stand, so the rivers are flooding now, every spring and the bright weed starts growing in the high lochs from the drain-off . . . Bright, bright change, all of it, across the ancient hills . . .

'Do you know what Margaret says,' Aly had told me, just before this story begins. 'She says it's the poor beasts she pities. With no one there to manage things, to make sure they're properly looked after on the hill, then taken out, properly, you know, with a good gun. Stalked properly and so on, things done in the right way . . .'

'I hadn't even thought –' I'd started then to speak, but couldn't. Even then, I'd been fiddling with my stupid baking, fiddling at the oven, at the stove because what could I say? Struck dumb with the image before me of four-wheel drives cutting over the same soft hills where Aly and his father before him had walked, with quiet knowledge and history, invisibly tracking the herd, picking out the oldest, the sick, the one with the game leg that would bring it down anyway for a long, slow death away from the others . . . Walking across the same land upon which I'd seen the animals coming through this morning, their easy, momentary flight . . . Now four-wheel drives and firing rifles out of open windows. No one knowing what they were doing. Aly and Margaret far, far away and the lodge opened up for a week or so every year as a sort of rich man's hotel.

'Helicopters even, some folk use,' Aly had said. 'Just firing down on them, while the deer are running, just random, scatter firing and wounding them, not finishing the job, leaving them there . . . Christ. You couldn't make it up.'

'I will write about all this, though,' I manage, as he's just about to go. 'There's this land futures book I've been asked to think about . . .'

Aly swings the door open and starts up the truck. 'Just remember it's not a story, that's all. Look after yourself, Beth,' he says as he starts to reverse into our drive to head back up the way, to Ben Mhorlaich. 'Give my best to the others. Tell Robbie I'll stop by one of these days soon and we'll have that dram.'

Index